Development Policies in Natural Resource Economies

Development Policies in Natural Resource Economies

Edited by

Jörg Mayer, Brian Chambers and Ayisha Farooq

*United Nations Conference on Trade and Development
(UNCTAD), Switzerland*

Edward Elgar

Cheltenham, UK • Northampton, MA, USA

Published in association with UNCTAD

Published by
Edward Elgar Publishing Limited
Glensanda House
Montpellier Parade
Cheltenham
Glos GL50 1UA
UK

Edward Elgar Publishing, Inc.
6 Market Street
Northampton
Massachusetts 01060
USA

A catalogue record for this book
is available from the British Library

Library of Congress Cataloguing in Publication Data

Development policies in natural resource economies / edited by Jörg
    Mayer, Brian Chambers, and Ayisha Farooq.
        Includes bibliographical references and index.
        1. Natural resources—Developing countries. 2. Developing
    countries—Economic policy. 3. Developing countries—Economic
    conditions. 4. Structural adjustment (Economic policy)—Developing
    countries. I. Mayer, Jörg, 1958–   . II. Chambers, Brian, 1943–
. III. Farooq, Ayisha, 1973–   .
    HC59.7.D477   1999
    333.7'09172'4—dc21   98–30463
                                                                              CIP

ISBN 1 84064 009 X ✓

Printed and bound in Great Britain by Biddles Ltd, Guildford and King's Lynn

Contents

PART THREE: NATIONAL EXPERIENCES WITH
RENEWABLE NATURAL RESOURCES

PART FOUR: NATURAL RESOURCE POLICY FROM A LOCAL AND
REGIONAL PERSPECTIVE

PART FIVE: CONCLUSIONS

Figures

Tables

Contributors

Abbas Alnasrawi, University of Vermont, Burlington, USA

Samuel K. Appiah, Timber Export Development Board, Takoradi, Ghana

Richard M. Auty, Lancaster University, Lancaster, UK

Brian Chambers, United Nations Conference on Trade and Development, Geneva, Switzerland

L.T. Chitsike, Africa Resources Trust, Harare, Zimbabwe

Ayisha Farooq, United Nations Conference on Trade and Development, Geneva, Switzerland

Raanan Katzir, Ministry of Agriculture and Rural Development, Tel-Aviv, Israel

Jörg Mayer, United Nations Conference on Trade and Development, Geneva, Switzerland

Modise D. Modise, Ministry of Finance and Development Planning, Gaborone, Botswana

F. Phillip Muema, Ministry of Agriculture, Nairobi, Kenya

Ligia Noronha, Tata Energa Research Institute, Goa, India

Rubens Ricupero, United Nations Conference on Trade and Development, Geneva, Switzerland

Rabbi Poobal Royan, Prime Minister's Department, Kuala Lumpur, Malaysia

Jeffrey D. Sachs, Harvard University, Cambridge, USA

Andrew M. Warner, Harvard University, Cambridge, USA

Adrian J.B. Wood, University of Sussex, Brighton, UK

Foreword

In the literature on economic development, the 'convergence hypothesis' implies that poor countries should be growing at a faster rate than richer countries, given the fulfilment of certain conditions relating to savings behaviour, technology and population growth. While this hypothesis has generally held over the past twenty to thirty years for those developing countries whose economies are based on manufactures, growth rates have often been disappointing for developing countries that are rich in natural resources. Does the poorer performance of these latter countries indicate that their comparative advantage in natural resources is more apparent than real? Is there a special challenge facing resource-based economies? Should the development policies of resource-rich countries differ from those of resource-poor countries? Such fundamental questions have become increasingly important for a large number of developing countries as the phenomena of globalization and liberalization impinge on their natural resource base and challenge the goal of sustainable development.

Since its creation over thirty years ago, the United Nations Conference on Trade and Development (UNCTAD) has sought to shed light on the problems and complexities of economic growth and to promote constructive international debate on emerging issues of particular concern to developing countries. Continuing this UNCTAD spirit of inquiry and debate, we convened a group of experts in order to examine the fundamental questions posed above. The group, which met in November 1996, was chaired by the then Ambassador and now Prime Minister of the Republic of Yemen, Dr Farag Bin Ghanem, and comprised some twenty distinguished experts and participants drawn from government, industry, academia and intergovernmental and non-governmental organizations. The present book draws largely on presentations prepared by members of the group and reflects, I believe, the high quality of the group's discussions as well as the skill of the editors in collating its work.

We recommend this publication to anyone interested in economic development. It contains a wealth of empirical analyses and practical experiences of natural resources and development policy. It opens new avenues of inquiry for researchers and poses new challenges for development planners, *inter alia* on the role of human capital and the inclusion of local communities. This publication is therefore not the last word on development policies in natural resource economies – indeed, it may be only a first step. But the reader should find ample reward in this since the first step is often the most difficult one to take.

RUBENS RICUPERO
Secretary-General of UNCTAD

Acknowledgements

The editors would like to acknowledge the contributions made by a number of people to the production of this publication. Those named in the list of contributors have all given generously of their time in preparing and reviewing material. In addition, the following people also participated in the work of the UNCTAD expert group on resource-based economies and contributed to discussions on which the introductory and concluding chapters of this publication are partly based: Carmen Alvarez, Corpoven, Venezuela; Sinan Al-Shabibi, UNCTAD secretariat, Geneva; Prasert Anupunt, Horticultural Research Institute, Thailand; Phillip Crowson, Rio Tinto, United Kingdom; Graham Davis, Colorado School of Mines, United States; Mohamed Hafiz-Khodja, OPEC secretariat, Vienna; Alberto Pasco-Font, Grupo de Análisis para el Desarrollo, Peru; and John Strongman, World Bank, Washington, DC.

In UNCTAD, Pauline Brady helped to organize the expert group and collate the experts' papers, and Chris MacFarquhar and Graham Grayston worked diligently on editing the text of this publication. The preparation of camera-ready copy was undertaken kindly and efficiently by Martin Best and Petra Hoffmann.

1. Introduction

Jörg Mayer[1]

This book will argue that the presence of an inverse statistical relationship between resource abundance and economic growth over the last three decades should not be taken to imply that natural resource abundance is a curse. There are examples of successful resource-based industrialization both in the late nineteenth century, such as in the United States and Sweden, and in the more recent past, such as most importantly in Chile, Israel and Malaysia. Drawing on these examples suggests that there is little inevitability about economic stagnation in natural resource economies. The ultimate effect on economic performance is decisively influenced by government policies and the outcome of institutional processes. Considering economic development as essentially a process of technological and organizational change suggests that the key policy question in natural resource economies is how to make the primary sector sufficiently productive to provide the resources for investment in both primary and non-primary sectors, with a view to initiating a process of gradual upgrading of skills and technology on the basis of capital deepening.

Substantial progress has been made over the past decade towards understanding the fundamental sources of long-run economic growth and economic development. The theoretical understanding of economic growth and development has been advanced most importantly by Romer's investigation (1986, 1990) of endogenous technical innovation and increasing returns to scale, Lucas's analysis (1988, 1993) of the causes and effects of different rates of human capital accumulation, Grossman and Helpman's study (1991) of the interaction of motives for the development of new technology, capital accumulation and international technology spillovers, and North's inquiry (1990) into the role of institutions in economic development. The empirical comparison of different growth and development experiences across countries has been greatly facilitated by the increasing availability of standardized data sets, notably the Penn World Tables data set of Summers and Heston (1991), as demonstrated by the dizzying number of studies on convergence, initiated by Barro (1991).

While these developments may be of particular interest only to economists, a wider audience has become interested in the sources of long-run economic growth and development as a result of the rapid economic growth in East Asia, which is in sharp contrast to the growth in most countries in the world economy. Policy makers thus face the question of what development policies to follow with a view to emulating the East Asian experience. Taking into account the theoretical developments above, Stiglitz (1996, p. 151) argues that 'East Asia's success was based on a combination of factors, particularly the high savings rate interacting with high levels of human capital accumulation, in a stable, market-oriented environment – but one with active government intervention – that was conducive to the transfer of technology'. By contrast, economic growth in many resource-rich countries has failed to take off despite the analyses and policy advice from international organizations and developed countries. Therefore, there is a need to re-examine the effectiveness of the economic policies proposed to the natural resource rich developing countries, in terms of stimulating economic growth and development.

The observation that over the last few decades countries with an abundance of natural resources have tended to do less well than other countries in terms of economic growth, exports, income and employment, and that such abundance has often been related to underdevelopment and an absence of economic dynamism, is at first somewhat puzzling. Theorists such as Malthus, Ricardo and Jevons expected that economic growth would eventually come to a halt because of limitations on the availability of natural resources. Moreover, the United States' assumption of economic leadership was clearly supported by its comparative advantage in natural resource endowments. The possession of natural resources is clearly an asset that increases national wealth and an economy's purchasing power as regards imports, and it might therefore be expected to stimulate a country's investment and growth rates. Figure 2.1 (p. 13) provides evidence regarding this negative statistical relationship from a cross-country perspective, while Table 1.1 provides similar evidence on a country-specific basis.

Some observers have offered explanations for this phenomenon. One pillar of pessimism regarding the contribution of the natural resource sector to economic development has been the long-term trend of commodity prices in relation to prices of manufactured goods. There has been a passionate debate about whether there exists a secular decline in commodity prices. This debate is unresolved, but the substantive decline in real commodity prices since the beginning of the 1980s, as evidenced in Figure 1.1, has lent support to the pessimists. Worse, according to projections by the World Bank (1995, p. 19), real non-oil commodity prices will decline on average by about 2 per cent over the coming decade, with timber being the only commodity group projected to benefit from real price increases. However, since the evolution of commodity prices is not usually amenable to policies adopted at the national level, on which this book focuses, demand-side issues will not be further addressed here.

Table 1.1 Natural resource abundance and economic growth

Natural resource abundant and high-growth countries or territories	Natural resource abundant and low-growth countries or territories	Natural resource scarce and high-growth countries or territories	Natural resource scarce and low-growth countries or territories
Algeria	Bolivia	Austria	Argentina
Botswana	Central African Rep.	Brazil	Australia
Cameroon	Chile	Burundi	Bangladesh
Cyprus	Comoros	Canada	Benin
Dominican Republic	Congo	Cape Verde	Burkina Faso
Ecuador	Costa Rica	China	Chad
Fiji	Côte d'Ivoire	Colombia	Guinea-Bissau
Guinea	El Salvador	Denmark	Haiti
Iceland	Gabon	Egypt	Mozambique
Indonesia	Gambia	Finland	Nigeria
Ireland	Ghana	France	Pakistan
Kenya	Guatemala	Greece	Panama
Malaysia	Guyana	Hong Kong, China	Sierra Leone
Mauritius	Honduras	India	Somalia
Morocco	Iran, Islamic Rep. of	Israel	Sweden
Netherlands	Jamaica	Italy	Switzerland
Singapore	Madagascar	Japan	Uruguay
Sri Lanka	Malawi	Jordan	
	Mali	Korea, Rep. of	
	Mauritania	Lesotho	
	New Zealand	Mexico	
	Nicaragua	Norway	
	Peru	Paraguay	
	Philippines	Portugal	
	Rwanda	Spain	
	Senegal	Syrian Arab Rep.	
	Togo	Taiwan Pr. of China	
	Trinidad and Tobago	Thailand	
	Uganda	Tunisia	
	Venezuela	Turkey	
	Zambia	United Kingdom	
	Zimbabwe	United States	

Notes: Natural resource abundance is measured by the share of primary commodity exports in GDP in 1970, while growth performance is measured by the average annual growth rate of real GDP per capita during 1970–90. The countries have been grouped according to the medians of the two variables. Within each group, the countries are listed in alphabetical order.

Source: Growth rates calculated from Penn World Tables; other data are from the UNCTAD database.

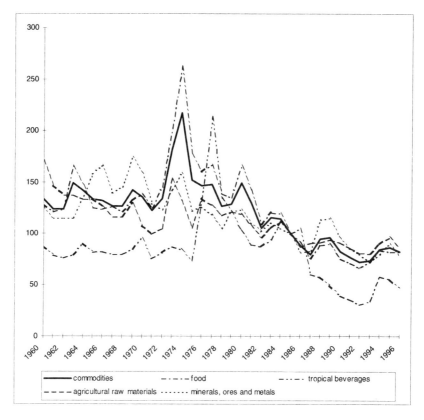

Note: Nominal price indices have been deflated by export unit values of manufactured goods from developed countries.

Source: UNCTAD database.

Figure 1.1 Real market-price indices of commodity groups (1985 = 100), 1960–96

A second explanation has been associated with a situation known as 'Dutch disease' – a situation of imbalance characterized by the coexistence of booming and lagging sectors in an economy. Dutch disease has most often been associated with a booming mining sector and shrinking manufacturing and agricultural sectors. The frequent existence of substantial rents (that is, revenues in excess of production costs and a normal return on capital) on mineral ores can lead to a strong appreciation of the real exchange rate, with the result that virtually no non-mining activity remains internationally competitive. Dutch disease effects can permanently damage a country's development prospects, for example when they cause once-and-for-all cessation of non-mineral activities or trigger excessive levels of protection. A country in which such activities cease will find it difficult to restart them, even after the mineral rents dry up and the real exchange rate returns to a lower level, because suppliers from other countries who have continued to enjoy learning effects associated with such activities and maintained business contacts will have become more competitive.

It has also been argued that resource rich countries may squander their resource advantage because mineral revenues may be taken for granted by government, with the result that no action is taken to prepare for alternative economic activities which become necessary once market demand for the resource falters or the non-renewable resources approach depletion. The resource advantage can also be squandered when an excessively optimistic estimation of export prospects leads to the pursuit of lax economic policies, giving rise to rent-seeking behaviour. Competition among the interest groups can lead to situations in which public subsidies and other forms of transfers grow more quickly than the increase in windfall income, with adverse effects on investment and the economy's aggregate growth rate. Eventually, the country as a whole may be worse off than before the windfall.

A fourth explanation is related mainly to agricultural commodities and is known as the 'fallacy of composition', or the 'adding-up problem'. This problem is associated with the low price elasticity of demand for many agricultural commodities; accordingly, total export revenue tends to fall when supply is increased. The significance of the adding-up problem is that – in the absence of booming global demand for a commodity – it is not possible for all resource-based economies producing a particular commodity to achieve high export-led growth.

A fifth explanation concerns the growth potential of resource-based economies over the long term. It is often argued that manufacturing is a much more efficient motor of economic development than resource-based activities, because of the greater forward and backward linkages and the higher learning-by-doing effects associated with manufacturing activities. If this explanation is correct, the loss of positive external economies associated with learning-by-doing effects and of the beneficial effects of increasing returns to scale coming from manufacturing would have detrimental effects on an economy's growth potential in the long term.

A final explanation concerning the development prospects of resource-based economies relates to non-renewable resources. If resources such as fuels and minerals are exploited to the full, a country's national patrimony may become depleted before the groundwork has been laid for sustainable development on the basis of other economic activities.

If the pessimism implied in these various explanations is valid, natural resource abundance may be seen as a curse rather than a blessing. By contrast, if such pessimism is not well founded, governments of resource-based economies would be ill-advised to allow it to influence policy decisions. This pessimism could very well lead governments to ignore their natural resource endowments and to proceed to a supposedly higher growth path via the production of other, non-resource-related goods. As a consequence, policy makers might adopt an anti-primary-sector, pro-industry policy without giving due consideration to the comparative advantage which resource abundant countries possess. In effect, several observers have stressed that the relationship between resource abundance and low economic growth is not a law; rather, it presents a challenge which appropriate policies can address in order to avoid the pitfalls.

There are in fact a number of countries which are characterized by natural resource abundance and which have achieved rapid economic growth. It has sometimes been overlooked that the country with the highest annual average growth rate of per capita income over the last 25 years is not one of the Asian tigers, but the resource-based economy of Botswana. In addition, the dynamism of other rapidly growing countries has often been supported by resource-based activities; several countries in South-East Asia and Latin America provide examples of this.

The question therefore arises: what are the lessons that can be learned from such success stories and how can their example be emulated by other resource-based economies?

It is clear that both price and non-price factors have played a role in the experience of successful countries. But whether price or non-price factors play the dominant role in the development of resource-based economies is still a matter of some controversy. Some countries have a long record of sound macroeconomic policies and have reacted very quickly whenever economic policies have started to create imbalances. Many other countries have adopted policy reform and taken important steps towards achieving a sustainable macroeconomic policy stance. In these countries, adjustment policies, particularly in agriculture, have tended to focus on increasing producer prices as well as the prices of inputs such as fertilizer, credit and water. This has been accompanied by changes in exchange rates and by institutional reform of parastatals, such as centralized marketing boards, which were generally the institutions through which the government taxed farmers. Although such policy adjustments have produced favourable short-term results, initial successes were not sustained in a number of cases. Some may argue that the slow supply response to the reform of price factors is due to policy slippages, while others would say that it is still too early to assess the impact of such reform.

In contrast to these views, it has also been argued that supply response has been hampered by other constraints, such as the inadequate availability of extension services and of infrastructure and yield-increasing technologies. It would appear, for example, that the availability of appropriate transportation and communication facilities, as well as of technology and human skills, has been crucial in the experience of successful countries. Since such factors are public goods, changes in relative market prices are not likely to increase their supply.

Participants in the debate on development policies in general, and the debate in natural resource economies in particular, may be divided into those who favour cross-country analysis with a view to identifying some general patterns of policies which have been found to further economic development, and those who argue that each country has its particularities and that only by studying these can valid inferences be made about how to emulate success in other countries. This book brings together both cross-country and country-case studies in an attempt to analyse what made the successful countries perform better than would be expected from cross-country analyses.

THEMES

Five sets of questions and issues are of central interest to the present study:

1. Is there a direct link between natural resource abundance and low economic growth, for example, because unskilled labour and natural resource intensive activities can be a technological dead end, unconducive to the productivity enhancement and indigenous learning upon which ongoing development is now generally believed to depend? Or is this statistical relationship driven indirectly through the increased difficulty in resource abundant countries in creating an appropriate institutional framework and set-up for policy making?
2. Do resource rich countries differ from other countries with respect to both the speed at which new technology is created and adopted and the accumulation of human capital, that is, two factors which have been prominent in the recent literature on economic growth?
3. Does trade liberalization in countries with natural resource abundance have adverse effects on their economic development since it tends to shift the allocation of resources towards activities which use natural resources intensively, while skill- and capital-intensive activities are a more powerful motor of economic growth? Or does trade liberalization have favourable growth effects because it removes the distortionary effects of trade barriers which hamper product upgrading and facilitates the transfer of technology, thereby increasing the demand for skill-intensive activities?
4. Is there a difference between mineral- and agriculture-based economies regarding an appropriate institutional set-up, given that minerals are non-renewable resources while agriculture uses renewable resources? Is a

  mineral revenue stabilization fund an appropriate and practicable instrument to avoid Dutch disease effects?
5.   How does the exploitation of natural resources affect the sustainability
      of economic activities, given that it may lead to an unequal distribution
      of environmental damage and socioeconomic benefits among different
      parts of the population?

PRESENTATION

This book has five parts. Part One concentrates on cross-section studies which
set the experience of individual countries in context. Part Two analyses development experiences of mineral economies, while Part Three emphasizes development experiences in agriculture. These three parts look at the issues of development policies in natural resource economies from a macroeconomic perspective, while Part Four is concerned with microeconomic issues, including those
relating to the sustainability of resource exploitation in environmental terms.
Part Five draws conclusions about how the successful performers have tackled
the above questions and discusses policy recommendations for natural resource
economies.

   Chapter 2, by Jeffrey Sachs and Andrew Warner, presents a cross-country
econometric analysis of the relationship between natural resource abundance
and economic growth. The authors point to direct and indirect effects through
which resource abundance has tended to depress growth over the past 20 years.
The direct effects are analysed in a dynamic Dutch disease model which stresses
production externalities and increasing returns to scale in education and on-the-
job training in manufacturing. The indirect effects are considered in a political
economy framework emphasizing the quality of institutions and policy choices,
including the degree of trade openness.

   In Chapter 3, Adrian Wood uses the often-disputed but widely used
Heckscher–Ohlin theory of trade to test whether cross-country differences in
export composition (manufactures, processed and unprocessed primary products) can be explained through differences in endowments with skills, labour
and natural resources. The influence of differences in the degree of trade openness is also analysed. The objective of this analysis is to see whether natural
resource rich countries can be advised to emulate the export-led industrialization development strategy which was successfully applied by the natural resource poor newly industrialized economies in East Asia.

   Part Two starts with Richard Auty's contribution, which provides the bridge
from cross-country to country case studies, as his chapter has features of both
methodologies. He focuses on the required policy adjustments during a mineral
economy's transition from a youthful stage, when mineral activities expand rap-

idly, through early maturity, which is marked by a sustained slow-down in mining expansion, to late maturity, when the mineral sector loses its major economic influence. The case studies discuss how such policy adjustments have been managed in Indonesia, Trinidad and Tobago, Botswana, Chile and Peru.

Modise D. Modise discusses in Chapter 5 how Botswana, whose economy depends heavily on the exploitation of diamond resources, has achieved very high annual average growth rates of per capita GDP over the last 25 years. He stresses the exceptional features of diamonds as a resource and discusses practical ways of managing mineral revenues with a view to avoiding Dutch disease effects.

In Chapter 6, Abbas Alnasrawi analyses the development experience of the oil-based economy of Iraq, focusing on the use of oil revenue and the impact of external shocks on the Iraqi economy.

Part Three contains country case studies related to renewable resources. In Chapter 7, Raanan Katzir outlines Israel's transition from extensive traditional agriculture to intensive export-oriented agriculture. He emphasizes the roles played by extensive agricultural research and the setting up of an institutional framework which guarantees close interaction between the government, farmers, researchers and extension workers on a continuous basis.

In Chapter 8, Rabbi Poobal Royan examines the transition of the Malaysian economy from natural resource dependence to industrialization. He focuses on research and rapid technological change in the natural resource sector and on the flexible adjustment of economic policies to changing circumstances and needs, which has been based on the perspective that the joint development of the natural resource sector and resource-based manufacturing offers dynamic complementarities.

Phillip Muema deals in Chapter 9 with Kenya's exports of horticultural products, which have been among the few categories in the natural resource sector to have experienced dynamic demand on world markets over the past few years. He also addresses tenure systems and ownership structures in agriculture.

Samuel Appiah examines in Chapter 10 the evolution of the forestry sector in Ghana, focusing on competitiveness in wood processing, sustainable forest management and the role of institutional factors, such as the competitive allocation of logging rights.

Part Four turns from the macroeconomic perspective to the local level. In Chapter 11, Ligia Noronha looks at mineral exploitation in the Indian province of Goa, stressing issues related to the fact that local communities are burdened with the adverse environmental and social impacts of resource exploitation, while the main economic benefits of the latter accrue at the national level.

In Chapter 12, L.T. Chitsike explains the rationale, objectives, institutional set-up and achievements of the Communal Areas Management Programme for

Indigenous Resources (CAMPFIRE) in Zimbabwe, which has become the most successful management system of a resource-based area in Africa.

Conclusions and policy implications are summarized in Part Five.

NOTE

1. The opinions expressed in this chapter are those of the author and do not necessarily reflect the views of UNCTAD.

REFERENCES

Barro, R. (1991), 'Economic growth in a cross section of countries', *Quarterly Journal of Economics*, **106**, 407–44.

Grossman, G. and Helpman, E. (1991), *Innovation and Growth in the Global Economy*, Cambridge (Mass.) and London: MIT Press.

Lucas, R. (1988), 'On the mechanics of economic development', *Journal of Monetary Economics*, **22**, 3–42.

Lucas, R. (1993), 'Making a miracle', *Econometrica*, **61**, 251–72.

North, D.C. (1990), *Institutions, Institutional Change and Economic Performance*, Cambridge: Cambridge University Press.

Romer, P. (1986), 'Increasing returns and long-run growth', *Journal of Political Economy*, **94**, 1002–37.

Romer, P. (1990), 'Endogenous technological change', *Journal of Political Economy*, **98**, S71–S102.

Stiglitz, J. (1996), 'Some lessons from the East Asian miracle', *World Bank Research Observer*, **11**, 151–77.

Summers, R. and Heston, A. (1991), 'The Penn world table (mark 5): an expanded set of international comparisons, 1950–1988', *Quarterly Journal of Economics*, **106**, 327–68.

World Bank (1995), *Global Economic Prospects and the Developing Countries*, Washington, DC: World Bank.

PART ONE

Resource Endowments and the Options
for Development Policy

2. Natural Resource Intensity and Economic Growth

Jeffrey D. Sachs and Andrew M. Warner[1]

One of the surprising features of economic life is that resource poor economies often vastly outperform resource rich economies in economic growth (Sachs and Warner, 1995b). The basic pattern is evident in Figure 2.1, where we graph each country's annual growth rate between 1970 and 1989 in relation to its natural-resource-based exports in 1971, measured as a percentage of GDP. Resource-based exports are defined as agriculture, minerals and fuels. On average, countries with a high value of resource-based exports to GDP tend to have a lower growth rate. In this chapter, we examine further what is responsible for this inverse relationship.

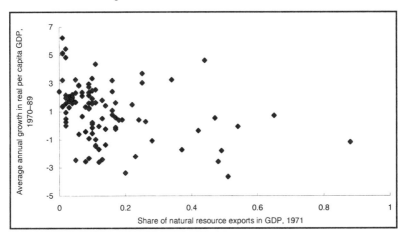

Figure 2.1 Natural resource abundance and economic growth

Before doing so, we should mention that many previous researchers have noted the problems of resource intensive economies in the 1970s and 1980s. Important earlier findings of the failures of resource-led development include several outstanding works, such as the volume of papers edited by Neary and van Wijnbergen (1986), a series of studies by Alan Gelb, culminating in Gelb (1988), and several key studies by Auty, most comprehensively in Auty (1990). These studies suggest many of the economic and political factors that may have played a role in the disappointing performance of resource abundant economies and so provide a basis for some of the hypotheses tested later in this chapter on the cross-country data.

A common element in much of the modern thinking on natural resource intensity is that resource abundance blocks countries from the kind of beneficial structural change that often accompanies the development process. In the first section of this chapter we discuss a formal model (the model itself is provided in Appendix 1) to demonstrate that this kind of effect can indeed happen in a general equilibrium growth model, and in so doing we point to some of the key assumptions required to sustain this argument. After presenting this evidence, we discuss some further reasons that may account for the result in Figure 2.1. The final section of this chapter presents empirical work that examines the evidence for several possible linkages between natural resources and slow growth.

RESOURCE ABUNDANCE AND SLOW GROWTH

There are a large number of hypotheses that can be formulated to account for the negative relationship shown in Figure 2.1 (in addition to the hypothesis, discarded in Sachs and Warner (1995b), that this negative relationship is purely spurious). One early explanation of the phenomenon is social: that easy riches lead to sloth. The sixteenth-century French political philosopher Jean Bodin asserted as much when he claimed that 'Men of a fat and fertile soil are most commonly effeminate and cowards; whereas contrariwise a barren country makes men temperate by necessity, and by consequence careful, vigilant, and industrious'.[2]

We see that the idea of a hidden curse attached to easy riches has been around for a long time. In the more modern theoretical literature, the curse often hinges on an assumption that large natural resource sectors or booms in commodity prices serve to draw economic resources away from growth-promoting activity. There are shades of this theme in development literature in the 1940s and 1950s, and in the Dutch disease models of the 1970s and 1980s, although these models typically analyse comparative static exercises rather than the growth process explicitly.

Related work by Hirschman (1958), Seers (1964) and Baldwin (1966) promoted the view that beneficial 'forward and backward linkages' between primary exports and the rest of the economy would be small. The basic idea was that manufacturing, as opposed to natural resource production, leads to a more complex division of labour and hence to a higher standard of living. This negative assessment of resource-based development in due course led to revisionist literature describing successful cases of staples-led growth, for example Roemer (1970) on Peru, and further success cases reviewed in Lewis (1989).

The global commodity price booms of the 1970s promoted additional research into the economics of natural resource booms. An excellent summary of the literature can be found in the volume edited by Neary and van Wijnbergen (1986). The salient issues were whether resource booms promoted de-industrialization, and the macroeconomic policy responses to natural resource booms. The relationship between natural resource abundance and growth was not an explicit focus of this literature, but inevitably there is a considerable amount of overlap between this question and the questions studied in the Dutch disease literature.

As emphasized in Dutch disease models, the existence of large natural-resource-producing sectors or booms in natural resource sectors will affect the distribution of employment throughout the economy. This points to one possible way in which natural resource abundance can affect growth. Matsuyama (1992) has provided an endogenous growth model of the related issue of the role of agriculture in economic development. In Matsuyama's model there are two sectors: agriculture and manufacturing. Manufacturing is characterized by learning-by-doing that is external to individual firms and is thus not properly taken into account in their decisions. The rate of human capital accumulation in the economy is proportional to total sectoral production, not to the production of an individual firm. Forces which push the economy away from manufacturing and towards agriculture lower the economy's rate of growth by reducing the learning-induced growth of manufacturing. This externality makes the market equilibrium inefficient. In this context, Matsuyama shows that trade liberalization in a land-intensive economy could actually slow economic growth by inducing the economy to shift resources away from manufacturing and towards agriculture.

In Matsuyama's model, the adverse effects of agricultural production arise because the agricultural sector directly employs the factors of production that would otherwise be used in manufacturing. Such a framework may be useful for studying labour-intensive production of natural resources, as in agriculture, but is less relevant for a natural resource sector such as oil production, which uses very little labour and therefore does not directly draw employment from manufacturing. However, it is not difficult to extend Matsuyama's point to a setting that is more appropriate for natural-resource-intensive economies, using the framework of the Dutch disease models.

We present such a model in Appendix 1 to this chapter. In our version of the Dutch disease model, the economy has three sectors: a tradable natural resource sector, a tradable (non-resource) manufacturing sector and a non-traded sector. Capital and labour are used in the manufacturing and non-traded sectors, but not in the natural resource sector. The greater the natural resource endowment, the higher the demand for non-tradable goods, and consequently the smaller the allocation of labour and capital to the manufacturing sector. Thus, when natural resources are abundant, tradables production is concentrated in them rather than in manufacturing, and capital and labour that otherwise might be employed in manufacturing are pulled into the non-traded goods sector. As a corollary, when an economy experiences a resource boom (either an improvement in the terms of trade or a resource discovery), the manufacturing sector tends to shrink and the non-traded goods sector tends to expand.

The shrinkage of the manufacturing sector is dubbed the 'disease', although there is nothing harmful about the decline in manufacturing if neoclassical competitive conditions prevail in the economy. The Dutch disease can be a real disease, however – and a source of chronic slow growth – if there is something special about the sources of growth in manufacturing, such as the 'backward and forward linkages' stressed by Hirschman and others, if such linkages constitute production externalities, or the learning-by-doing stressed by Matsuyama. If manufacturing is characterized by positive externalities in production, the shrinkage of the manufacturing sector caused by resource abundance can lead to a socially inefficient decline in growth. The economy loses the benefits of the external economies or increasing returns to scale in manufacturing. In the model in Appendix 1, the key assumption for this effect is equation (8), which has the rate of growth of human capital depending on the share of value added in the manufacturing sector.

We now summarize two main points that emerge from the model. First, quite simply, economies with larger resource sectors will grow more slowly, assuming that no resource boom occurs. Second, a temporary resource boom can lead to patterns in the path of GDP as illustrated in Figure 2.2. In this figure, the boom causes short run euphoria as GDP jumps up, but it also sets in motion a period of slow growth. The adverse effect of this on GDP is only gradually apparent, as the formerly booming economy successively looses ground to other economies without natural resources. Even if the booming economy eventually reverts to its pre-boom growth rate, it may still have a permanently lower level of GDP than the other economy. Measured growth will also probably be lower, although one can see from the figure that there are important issues about the period over which growth is measured and the appropriate way to control for natural resource booms.

It is important to stress, however, that the negative effect of large resource endowments on growth need not depend on the presence of production externalities in manufacturing, but instead could result from increasing returns to scale in education or job training. Consider the following simple example. Suppose that an increase in workers' education increases the productivity of labour

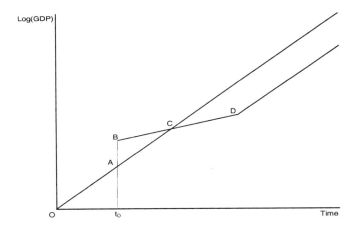

Figure 2.2   Resource boom and economic growth

in manufactures, but not in the non-tradable sector. Thus, a young person incurs the costs of education only if he or she expects to be employed in the manufacturing sector. Suppose further that the education production function is such that the skill level of a school graduate is a multiple, greater than one, of the skill level of the teacher (herein lie the increasing returns). In an overlapping generations model, a resource rich economy can arrive at a stationary state in which each generation chooses to forgo education and to work directly in the non-tradable sector, since the price and hence market wage in that sector are above the marginal product of labour in manufacturing. In a resource poor economy, by contrast, workers will move into manufactures and will have the incentive to invest in education, since higher-skilled manufacturing workers earn a premium over uneducated workers. The education process will produce not only skilled workers, but also more skilled teachers in the next generation. This in turn will lead to yet greater skills among the school graduates of the following generation. It is easy to see that a virtuous circle of endogenous growth can result, in which each generation chooses to become educated and each thereby reaches a higher level of skills than the preceding generation.

Another famous set of arguments focuses not on the domestic-economy consequences of natural resource abundance, but instead on the global conditions of the natural resource industry. For one reason or another, the general theme has been that natural resources were likely to be a declining industry at the world level. The famous hypothesis of Raul Prebisch (United Nations Economic Commission for Latin America, 1950) and Hans Singer (1950) of a secular decline in the terms of trade of primary commodities *vis-à-vis* manufactures can be put into this category. They argued that resource-based growth would be frustrated by this secular decline in the terms of trade. Closely related views stated that world demand for primary products would inevitably fall behind world demand for manufactures or that productivity growth would be faster in manufacturing than in natural resource production.

The 'Prebisch hypothesis' of declining relative prices of raw materials was widely taken to mean that developing countries should avoid their dependence on natural resource exports by promoting industrialization. The great historical mistake in this thinking, promoted for example by the United Nations Economic Commission for Latin America, was to recommend industrialization through prolonged import substitution behind tariff and quota barriers, rather than through export promotion. Inward-looking state-led industrialization foundered almost everywhere it was attempted (see Sachs and Warner, 1995a, for a recent cross-country analysis of the adverse effects of this long-term growth strategy).

An alternative approach lies in the area of political economy. Natural resource production typically generates very high economic rents. Some have argued that this inevitably leads to greater corruption and inefficient bureaucracies. Gelb (1988), in particular, stresses that governments typically earned most of the rents from natural resource exploitation. Lane and Tornell (1995) have argued in a formal model that resource rich economies are subject to more extreme rent-seeking behaviour than resource poor economies, as national politics are oriented towards grabbing the rents earned by natural resource endowments. In their model, a windfall coming from terms-of-trade improvement or the discovery of natural resource deposits can lead to a 'feeding frenzy' in which competing factions fight for the natural resource rents and end up inefficiently exhausting the public good. The case studies in Gelb (1988) and Auty (1990) lend support to the existence of these political channels of influence.

A final set of arguments focuses not on the size of the resource endowment but on the world price volatility that is associated with natural resources. It is well known that world prices for primary commodities have been more volatile than world prices for other goods. This probably translates into greater *ex ante* uncertainty for primary commodity producers. Greater uncertainty can reduce factor accumulation as a result of greater risk or because it raises the option value of waiting. There is also the related idea that commodity price forecasts in the 1970s and 1980s turned out to be systematically biased, specifically too optimistic, and this served to encourage large public investments in projects that were hugely inefficient when the price forecasts turned out to be incorrect. As a result, the argument goes, the natural resource intensive economies ended up with more inappropriate capital on their hands than other economies.

Having summarized a number of theoretical arguments on the links between natural resource abundance and growth, we examine in the next section cross-country evidence regarding possible channels of influence in a preliminary attempt to narrow the range of theoretical possibilities identified in this section.

PATHWAYS CONNECTING RESOURCE INTENSITY AND ECONOMIC GROWTH

In this section we present some preliminary evidence to better understand what lies behind the negative relationship between natural resource intensity and growth. We start by listing a number of possible channels. One hypothesis is that high natural resource abundance leads to increased rent-seeking, corruption and poorer overall government efficiency. In this connection, we note that Political Risk Services, the company that produces the rule of law index, also produces an index for bureaucratic quality. The simple correlation between this variable and the rule of law variable is 0.98, and so the variables are nearly identical from a statistical point of view, even though they are given different labels. Hence, the data do not permit sharp distinctions between rule of law and bureaucratic quality, and it is best to regard the rule of law variable as a general index for the efficiency of legal and government institutions. In any case, we will see if there is any evidence that resource intensity works through this variable in affecting growth. We allow for the fact that poor government institutions may depress growth directly or indirectly by depressing investment demand.

A second hypothesis is that great resource wealth has encouraged developing countries to pursue protectionist, state-led development strategies as they try to combat the Dutch disease effects of resource abundance. This inward-looking development may result in lower investment rates and/or low growth rates directly, even controlling for investment rates. A third hypothesis is that countries with higher natural resource abundance would have higher overall demand and higher relative prices of non-traded goods. This might affect the relative prices of investment goods (which have a large traded component), with effects on investment rates and growth. A final hypothesis is that high resource abundance leads to increased aggregate demand that shifts labour away from sectors with high learning-by-doing and thus depresses growth in labour productivity, as in the Dutch disease-cum-learning model in Appendix 1. This effect, as well as further unspecified effects, may be captured by a variable representing resource abundance (SXP in the growth equation below) that enters directly into the growth equation, after controlling for trade policy and the quality of government institutions.

We summarize this discussion of the direct and indirect effects of resource intensity on growth with the following set of equations. We view this model as a starting point for exploration, rather than as a definitive structural model of the pathways from resource abundance to growth (see Appendix 2 for a full description of the variables):

$$GEA7089 = \alpha_0 + \alpha_1 * SXP + \alpha_2 * SOPEN + \alpha_3 * INV7089 + \alpha_4 * RL + \alpha_5 * LGDP70 + \alpha_6 DTT7189 + \varepsilon_1$$

$$INV7089 = \beta_0 + \beta_1 * LPIP70 + \beta_2 * RL + \beta_3 * SOPEN + \beta_4 * SXP + \varepsilon_2 \qquad (1.2)$$

$$SOPEN = \theta_0 + \theta_1 * SXP + \theta_2 * SXP^2 + \theta_3 * LAND + \varepsilon_3 \qquad (1.4)$$

$$RL = \eta_0 + \eta_1 * SXP + \eta_2 * LGDP70 + \varepsilon_4 \qquad (2.4)$$

$$LPIP70 = \gamma_0 + \gamma_1 * SXP + \gamma_2 * LGDPEA70 + \gamma_3 * SOPEN + \varepsilon_5 \qquad (2.4)$$

In the first regression, which is discussed in detail in Sachs and Warner (1995b), growth per economically active population between 1970 and 1990 (GEA7089) is regressed on the log of initial GDP per economically active population (LGDPEA70) and the share of primary exports in GDP in 1971 (SXP). SOPEN measures the fraction of years between 1965 and 1989 that the country was integrated with the global economy (see Sachs and Warner, 1995a, for details on the formal criteria). A country that was open every year between 1965 and 1989 received a value SOPEN = 1. A country that was always closed during these years received a value SOPEN = 0. The other variables in the first equation are designed to control for capital accumulation, institutional quality and global commodity price shocks. The variables considered are INV7089, the investment to GDP ratio averaged over the period 1970–89; RL, the rule of law variable used in Knack and Keefer (1994); and DTT7189, the log change of the ratio of export to import prices between 1971 and 1989 (we do not use 1990 data, so as to avoid the temporary spike in oil prices associated with the Gulf crisis).

The numbers of the other equations correspond to regressions in two tables, Tables 2.1 and 2.2. For example, the second equation above is given the number (1.2) because these estimates are reported in Table 2.1, regression 2. LPIP70 is the log of the ratio of the investment deflator to the overall GDP deflator in 1970. This variable measures the price of investment goods relative to overall prices. Several recent studies, for example Warner (1994) and Taylor (1994), have found this or similar variables to be significant determinants of investment rates, with a higher price of investment goods associated with a lower rate of investment relative to GDP. Both price indexes, for investment goods and for the GDP deflator, are taken from version 5.6 of the Summers and Heston (1991) data.

Clearly, this is an oversimplified model, with particularly inadequate explanations for RL and SOPEN. We present the results merely as an initial foray into a more structured assessment of the pathways from SXP to growth. We have tried to estimate this as a system with instrumental variables, but it turns out that the instruments suggested by the model above do not have sufficient sample variation to obtain meaningful estimates. Estimation as a system without instrumental variables yields estimates which are close to the single-equation least squares estimates. For simplicity, we present least squares estimates, viewing

Table 2.1   Associations between natural resource abundance and other explanatory variables

	Dependent variables				
	National saving % GDP 1970–89	Investment ratio % GDP 1970–89	Human capital accumulation change 1970–90	Share of years open 1965–89	Relative price of investment goods 1970–89
	(NS7089)	(INV7089)	(DTYR7090)	(SOPEN)	(LPIP70)
	(1.1)	(1.2)	(1.3)	(1.4)	(1.5)
LGDP70	6.23 (7.84)	–	0.09 (0.86)	–	–0.23 (–4.64)
SXP	8.07 (1.65)	0.09 (1.56)	–0.24 (–0.32)	–1.99 (–2.65)	0.20 (0.92)
SXP^2	–	–	–	3.50 (3.30)	–
SOPEN	–	0.06 (2.88)	–	–	–0.31 (–2.94)
RL	–	0.01 (2.65)	–	–	–
LPIP70	–	–0.05 (–2.97)	–	–	–
LAND	–	–	–	–0.09 (–3.51)	–
Adjusted R^2	0.39	0.59	–0.01	0.20	0.45
Sample size	103	75	86	102	99
Standard error	7.30	0.05	0.82	0.40	0.35
Mean dep. var.	16.35	0.21	1.54	0.39	0.43

Note: The numbers in parentheses are *t*-statistics.

Table 2.2   Associations between quality of institutions and natural resource intensity

	Dependent variables				
	Government repudiation of contracts	Risk of expropriation	Corruption	Rule of law	Bureaucratic quality
	(GRC)	(RE)	(CORR)	(RL)	(BQ)
	(2.1)	(2.2)	(2.3)	(2.4)	(2.5)
Log Real GDP 1980	0.70	0.73	1.38	1.43	1.43
	(3.49)	(2.87)	(9.81)	(9.76)	(10.26)
SXP	–3.79	–4.93	–3.66	–4.98	–5.29
	(–3.73)	(–3.86)	(–4.16)	(–5.43)	(–6.07)
Adjusted R^2	0.22	0.20	0.56	0.58	0.61
Sample size	64	64	84	84	84
Standard error	1.35	1.70	1.30	1.35	1.29

Notes: The numbers in parentheses are *t*-statistics. The five measures of institutional quality are indexes constructed by the Center for Institutional Reform and the Informal Sector from data collected by Political Risk Services. They are based on survey data taken around 1982; hence we use real GDP in 1980 as the income variable. They are measured on the following scale, from low to high: government repudiation of contracts (0–10); risk of expropriation (0–10); corruption (0–6); rule of law (0–6); bureaucratic quality (0–6). The correlations between these institutional measures are all above 0.6. SXP is measured as a fraction, and so a unit increase in this variable is equivalent to an increase in the share of primary exports in GDP from 0 per cent to 100 per cent.

them as imperfect but still informative estimates of the pathways from natural resource abundance to growth.

Estimates of these equations, and related results, are in Tables 2.1 and 2.2. We have already seen some empirical support for the idea that the quality of legal and government institutions is positively associated with growth (Sachs and Warner, 1995b), although admittedly some estimated effects are only marginally significant. In Table 2.2 we present additional evidence that resource abundant countries have poorer scores on a variety of measures of institutional quality. (We should note that the five regressions in Table 2.2 do not represent independent information, because the dependent variables are highly correlated with each other.)

We also find evidence that natural resource abundance may affect growth indirectly through the extent of trade openness. First, we postulate, and find supporting evidence for, a U-shaped relationship between openness (measured as SOPEN, on the vertical axis) and resource intensity (measured as SXP, on the horizontal axis). Our reasoning is as follows. Resource abundance squeezes the manufacturing sector, as in the Dutch disease. In almost all countries, the squeeze of manufactures provokes some protectionist response that aims to promote industrialization despite the Dutch disease effects. For the most highly resource endowed economies, however, such as the oil-rich states of the Middle East, the natural resource base is so vast that there is no strong pressure to develop an extensive industrial sector (other than in oil-based sectors such as petrochemicals and refining). Thus, for the most extreme resource-based cases, openness to trade (SOPEN) would tend to be high. The overall effect would therefore be a U-shaped relationship between SXP and SOPEN.

There is statistical support for this idea in regression 1.4, where we find a negative estimated coefficient on the level of SXP and a positive coefficient on SXP^2. The dependent variable SOPEN is a fraction that ranges between 1 (if a country was open for the whole period 1965–89) and 0 (if a country was never open). The estimated trough of the 'U' is when the share of primary exports in GDP equals 0.28. For countries below that value – which is almost all countries in the sample – higher primary exports tend to promote economic closure (that is, a low value of SOPEN). Above that threshold, higher SXP tends to promote openness. Two interesting examples on the positive part of the U are Malaysia and Saudi Arabia. These countries are extremely resource rich, and also have had a long tradition of open trade. Note that for regression 1.4 explaining SOPEN, we exclude Somalia because it is an extreme outlier. The next two extreme outliers, as ranked by the DFITS criteria (see Belsley *et al.*, 1980, for these criteria), are Saudi Arabia and Australia. If we also exclude these countries, the estimated coefficients on SXP and SXP^2 both rise and are still statistically significant. Moreover, the estimated trough of the U remains at about 0.28, even with these countries excluded.

Since the vast majority of our countries have SXP values on the negatively sloped part of the U relationship, we evaluate the effect of SXP growth via SOPEN at the mean of SXP (0.128) along the negatively sloped part of the U-shaped relationship. Starting from the mean of SXP, our estimates imply that a unit standard deviation increase in SXP (that is, from 0.128 to 0.260) reduces SOPEN by 0.08. Since SOPEN measures the percentage of years between 1965 and 1989 that a country is rated as open, this estimate implies that a country with a value of SXP one standard deviation above the mean would have been open for two years less on average than a country with the mean value of SXP.

We also look at the cross-country relationship between natural resource abundance and four other variables: savings rates, investment rates, rates of human capital accumulation and the relative price of investment goods. First, regarding savings rates, we do not find strong evidence that resource abundant economies have higher savings rates. Simple bivariate data plots show that only three resource abundant economies, namely Gabon, Kuwait and Saudi Arabia, had unusually high average savings rates (over the period 1970–89). Another resource abundant country, Somalia, had an extremely low average saving rate. But if we exclude these four countries, there is no clear cross-country relationship. Moreover, even with the three high-savings countries included in the sample, and the low-saving country, Somalia, excluded, a regression of average saving rates on the level of GDP and SXP does not yield a significant coefficient on SXP (see regression 1.1 in Table 2.1). Therefore, although it is possible that a more elaborate study would change this conclusion, the simple evidence does not support a positive association between resource abundance and average savings.

We reach similar conclusions when we examine the data on investment and human capital association. As we show in regression 1.2 in Table 2.1, average investment rates are not significantly associated with natural resource abundance. There is some evidence of a positive relationship between investment and openness and the rule of law variable, and some evidence of a negative relationship with the relative price of investment goods, but after controlling for these variables no significant effect of natural resource intensity emerges. We also find little direct evidence that more resource-intensive countries have had significantly lower rates of human capital accumulation, as shown in regression 1.3. We have tried excluding outliers (Bahrain, the Republic of Korea and Kuwait) from the human capital regression and estimating stock-adjustment equations where the change in the human capital stock is regressed on the initial level of human capital, SXP and initial income, but we still find no effect of SXP on human capital accumulation.

In summary, we have attempted to find evidence for indirect effects of resource intensity on growth by looking at the cross-country relationship between resource intensity and possible explanatory variables in growth regressions. We find evidence that resource intensity has been related to institutional quality (as summarized by the variables in Table 2.2) and broad policy choice (as summarized by the SOPEN variable), but we find little evidence that it is related to human or physical capital accumulation or savings rates. We now turn to some simple calculations in an attempt to quantify both the direct and the indirect impact of resource intensity on growth.

One approach to determining the magnitude of the indirect effects of resource abundance on growth is to examine the size of the estimated SXP coefficient as we successively control for the additional variables. As reported in

Sachs and Warner (1995b) the estimated SXP coefficient is –5.38 in the growth regression that controls only for initial income; and –5.54 in the growth regression that controls for an additional seven variables. This evidence suggests that the indirect effects are not large; otherwise, the additional controls should drive the estimated coefficient on SXP towards zero as more variables are added to the growth regression.

Another approach is to calculate the size of the indirect effects using the estimated coefficients. We first consider the rule of law variable. Suppose we were to increase SXP by a unit standard deviation (0.13). The coefficient estimate in Table 2.2 implies that this would be associated with a reduction in the rule of law index of –0.65 (= 0.13*–4.98). To calculate the effect on GDP, recall that the dependent variable in the growth regression in Sachs and Warner (1995b) is 100/19*[ln(GDP89) – ln(GDP70)]. If we multiply both sides of the equation by 19/100, the estimated coefficient on RL in the growth equation times 19/100 is an estimate of δln(GDP89)/δRL, holding constant GDP in 1970. The 0.27 coefficient in the growth regression implies that δln(GDP89)/δRL = 0.05. Therefore, the full effect of a unit standard deviation increase in SXP on ln(GDP89) would be –0.65 * 0.05 = –0.033, equivalent to a reduction of only about 3.3 per cent in GDP89. Thus, according to this calculation, the indirect effect of resource intensity operating through the quality of legal and government institutions is not large.

We also examine the size of indirect effects operating through openness policy, as summarized by our SOPEN variable. If we allow SXP to rise one standard deviation from its mean, that is from 0.13 to 0.26, the estimates in regression 1.4 imply that δln(GDP89) would be –0.08 * 0.27 = –0.022, equivalent to a reduction of only about 2.2 per cent in GDP89. Again, this is not large. Even if we used one of the larger estimates of the SOPEN coefficient, such as 2.70 in regression 1.3, the full effect would rise to only –0.04.

Our main conclusion is that the estimated direct effect of SXP on growth is large in comparison with these estimates of the indirect effects. These results lend tentative support to the view that the dynamic Dutch disease effects we emphasize in the growth model in Appendix 1 of this chapter are quantitatively important. However, it may also be the case that the normal downward bias in estimated regression coefficients, due to measurement errors in the independent variables, serve to depress the estimated indirect effects more than the direct effects. Of course, we cannot precisely separate true effects from measurement bias with the data we have at hand.

SUMMARY AND CONCLUSIONS

What is the reason for the apparent curse of natural resources? Much remains uncertain, but we find evidence that resource intensive economies are more likely to have been closed to international trade and have particularly poor scores on international measures of bureaucratic efficiency and institutional quality. We find less evidence that resource abundant economies have lower investment rates or lower levels of human capital attainment.

We do not agree that this curse of natural resources is an iron law of political economy. First, in related research in progress, we find that this curse does not hold true as regards the nineteenth century or earlier decades of the twentieth century. Our hypothesis is that the crucial natural resources in these periods (coal and iron ore) were more costly to transport and therefore it was more important in the past to be located near the sources of natural resources. Today, Japan and the Republic of Korea can import crude oil at much lower cost, so it is not an important disadvantage.

We also think that there is much to be learned from studying the resource abundant developing economies that have done well in the recent past: Botswana, Chile, Malaysia and Mauritius. What, if anything, distinguishes these countries from other slow-growing resource intensive economies? One common fact is that these countries did not attempt aggressively to alter the composition of their exports away from natural resources. Malaysia and Mauritius, in particular, focused policy on export promotion rather than attempting to develop a domestic manufacturing base behind protectionist trade policies, as so many other developing countries did. Which is worse: the natural resource curse, or the policy errors made as countries attempt to avoid the curse?

In conclusion, although this chapter does find evidence for a negative relationship between natural resource intensity and subsequent growth, it would be a mistake to conclude that countries should subsidize or protect non-resource-based sectors as a basic strategy for growth. First, although the results here using highly aggregated data are suggestive, they are far from definitive. Second, as argued in Sachs and Warner (1995a), the evidence from the recent past suggests that there are simpler and more basic policies that can be followed to increase national growth rates, especially open trade. Third, the welfare implications of resource abundance can be quite different from the growth implications. Resource abundance may be good for consumption even if not good for growth; policies might be good for GDP growth, while reducing real consumption. Put differently, government policies to promote non-resource industries would entail direct welfare costs of their own, and these could easily be larger than the benefits from shifting out of natural resource industries.[3] We therefore regard the issue of appropriate growth-oriented policies for resource abundant countries as an open and important topic for further analysis.

APPENDIX 1: A MODEL OF RESOURCE ABUNDANCE AND SLOW GROWTH

The model is an overlapping-generations model where people live two periods: working and receiving a wage in the first period; and retiring in the second period. We first describe the supply side and then the demand side. This is followed by a section that describes the equilibrium and the dynamic solution of the model and finally the main propositions about the effects of a richer natural resource endowment on the path of GDP.

Supply Side

The production side of the model has three sectors: a traded manufacturing sector, for which we use the superscript m, a non-traded sector, for which we use the superscript n, and a natural resource sector described by R or the superscript r. The natural resource sector produces a constant flow of natural resources in each period, which we denote by R. Production in this sector employs no capital or labour, and the resource output can be sold on world markets at an exogenous world price of p^r. For convenience, we choose units of R so that this price term need not appear in our equations. This model makes no distinction between resource booms that come about because of discoveries and resource booms that come about because of increases in resource prices.

In the two sectors that employ labour and capital, production functions are given by

$$X^m = G(L^m, K^m) \tag{1}$$

$$X^n = F(L^n, K^n) \tag{2}$$

The source of growth in this model is labour-augmenting technical change. We introduce a human capital variable, H, which can be thought of as the stock of knowledge in the economy. The key assumption is that the accumulation of knowledge is generated as a byproduct of employment in the traded manufacturing sector. This stock of knowledge raises the amount of effective labour by the same amount in *all* sectors, not just the traded sector. Hence the variable H multiplies the employment variables in each of the production functions. Normalizing the total labour force to 1, and letting the variable θ represent the *share* of labour in the traded sector, the production functions above may be written in the following way.

$$X^m = G(\theta H, K^m) \tag{3}$$

$$X^n = F((1-\theta)H, K^n) \tag{4}$$

We further assume that these functions are homogenous of degree one and can therefore be written in intensive form as

$$x^m = g(k^m) \tag{5}$$

$$x^n = f(k^n) \tag{6}$$

where lower case variables are denominated in units of effective labour. For example,

$$k^m = \frac{K^m}{\theta H}, \quad k^n = \frac{K^n}{(1-\theta)H}. \tag{7}$$

Having defined θ as the share of labour in the traded sector, we can now state explicitly the assumption that the accumulation of knowledge capital depends on the share of labour employed in the traded sector.

$$H_t = H_{t-1}(1+\theta_{t-1}) \tag{8}$$

Since the production functions can be written in intensive form, capital market equilibrium requires that capital is employed in each sector up to the point where the marginal product of capital per effective worker equals the world real interest rate. There are no adjustment costs in achieving the desired capital stocks.

$$p^n f'(k^n) = r \tag{9}$$

$$g'(k^m) = r \tag{10}$$

The price p^n is the ratio of the price of the non-traded good to the price of traded manufactures. The price of manufactures is the numeraire and is thus set equal to 1. The relative price p^n is determined later in the model, but once determined, the equations immediately above will determine the equilibrium capital-labour ratios in each sector.

Competition and free entry in both sectors ensures that there are zero profits. These conditions are written below with $b(w,r)$ denoting the unit cost functions. For given values of the world real interest rate, these equations can be used to solve for the wage rate, w, and p^n as functions of r and the world price of the traded good, p^m, set to 1 below.

$$p^n = b_w^n(w,r)w + b_r^n(w,r)r \tag{11}$$

$$1 = b_w^m(w,r)w + b_r^m(w,r)r \tag{12}$$

Demand Side

Consumers solve the following inter-temporal consumption problem. Each generation works and receives a wage when young. It is also assumed that the government obtains the revenue from sale of the natural resource and simply transfers this in lump-sum fashion to each member of the young generation. The variable R measures the size of this resource transfer per effective worker of the young generation. Consumers can save for retirement at the world rate of interest to spread consumption across time.

$$Max\ U = \left[\ln(c_t^m) + \beta\ln(c_t^n)\right] + \delta\left[\ln(c_{t+1}^m) + \beta\ln(c_{t+1}^n)\right] \tag{13}$$

$$s.t.\ \ c_t^m + p_t^n c_t^n + \frac{1}{1+r}\left(c_{t+1}^m + p_{t+1}^n c_{t+1}^n\right) = w_t + R_t \tag{14}$$

This produces the following demand functions for each generation.

$$\frac{C_t^m}{H_t} = c_t^m = \frac{1}{(1+\beta)(1+\delta)}(w_t + R_t) \tag{15}$$

$$\frac{C_t^n}{H_t} = c_t^{\ n} = \frac{1}{p_t^{\ n}} \frac{\beta}{(1+\beta)(1+\delta)}(w_t + R_t) \tag{16}$$

$$\frac{C_{t+1}^m}{H_t} = c_{t+1}^{\ m} = \frac{\delta(1+r)}{(1+\beta)(1+\delta)}(w_t + R_t) \tag{17}$$

$$\frac{C_{t+1}^n}{H_t} = c_{t+1}^{\ n} = \frac{1}{p_{t+1}^{\ n}} \frac{\delta\beta(1+r)}{(1+\beta)(1+\delta)}(w_t + R_t) \tag{18}$$

To obtain total demand for each good in any given period, we sum these demand functions across generations. A complication is that with human capital accumulation, the amount of effective labour is increasing in each period. Since we choose to express the quantities in terms of units of effective young workers, this means that we have to convert the expressions that are implicitly in units of old workers to units of young workers. Specifically, if c^o is consumption of the old per old worker, then $H_{t-1}/H_t\, c^o$ would be consumption of the old, per young worker.

The equation below sums the demands across the two generations for the non-traded good in a given period. Total demand is expressed per units of effective young workers, with the term $1/1+\theta_{t-1}$ reflecting the adjustment from old to young workers.

$$c_t^{\ n} = \frac{1}{p_t^{\ n}} \frac{\beta}{(1+\beta)(1+\delta)}\left[w_t + R_t + \frac{\delta(1+r_{t-1})}{1+\theta_{t-1}}(w_{t-1} + R_{t-1})\right] \tag{19}$$

Equilibrium

The last equation needed to solve the model is that supply must equal demand in the non-traded sector.

$$c_t^{\ n} = f(k^n)(1-\theta_t) \tag{20}$$

The reason for the extra $1-\theta$ term on the right hand side of this equation is that c'' is in units of young workers in the whole economy, but $f(k'')$ is in units of young workers only in the non-traded sector, so $f()$ must be reduced to express the right hand side in units of total young workers. Substituting the expression for total non-traded demand from above, the non-traded equilibrium can be written explicitly as:

$$\frac{1}{p_t^n} \frac{\beta}{(1+\beta)(1+\delta)}\left[w_t + R_t + \frac{\delta(1+r_{t-1})}{1+\theta_{t-1}}(w_{t-1}+R_{t-1})\right] - f(k^n) + f(k^n)\,\theta_t = 0 \qquad (21)$$

For later reference it is convenient to write this function as:

$$\phi(R_t, R_{t-1}, \theta_t, \theta_{t-1}) = 0 \qquad (22)$$

We first consider the solution to the model for the case where there is no natural resource production. Equations 11 and 12 determine the real wage and the relative price of non-traded goods for given values of r. Given the non-traded price, equations 9 and 10 then determine the equilibrium capital labour ratios in each sector. To determine θ, note first that equation 21 (or 22) above is a first order, non-linear difference equation in θ, so that we can define a steady state value for θ implicitly by $\phi(0,0,\theta^{ss},\theta^{ss})=0$. However, we now check to see if the dynamics that this equation implies for θ are locally stable. To see this we calculate

$$\frac{d\theta_t}{d\theta_{t-1}} = \frac{\dfrac{1}{p_t^n}\dfrac{\delta\beta(1+r)}{(1+\beta)(1+\delta)(1+\theta^{ss})^2}(w_t)}{f(k^n)} \qquad (23)$$

Local stability requires that this derivative lies between zero and one. The expression is clearly positive. It is also less than one, as can be seen in the following way. If one multiplies both numerator and denominator by $H(1-\theta)$, then the denominator equals total production in the non-traded sector. Referring back to equation 18, the numerator becomes total consumption of non-traded goods by the older generation, multiplied by a term, $(1-\theta)/1+\theta)$, which is less than one. Since total production must exceed consumption by the older generation, the denominator must exceed the numerator and the expression must be less than one.

Stability guarantees that although θ will not jump immediately to its new equilibrium following a shock, it will do so gradually in a step by step fashion. Furthermore, with θ following dynamic step-by-step adjustment, it can be seen from 8 that the human capital variable H will also follow dynamic step-by-step adjustment. Once θ has reached its new steady state value, H will then grow continuously at the constant rate θ.

Growth of H then determines growth of other key variables. From the equations in (7) we know that once H is growing at rate θ and θ itself is fixed at its steady state value, the capital stocks in the two sectors will also grow at rate θ. Furthermore, since the production functions are homogenous of degree one, and both factors are growing at rate θ, output in both sectors will grow at rate θ.

To evaluate GDP growth we use the factor income decomposition of GDP.

$$GDP = R + wH + r(K^n + K^m) \qquad (24)$$

Since all terms except R grow at rate θ in the steady state, it is clear that the non-resource economy also grows at rate θ. However, because of the presence of the non-growing resource sector, total GDP grows at rate $\alpha\theta$, where α is the fraction of GDP in all sectors outside the natural-resource sector.

To evaluate effects on the level, as opposed to the growth, of GDP, we substitute for K^n and K^m in equation 23 and rearrange to obtain

$$GDP = R + H(w+r)[k^n + \theta(k^m - k^n)] \qquad (25)$$

With the model described in the equations above, we can now establish the main propositions.

Proposition 1. Economies that experience a temporary resource boom, will have a lower rate of growth for several periods after the boom than otherwise identical economies without resource booms.

This can be established by considering the effects of a one shot resource boom. Suppose R_1 is positive and all other R's are 0. If all world prices are constant, during the period up to and including period 0 the share of labour in manufacturing and therefore the growth of the economy will be determined by θ^{ss}. In period 1, θ_1 will be determined implicitly by $\phi(R_1, 0, \theta_1, \theta^{ss}) = 0$. With the younger generation wealthier in period 1 because of the resource boom, as long as they wish to spend some of their increased wealth in the first period on non-traded goods, demand will rise and draw labour from the traded sector to the non-traded sector. That is, θ_1 will be lower than θ^{ss}. In period 2, θ_2 will be determined implicitly by ϕ $(0,R_1,\theta_2,\theta_1) = 0$. There is again a direct demand effect on non-traded goods in period 2 from the resource boom in period 1. Now, the beneficiaries of the resource boom are the older generation. As long as they spend some of their higher wealth on non-traded goods in period 2, this direct demand effect will act to depress θ_2 relative to θ^{ss}. But there is also a second effect in period 2. That is, with a lower θ_1, there will be less effective people in the young generation in period 2 and demand by the wealthier old generation will carry a higher weight in economy-wide demand. This effect also serves to raise demand for the non-traded good relative to the case where there is no resource boom.

Since the magnitude of the direct demand effects in the two periods depend on preferences regarding inter-temporal consumption smoothing, we cannot establish which one is larger. Because of this, we cannot establish whether θ_1 exceeds θ_2, even though there is the additional effect depressing θ_2 in period 2. But it is clear that θ_2 will be less than θ^{ss}, because the direct demand effect cannot fall below 0, and the indirect effect works to depress θ. After period 2, the dynamics of θ take over and θ returns gradually to θ^{ss}. Overall, θ will fall below θ^{ss} for several periods after the resource boom in period 1, and the economy will grow slower than similar economies without resource booms.

Proposition 2. The effect of a rise in the natural resource endowment in period 1 on the level of non-resource GDP in period 1 depends on the capital intensities of the two sectors.

This can be seen by differentiating the expression for GDP in equation 24 with respect to R_1.

$$\frac{\partial GDP_1}{\partial R_1} = 1 + H_1(w+r)\frac{\partial \theta_1}{\partial R_1}(k^m - k^n) \tag{26}$$

The effect of a rise in R_1 on non-resource GDP is given by the second term on the right hand side. We know from proposition 1 that $d\theta_1/dR_1$ is negative. Hence non-resource GDP will initially rise with a rise in the resource endowment if the non-traded sector is more capital intensive than the traded sector, $k^n > k^m$.

The effect of an increase in natural resource intensity
We can now demonstrate what happens when an economy has a one-shot increase in the natural resource endowment R in period 1. Recalling the equations from above, we have the factor income decomposition of total GDP,

$$GDP = R + wH + r(K^n + K^m) \tag{27}$$

and after substituting for K^n and K^m and rearranging, we have:

$$GDP = R + H(w+r)[k^n + \theta(k^m - k^n)] \tag{28}$$

The one-shot rise in R will of course directly increase GDP in period 1, but it will also have a more subtle and prolonged effect on growth in subsequent periods. Suppose that the proceeds from the resource boom are transferred to the younger generation in period 1. The increase in wealth will raise demand in period 1, and some of the increased demand will fall on the non-traded good. This will draw labour from the manufacturing sector, that is θ will decline. We can see from the definition of GDP above that the decline in θ will have a contemporaneous effect on the level of GDP depending on the capital intensities in the two sectors. For example, if the non-traded sector is more capital intensive than the manufacturing sector, then the rise in employment in that sector will raise GDP by more than the decline in employment in manufacturing will lower GDP.

The change in sectoral employment will also have a more prolonged effect on accumulation of human capital and future growth. With a lower θ_1, human capital will be lower in period 2 than it would have been without the resource boom. Furthermore, even though the resource boom will have ended by period 2, the wealthier generation will still be living in period 2, and demand will still be higher than without the resource boom. This means that θ_2 will again be lower than otherwise and human capital accumulation will again be lower in period 3. Thereafter, as described above, θ will climb gradually back to the steady state level but, of course, human capital accumulation, physical capital accumulation, and growth will be slower in the intervening period.

It is possible then, that the full effect of the one-shot resource boom is to raise the level of GDP initially, but reduce the growth rate by enough that the level of GDP eventually falls below that of a non-booming economy. This case of long-run immiseration as a result of a resource boom is illustrated in Figure 2.2. Initially, both economies start with the same level and growth rate of GDP, so that the log of GDP follows the straight line between points O and A. Then, at time t_0, the resource boom causes the level of GDP in one economy to rise immediately, say to point B. But the resource boom also ushers in a period of slower growth, so that it is possible for GDP to fall below that of the other economy, illustrated by point C. Starting at point D, the two economies again have the same growth rate, but the economy which formerly had the resource boom will have a permanently lower level of GDP.

APPENDIX 2: DESCRIPTIONS AND SOURCES OF VARIABLES

LGDPEA70   Natural log of real purchasing-power-parity-adjusted GDP per economically active population in 1970. GDP data from Summers and Heston Penn World Tables version 5.6 (in 1985 international prices); economically active population (defined as ages 15–64) from the World Bank, *World Data, 1995*.

GEA7089   Average annual growth in real GDP per economically active population between 1970 and 1989. Based on the same sources as LGDPEA70.

SXP   Share of natural resource exports in GDP in 1971. Taken from the World Bank, *World Tables, 1993* data diskette. Both numerator and denominator are measured in nominal dollars. The dollar GDP data in the *World Tables* uses a smoothed exchange rate to convert local currency GDP to dollars. Primary exports are the sum of the categories 'nonfuel primary products' and 'fuels'. Non-fuel primary products cover Standard International Trade Classification (SITC) categories 0, 1, 2, 4 and 68. Fuels cover SITC category 3. These categories are from revision 1 of the SITC.

SOPEN   The fraction of years during the period 1965–89 in which the country is rated as an open economy according to the criteria in Sachs and Warner (1995).

INV7089   Ratio of real gross domestic investment (public plus private) to real GDP, averaged over the period 1970–89. Source: Barro and Lee (1994), who in turn used Summers and Heston (Penn World Tables) version 5.5.

RL   Rule of law index. This is an index constructed by the Center for Institutional Reform and the Informal Sector (IRIS) from data printed in the *International Country Risk Guide*, published by Political Risk Services. This variable 'reflects the degree to which the citizens of a country are willing to accept the established institutions to make and implement laws and adjudicate disputes'. Scored 0 (low) to 6 (high). Measured as of 1982. See Knack and Keefer (1994) for further details.

BQ   Bureaucratic quality index. See the sources for RL. A high score means 'autonomy from political pressure', and 'strength and expertise to govern without drastic changes in policy or interruptions in government services'. Scored 0–6.

CORR   Corruption in government index. See the sources for RL. A low score means 'illegal payments are generally expected

	throughout . . . government' in the form of 'bribes connected with import and export licenses, exchange controls, tax assessments, police protection, or loans'. Scored 0–6.
RE	Risk of expropriation index. See RL for sources. Scored 0–10, with lower scores for high risk of 'outright confiscation' or 'forced nationalization'.
GRC	Government repudiation of contracts index. See RL for sources. Scored 0–10, with a low score indicating high 'risk of a modification in a contract taking the form of a repudiation, postponement or scaling down'.
DTT7189	Change in the log of the external terms of trade between 1971 and 1989. DTT7189 = LN(TT89) – LN(TT71), where TT is the ratio of a US dollar export price index (1987 = 100) to an import price index in similar units. Source: World Bank, *World Tables, 1993*. Data for Taiwan Province of China were obtained from the *Taiwan Statistical Data Book, 1992*. Data for South Africa were obtained from *Bulletin of Statistics*, Pretoria, December 1972 and June 1992.
ASIA	Dummy variable equal to 1 for Asian countries, 0 otherwise.
SSAFRICA	Dummy variable equal to 1 for sub-Saharan African countries, 0 otherwise.
LAMERICA	Dummy variable equal to 1 for Latin American countries, 0 otherwise.
LAND	The log of the ratio of total land area to population in 1971. The land data are from Table 1 of the Food and Agriculture Organization's (FAO) 1971 *Production Yearbook*. For a few countries with incomplete data in that publication, we use the data in the 1993 *Production Yearbook*.
NS7089	National saving as a percentage of GDP. Source: World Bank, *World Data, 1995*, CD-Rom.
LPIP70	The log of the ratio of the investment deflator to the GDP deflator in 1970. The deflators are the PPP deflators reported in version 5.6 of the Penn World Tables (see Summers and Heston, 1991, for a description of an earlier version of these data). In the Summers and Heston notation, LPIP70 = ln(PI/P), using 1970 data.
DTYR7090	Change in the total years of education in the population over the age of 15 from 1970 to 1990. Source: Barro and Lee (1996).

NOTES

1. This chapter draws on our earlier paper 'Natural resource abundance and economic growth', National Bureau of Economic Research Working Paper no. 5398, Cambridge (Mass.), 1995. The reader is referred to that paper for the evidence documenting an inverse relationship between natural resource abundance and economic growth. We are grateful to Richard Auty, William Easterly, Jörg Mayer, Alan Taylor, Jeffrey Vincent and participants in the UNCTAD expert meeting on 'Development Policies in Resource-based Economies, Geneva, 21-22 November 1996.
2. Cited in Holmes (1995, p. 109).
3. Nor should our results be taken to deny that there are benefits from good policies regarding natural resource exploitation. Compare, for example, the experiences of the primary producers in Asia, namely Malaysia, Indonesia and Thailand, with those in Africa (see Roemer, 1994).

REFERENCES

Auty, R.M. (1990), *Resource-based Industrialization: Sowing the Oil in Eight Developing Countries*, New York: Oxford University Press.

Baldwin, R.E. (1966), *Economic Development and Export Growth: A Study of Northern Rhodesia, 1920-1960*, Berkeley and Los Angeles: University of California Press.

Barro, R.J. and J. Lee (1994), *Data Set for a Panel of 138 Countries*, available on the Internet (http://www.nber.org/pub/barro.lee).

Barro, R.J. and J. Lee (1996), 'International data on education', mimeo, Cambridge (Mass.): Harvard University, January.

Belsley, D.A., E. Kuh and R.E. Welsch (1980), *Regression Diagnostics*, New York: John Wiley.

Bodin, J. (1962), *The Six Books of a Commonwealth* [Les six Livres de la République], trans. R. Knolles, ed. K.D. McRae, Cambridge (Mass.): Harvard University Press.

Gelb, A.H. (1988), *Windfall Gains: Blessing or Curse?*, New York: Oxford University Press.

Hirschman, A.O. (1958), *The Strategy of Economic Development*, New Haven (Conn.): Yale University Press.

Holmes, S. (1995), *Passions and Constraints*, Chicago: University of Chicago Press.

Knack, S. and P. Keefer (1994), 'Institutions and economic performance: cross-country tests using alternative institutional measures', IRIS Working Paper 109, University of Maryland, Center for Institutional Reform and the Informal Sector.

Lane, P. and A. Tornell (1995), 'Power concentration and growth', Discussion Paper 1720, Cambridge (Mass.): Harvard Institute of Economic Research.

Lewis, S.R. (1989), 'Primary exporting countries', in H. Chenery and T.N. Srinivasan (eds), *Handbook of Development Economics*, vol. II, Amsterdam: North-Holland.

Matsuyama, K. (1992), 'Agricultural productivity, comparative advantage, and economic growth', *Journal of Economic Theory*, **58**, pp. 317–34.

Neary, P.J. and S. van Wijnbergen (eds) (1986), *Natural Resources and the Macroeconomy*, Cambridge (Mass.): MIT Press.

Roemer, M. (1970), *Fishing for Growth: Export-led Development in Peru, 1950–1967*, Cambridge (Mass.): Harvard University Press.

Roemer, M. (1994), 'Asia and Africa: towards a policy frontier', Consulting Assistance on Economic Reform (CAER) Discussion Paper 23, Cambridge (Mass.): Harvard Institute for International Development (HIID).

Sachs, J.D. and A.M. Warner (1995a), 'Economic reform and the process of global integration', *Brookings Papers on Economic Activity*, **1**, pp. 1–118.

Sachs, J.D. and A.M. Warner (1995b), 'Natural Resource Abundance and Economic Growth', Working Paper 5398, Cambridge (Mass.): National Bureau of Economic Research (NBER).

Seers, D. (1964), 'The mechanism of an open petroleum economy', *Social and Economic Studies*, **13**, pp. 233–42.

Singer, H.W. (1950), 'The distribution of trade between investing and borrowing countries', *American Economic Review*, **40**, pp. 473–85.

Summers, R. and A. Heston (1991), 'The Penn world table (mark 5): an expanded set of international comparisons, 1950–1988', *Quarterly Journal of Economics*, **106**, pp. 327–68.

Taylor, A.M. (1994), 'Domestic saving and international capital flows reconsidered', Working Paper 4892, Cambridge (Mass.): National Bureau of Economic Research.

United Nations Economic Commission for Latin America (1950), *The Economic Development of Latin America and its Principal Problems*, Lake Success (New York): United Nations Department of Economic Affairs, document E/CN.12/89/rev.1.

Warner, A.M. (1994), 'Mexico's investment collapse: debt or oil?', *Journal of International Money and Finance*, **13**, pp. 240–56.

3. Natural Resources, Human Resources and Export Composition: a Cross-country Perspective

Adrian J.B. Wood[1]

What determines the division of a country's exports between manufactures and primary products, and, within the latter category, between processed and unprocessed primary products? This chapter argues, on the basis of an economic theory and data for about 100 countries, that this division of exports is largely determined by the relative availability of different resources (or 'factors of production'), and in particular by a country's 'endowments' of natural resources (or 'land'), labour and skill.

The first section introduces the theory and the data. An analysis of the division of exports between manufactures and primary products is presented in the subsequent section, and is then extended by subdividing primary exports between processed and unprocessed items. The final section discusses the possible implications of the results for development policy in natural resource based economies.

THEORY AND DATA

The trade theory on which this chapter is based, which is to be found in all economics textbooks, is that of Heckscher and Ohlin. The central insight of these two Swedish economists was that countries tend to export types of goods whose production requires the intensive use of factors of production with which they are relatively abundantly endowed. Conversely, the goods which countries tend to import are those whose production requires intensive use of factors which are relatively scarce at home.

To put the theory in other words, trade is seen as a response to the fact that the mix of goods (and hence indirectly of factors) which people want to consume varies much less among countries than the mix of factors which countries possess, and hence the mix of goods which they can produce most cheaply.

Goods are thus essentially a way of packaging factors, with each country exchanging packages containing factors of which it has more than it wishes to consume at home (its exports) for packages containing factors of which it has less than it wishes to consume at home (its imports).

Heckscher–Ohlin (H–O) theory depends on some large assumptions, the most important of which are that the preferences of consumers are similar among countries, and that the production of each good everywhere uses the same mix of factors (that is, that technology is similar in all countries). These assumptions are especially inaccurate when goods and factors are narrowly defined – particular types of car, for example, or particular types of engineer – and for this reason H–O theory is not helpful in explaining the pattern of trade at a high level of detail. However, these assumptions are more plausible for broadly defined goods, such as manufactures and primary products, and for broadly defined factors, such as land and labour, and thus it is at this level of aggregation, used in the present paper, that H–O theory is most useful in practice.

Three Goods

The definition of *manufactures* used in this chapter is the narrow one of trade statisticians: categories 5–8 less 68 (non-ferrous metals) of the Standard International Trade Classification (SITC), with all other goods defined as *primary products* (processed plus unprocessed). Production and employment statisticians use a much broader definition of manufacturing: category 3 (now division D) of the International Standard Industrial Classification (ISIC). This includes, in addition to narrowly defined manufactures (for example garments, shoes, toys, pharmaceuticals and aircraft), what are defined here as *processed primary products*, which are goods whose production, though undertaken in factories, uses large inputs of local raw materials: for example, canned tuna, beer, cigarettes, paper, gasoline and aluminium ingots. (To put it another way, processed primary products are the goods which the ISIC classifies as manufactures but the SITC as primary products.) The present definition of *unprocessed primary products* is thus those which the ISIC classifies (much more narrowly than the SITC) as agricultural and mineral, namely goods in the state in which they leave the farm or the mine.[2]

Data on exports, divided into these three categories, were derived partly from the UNCTAD *Handbook of Trade and Development Statistics* (which uses the SITC classification) and partly from the UNIDO database (which uses the ISIC classification). The data cover rather more than 100 countries, at all levels of development, and mainly refer to a single year, 1989.

Three Factors

In textbooks, H–O models usually have two factors of production: capital (labelled K, and referring here only to financial or physical capital), and labour (labelled L, and meaning simply the total number of workers). This chapter will bring in two more factors: skill (labelled H for human capital), which is an aggregate of all sorts of education and training; and land (labelled N for natural resources), which is likewise an aggregate of all sorts and qualities of natural resources. But it will leave out K, on the grounds that capital is internationally mobile – meaning that differences in its availability cannot affect the comparative advantage of particular countries. The number of factors in the present analysis is thus reduced to three: skill, labour and land.

Skill is measured by years of schooling. More specifically, skill per worker is proxied by the average number of years of schooling of the adult (over 25) population (from Barro and Lee, 1993). Hence the stock of skill in a country is measured as its total number of person-years of schooling, obtained by multiplying average years of schooling by the number of adult citizens, the latter being the present measure of the country's stock of the second factor – labour. The third factor – land – is measured by the total land area of each country (and land per worker as land area divided by adult population). The obvious limitations of these measures of skill and natural resources merit immediate discussion.[3]

Years of schooling has two defects as a measure of skill. One is that it takes no account of cross-country differences in the quality of schooling – how much (and what) the student learned in the years concerned. The other is its neglect of sources of skill acquisition other than schooling – both formal classroom training and experience (or on-the-job training). For statistical purposes, however, these defects are less serious than they may appear, because there is a strong cross-country correlation between years of schooling and these other aspects of skill; that is, countries with longer schooling tend also to provide better-quality schooling and more training.

Total land area is an unbiased measure of natural resource availability, in the sense that what each country has, per square kilometre of its surface area, in terms of soil fertility, water resources, minerals and so on, can be regarded as the outcome of a random draw. It is clearly not an ideal indicator, since in principle it could be much improved by allowing for variation among countries in the composition and quality of their land. In practice, however, attempts to achieve such an improvement, using data on several types of land (arable, pasture and forest), on water resources, and on metal, oil, gas and coal reserves, have been largely unsuccessful (Wood and Berge, 1994; Owens and Wood, 1997).

MANUFACTURED VERSUS PRIMARY EXPORTS

It is convenient to begin with an explanation of cross-country differences in the division of exports between two categories of goods: manufactures (narrowly defined) and primary products (broadly defined to include both processed and unprocessed items). It is particularly convenient to do so because these differences can be explained largely in terms of differing endowments of only two of the three factors: skill and land. (A fuller account of the analysis in this section is in Wood and Berge, 1994, 1997.)

Labour can be left out because there is, on average, no clear difference in labour intensity between manufacturing and primary production.[4] Both sectors employ substantial numbers of workers, but it is hard to generalize about which employs more relative to their combined use of the other two factors (skill plus land). In poorer developing countries, agriculture is more labour-intensive than manufacturing, but in some developed countries it is the other way round, and in many countries there is little difference. Mining is usually less labour-intensive than manufacturing (and hence the direction of the difference between manufacturing and primary production may depend on the composition of a country's natural resources).

What distinguishes manufacturing from primary production much more clearly and generally is another sort of difference in factor proportions, namely that the ratio of skill to land is always higher in manufacturing than in primary production. Manufacturing is much more compact than agriculture, since it is carried out on fairly small sites and in cities, whereas farming needs large tracts of land. Skill requirements also differ: illiterate people can work as farmers, whereas even 'unskilled' work in modern manufacturing requires a basic education. Mining can be carried out on small sites, sometimes with a skilled labour force, but the relative cost structure of mining resembles that of agriculture, with a higher ratio of rent (for land or other natural resource use) to skilled wages than in manufacturing.

Given this difference in factor proportions, what determines a country's comparative advantage between manufactures and primary products is its relative endowments of skill and land. In the absence of trade, the relative price of skill and land would vary among countries, depending on the relative scarcity of these two factors. For example, in a country with a large amount of natural resources and few skilled workers, land would be cheap relative to skill. These variations in relative factor prices would cause corresponding variations in product prices: manufactures would cost more, relative to primary products, in a country with a low ratio of skill to land. Given the opportunity to trade, such a country will tend to export primary products and import manufactures – and vice versa for a country with a high ratio of skill to land.

The hypothesis is thus that countries with high skill–land ratios tend to export manufactures, while those with low skill–land ratios tend to export primary products. This is tested by running a cross-country regression of the form:

$$(X_m/X_p)_i = a + b(H/N)_i + u_i \tag{1}$$

where X_m and X_p are gross exports of manufactures and primary products, H and N are our measures of skill and land (so that H/N is person-years of schooling per square kilometre), u is the error term, and the subscript i identifies the country.[5] The ratios on both sides of the equation are in logarithms. An expanded version of this regression, including labour, was also tried: it confirmed that the exclusion of labour was justified (in the sense that including it added little to the explanation based on skill and land only).

The results are strongly supportive of the hypothesis. The coefficient b is positive (its value is about 0.75, using data for 1989) and highly statistically significant, and the regression explains more than half the cross-country variation in the export ratio ($R^2 = 0.57$). The strength of the relationship is apparent from the scatter plot of the data in Figure 3.1. There is considerable dispersion, but countries with high skill–land ratios clearly tend to have high ratios of manufactured to primary exports, and vice versa. Similar results were obtained using data for 1960 and 1975, although the proportion of variance explained in these earlier years is somewhat lower.

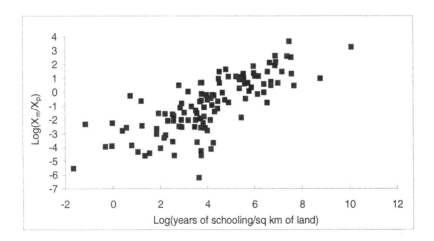

Figure 3.1 Export structure and resources: cross-country pattern

Figure 3.2 is based on the same data as Figure 3.1, but shows the regression line and the average values of the dependent and independent variables for six country groups: developed countries, the four main developing country regions (Africa, Latin America, South Asia and East Asia), and the seven 'high-performing' developing countries which were the subject of the World Bank's *East Asian Miracle* study. It reveals a striking cross-regional replication of the cross-country pattern in Figure 3.1, regional differences in the ratio of manufactured to primary exports being strongly correlated with regional differences in skill–land ratios. The sharpest contrast is between Africa and high-performing East Asia (HPEA), at the two ends of the regression line, but Latin America is also below average with respect to both variables (and by comparison with both Asian regions). The developed group is the only one which deviates to a statistically significant extent from the regression line (with a higher ratio of manufactured to primary exports than its skill–land ratio would predict).

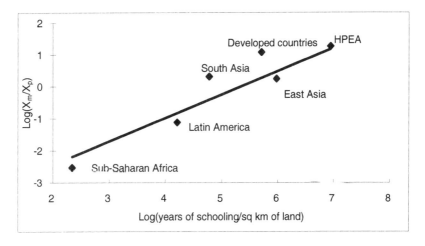

Figure 3.2   Export structure and resources: regional pattern

Further tests using the data in Figures 3.1 and 3.2 were conducted to discover whether differences among countries in their trade policies might explain that part of the variation in export composition which is not explained by differences in skill–land ratios. These tests were hampered by limited data on trade policy, but suggested that the contribution of trade policy differences is minor.[6] However, the lower proportion of the variation in export composition explained by variation in the skill–land ratio in 1960 and 1975 is probably partly a reflection of the greater influence of trade policy in these earlier years, when various developing countries that now export mainly manufactures had inward-oriented trade regimes which limited their exports mainly to primary products.

PROCESSED VERSUS UNPROCESSED PRIMARY EXPORTS

The analysis will now be extended to the division of exports into three categories – distinguishing processed from unprocessed items within the primary category. To do this, it is necessary also to bring labour back into the analysis; that is, to work with three factors, as well as with three goods. The reason is that, although there is no general difference in labour intensity between manufactures and primary products as a whole, there is a systematic difference in labour intensity within the primary category between processed and unprocessed products.

More specifically, processed primary products are generally less labour-intensive than both unprocessed primary products and manufactures. This is because primary processing requires, per unit of output, large inputs of both land and skill (the former to provide the materials to be processed, the latter for the processing), while each of the other two goods requires a large input of only one of these two factors (land for unprocessed primary products, and skill for manufactures). There are undoubtedly exceptions to this generalization for specific goods within each of these three categories, but earlier studies of primary processing also noted its relatively low labour intensity (for example, Roemer, 1977).

To investigate the influence of differing factor endowments on this three-way division of exports, Owens and Wood (1997) use a set of regressions:

$$(X_m/X)_i = a_1 + c_1 h_i - d_1 n_i + u_{1i} \tag{2a}$$

$$(X_{pp}/X)_i = a_2 + c_2 h_i - d_2 n_i + u_{2i} \tag{2b}$$

$$(X_{up}/X)_i = a_3 + c_3 h_i - d_3 n_i + u_{3i} \tag{2c}$$

each of which is similar in principle to regression (1) above, but with two differences. The first is that the dependent variable makes exports of the good concerned a ratio of total exports (rather than of another category of exports); for example, X_{pp}/X is the share of processed primary products in total exports, and X_{up}/X the share of unprocessed primary products. The second difference is that instead of having a single factor ratio (H/N) as the independent variable, regressions (2) have two separate factor ratios which between them measure endowments of all three factors: h is skill per worker (H/L) and n is land per worker (N/L).

The results for regressions (2a) and (2c) are strikingly symmetrical. The pattern of signs on the independent variables is (as expected) positive on h and negative on n in the manufactured export regression, and vice versa in the unprocessed primary export regression. In other words, a high level of skill per worker in a country raises the export share of manufactures and reduces that of unprocessed primary products, while a large endowment of land per worker does the opposite. (All four of these coefficients are also similar in absolute size – roughly 0.4.)

The results for processed primary exports (regression (2b)) are entirely different, with the coefficients on h and n both being positive, implying that primary processing requires both more skill and more land per unit of labour input than exports in general (and thus confirming that processed primary products are less labour-intensive than other exports). Further analysis reveals that processed primary products are not just more skill-intensive than unprocessed primary products, but are of much the same skill intensity as manufactures. This finding is consistent with earlier studies of 'resource-based industrialization', which found that primary processing has skill requirements similar to those of narrowly defined manufacturing (for example, Roemer, 1977; Wall, 1987).

Group averages of the data used in these regressions are presented in two figures, using the same country groupings as before (that is, as in Figure 3.2). Figure 3.3 shows the average factor endowments of each region (within each of which there is, of course, considerable variation). The level of skill per worker is high in developed countries, intermediate in East Asia and Latin America, and low in South Asia and Africa. Land per worker is low in Asia (East and South), intermediate in developed countries and Latin America, and high in Africa. If the Africa point were shifted to the left to allow for the poor quality of much of its land, the four developing regions would thus lie in the four cells of a 2 x 2 matrix of (low and intermediate) skill and land per worker. (The skill–land ratio of each region is measured by the slope of a ray from the origin through its point: high-performing East Asia obviously has the highest skill–land ratio, and Africa the lowest.)

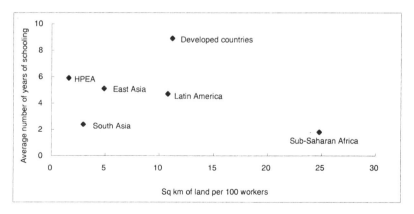

Figure 3.3 Regional factor endowments

Figure 3.4 shows the average composition of each region's exports, which is in accordance with what would be predicted from regional differences in factor endowments and from the relative factor intensities of the three goods. In particular, since primary processing is intensive both in skill and in land relative to labour, it is not surprising that, among the four developing regions, the share of processed primary products in exports is highest in Latin America, which is well endowed with both skill and land. Conversely, it is not surprising that the share of processed primary products is lowest in South Asia, which is poorly endowed with both skill and land. The other two developing regions are well endowed with one of these factors, but not the other, and so one expects their processed primary export shares to be somewhere in between, as indeed they are.

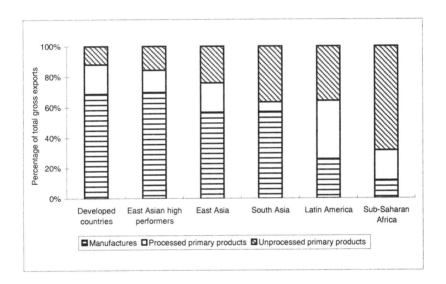

Figure 3.4 Regional exports

Another way of looking at Figure 3.4 is to ask how making the distinction between processed and unprocessed primary products alters the impression of interregional differences in export shares derived earlier from Figure 3.2 (in which both sorts of primary products were combined), particularly for the two regions with abundant natural resources. There is a large change in the relative position of Latin America, where, although manufactures are a small share of exports, processed primary products are a large share, and hence unprocessed primary products are also a small share – no greater than in South Asia, for example, and not much greater than in East Asia.

By contrast, the relative position of Africa is hardly affected: most of its large primary export share is unprocessed. This is because Africa's factor endowments combine low skill per worker with high (or intermediate) land per worker. Neither of these endowment ratios on its own would be sufficient to cause specialization in unprocessed primary exports: South Asia also has low skill per worker, but this is offset by low land per worker (resulting in a middling skill–land ratio); and Latin America too has high land per worker, but this is offset by higher skill per worker (causing a larger share of primary exports to be processed). Together, however, these two features of Africa's factor endowments fix its export pattern: high land per worker causes most exports to be primary, and low skill per worker causes most of these primary exports to be unprocessed.

IMPLICATIONS FOR TRADE AND DEVELOPMENT POLICY

To summarize the results of the two previous sections, differences among countries in the composition of their exports (the shares of manufactures, processed primary products and unprocessed primary products) are rather well explained by inter-country differences in the availability of three broad factors of production – skill, labour and land – in accordance with the predictions of Heckscher–Ohlin trade theory. Moreover, this analysis is not just an elaborate way of proving the obvious: it is indeed self-evident that natural resource availability has a positive influence on primary exports, but the ways in which the outcome depends also on the availability of labour and of education are obvious only in retrospect.

It is also important to emphasize the limitations of these results. They do not include any subdivision of manufacturing (a fuller analysis should distinguish between more and less skill-intensive manufactured goods), and they omit trade in services. The measures of skill and land endowments are crude, and the results leave a large minority of inter-country variation in export composition unexplained. In analysing the situation of any specific country, it is useful to place it in the context of the regressions and figures discussed above, but one must also recognize that many countries deviate substantially from their predicted values. In some cases, such deviations are explained by the deficiencies of the resource measures (for example where an oil exporter is far below the regression line in Figures 3.1 or 3.2 because the extent of its natural resources is underestimated by the land area measure) or by trade policy interventions, but in other cases the deviations are harder to reconcile with H–O theory.

What are the implications of these results for trade and development policy in 'resource-based economies' – meaning countries where natural resources are abundant relative to labour (a high land–labour ratio) or to skill (a low skill–land ratio)? The answer varies widely, depending on one's view of the nature and causes of economic development.

Two Extreme Positions

Those who see market forces as the key to development would probably argue that these results have no implications whatsoever for policy, in the sense that they do not imply the need for any government action beyond the basic functions assigned to the state by the Washington Consensus. A person with this view might find the results encouraging, because they suggest that the pattern of trade is only minimally distorted by trade policy interventions, and even helpful, because they provide a better basis for predicting and evaluating the trade pattern of particular countries. But from this point of view, the results provide no reason for departing from the principle of free trade and specialization according to the comparative advantage given by resource endowments: for some countries, the best route to development lies in exporting manufactures, and for others in exporting primary products, and experience has shown that it is a costly mistake to try to change this state of affairs by interventionist trade policy. Nor, from this point of view, do these results add anything to the case for investing in education in developing countries.

At another extreme, those in the long tradition of development economists which has seen industrialization as the key to development would probably argue that these results imply the need for protection of manufacturing in countries with low skill–land ratios. Otherwise, such countries will be confined to primary production (which has little growth potential because of its low income elasticity of demand, slow technical progress and few opportunities for learning), and will thus stay poor and underdeveloped.

More specifically, an advocate of import-substituting industrialization would find in these results a powerful weapon with which to attack the Washington Consensus view that the development success of East Asia proves the merits of open, export-oriented trade policies. These policies were beneficial in East Asia because the region had a special combination of resource endowments (a high level of education and few natural resources, and thus a high skill–land ratio) which gave it a comparative advantage in manufacturing. For East Asia, therefore, openness to trade did indeed promote development, because it stimulated manufacturing, but for other regions, with different resource endowments (particularly for those with low skill–land ratios), greater openness to trade retards development by causing manufacturing to contract.

An Intermediate Position

My own view of the policy implications of these results is different from both these two positions, though in some respects it overlaps with them. I see the key to development as being skill acquisition – raising the level of economically useful knowledge embodied in a country's labour force – a proposition which seems to me to be consistent with most of what is known both about the causes of the cross-sectional gaps in income between rich and poor countries and about the causes of East Asia's remarkable success in catching up over time. I also see scope for government intervention to accelerate the process of skill acquisition, not only through improvement of education and training, but also through trade and industrial policy.

Manufacturing is neither a necessary nor a sufficient condition for skill acquisition. It is not necessary, because primary production includes activities of high- as well as low-skill intensity – not only in mining and primary processing, but also in agriculture (as can be seen, for example, from Israel and the Netherlands). It is not sufficient, because some manufacturing is of low-skill intensity (there is not much to be learned from stitching shirts). Nor does exporting manufactures provide any more of an automatic path to prosperity than exporting primary products: strong competition in world markets has been driving down prices and wages in labour-intensive manufacturing, just as for many primary commodities.

However, manufacturing is on average more skill-intensive than primary production, and processed primary products are more skill-intensive than unprocessed ones. There is thus bound to be an association between skill acquisition and shifts in the sectoral structure of production. Moreover, this association reflects causation in both directions, because there is undoubtedly greater scope for learning-by-doing in more skill-intensive activities: the expansion of more skill-intensive sectors (and of more skill-intensive activities within sectors) thus raises the skill level of the labour force as well as being raised by it. This causal linkage is probably behind the well-established finding that countries with abundant natural resources grow more slowly than those with few natural resources.

One policy implication of the results in this chapter, I think, is thus to reinforce the case for investing in education and training in resource-based economies. By raising their skill–land ratios, such investment in human resources will tend to shift their comparative advantage and output structure away from unprocessed towards processed primary production, and away from primary production towards manufacturing, and so speed up their learning-by-doing. Historically, this strategy of expansion of education alongside use of abundant natural resources was successfully followed by, for example, the United States

and Scandinavia. In the contemporary context, however, three important qualifications must be noted:

1. Investing in education and training is easier said than done, especially
    for poor countries or those experiencing financial crises, and is at best
    likely to take a considerable time. Moreover, what matters is not, as the
    results in this chapter might seem to imply, simply increasing the number
    of years of schooling: the quality of that schooling is also crucial, and
    often harder to improve than its quantity.
2. Comparative advantage means what it says. A country can shift its
    comparative advantage into more skill-intensive activities only if it accu-
    mulates skills more rapidly than other countries. This increases the mag-
    nitude of the educational challenge for resource-based economies, since
    educational levels are rising throughout the world.
3. Supply-side efforts to expand education and training may not be suffi-
    cient to raise the skill level of the labour force. There must also be a
    demand for skilled labour, without which parents will be reluctant to send
    their children to school and firms to send their workers for training. But
    in countries whose pattern of trade is such that they are specialized in
    sectors and activities of low-skill intensity, this demand for skilled labour
    may well be lacking. In other words, producing in accordance with com-
    parative advantage can trap such a country in a low-skill equilibrium.

There is thus a case for using restrictions on trade or industrial policy to promote skill-intensive sectors and hence create the necessary demand. Indeed,
this is essentially what the successful East Asian countries did, through a combination of rapid educational expansion and protection of a sequence of industries of increasing skill intensity (with later incentives for these industries to
export). This was effective in expanding the stock of skills because it caused the
demand for educated labour to rise in line with its supply and gave educated
young people opportunities for employment in which they could add vital practical experience. It would make no sense for resource-based economies to attempt
to follow this East Asian path in detail, because their comparative advantage
lies in different sectors, but they could still apply the same general principle,
namely that accelerating skill acquisition requires a cumulative sequence of
policy actions on both the supply side and the demand side of the labour market.

NOTES

1. The research summarized in this chapter was undertaken in collaboration with Kersti Berge and Trudy Owens, and financed by the United Kingdom Overseas Development Administration (through ESCOR Research Scheme R5037 and its accountable grant to the Institute of Development Studies). Comments and suggestions for improvement from many other colleagues, too numerous to list here, are also gratefully acknowledged.
2. For a fuller explanation of these categories and of the sources of the trade data, see Owens and Wood (1997).
3. There is, incidentally, an inverse cross-country correlation between land per worker and average years of schooling (for the most recent year, with both variables in logs, R = – 0.38).
4. This is because, in a H–O model, trade arises from the combination of two sorts of differences: inter-country differences in factor endowments and inter-product differences in factor proportions. Thus if all products happened to have the same factor proportions, there would be no reason in H–O theory for trade, even if countries had different factor endowments. By extension of this logic, it can be shown that if products are similar in their use of one particular factor, such as labour, differences among countries in their endowments of that factor do not affect the composition of trade, and so there is no need to include it in the model.
5. This regression is based on gross exports, whereas H–O theory refers to net exports (that is, gross exports minus imports). However, similar results are obtained when the gross export ratio is replaced by a net export ratio. The reason for the similarity is that the ratio of manufactured to primary imports, though it varies among countries, is uncorrelated with variations in their skill–land ratios, probably because imports are highly diversified among different specific types of manufactures and primary products.
6. Further analysis of the contribution of trade policy is undertaken in Mayer (1997) and Ridao-Cano (1996).

REFERENCES

Barro, R. and J.W. Lee (1993), 'International comparisons of educational attainment', *Journal of Monetary Economics*, **32**, pp. 363–94.

Mayer, J. (1997), 'Is having a rich natural resource endowment detrimental to export diversification?', Discussion Paper 124, Geneva: UNCTAD.

Owens, T. and A. Wood (1997), 'Export-oriented industrialisation through primary processing?', *World Development*, **25**, pp. 1453–70.

Ridao-Cano, C. (1996), 'Does openness to trade speed adjustment: a dynamic panel data analysis', Brighton: Institute of Development Studies, mimeo.

Roemer, M. (1977), 'Resource-based industrialisation in the developing countries: a survey of the literature', Discussion Paper 21, Cambridge (Mass.): Harvard Institute of International Development.

Wall, D. (1987), 'Processing primary products: a review of some case studies', Discussion Paper 43, Brighton: International Economics Research Centre.

Wood, A. and K. Berge (1994), 'Exporting manufactures: trade policy or human resources?', Working Paper 4, Brighton: Institute of Development Studies.

Wood, A. and K. Berge (1997), 'Exporting manufactures: human resources, natural resources and trade policy', *Journal of Development Studies*, **34**, pp. 35–59.

PART TWO

National Experiences with Non-renewable
Natural Resources

4. The Transition from Rent-driven Growth to Skill-driven Growth: Recent Experience of Five Mineral Economies

Richard M. Auty

MINERAL ECONOMIES: A SUBGROUP OF LOW-GROWTH RESOURCE-RICH COUNTRIES

The mineral economies might be expected to outperform other developing countries, given the additional import capacity and extra investment resources which mineral exports provide (Sachs and Warner, 1995). Yet most, but not all, of the mineral economies have performed disappointingly. Figure 4.1 shows growth in per capita GDP during the period 1960–90 for countries classified according to their dependence on mineral exports. The (resource-deficient) manufactured goods exporters achieved the highest mean per capita GDP growth rate and the hard mineral exporters the lowest rate. Moreover, Botswana alone accounts for half the mean growth rate for the hard mineral exporters, and its exclusion from that group (on the grounds that its diamond resource has more in common with oil-driven growth) lowers the mean growth rate of the remaining hard mineral exporters to only 0.3 per cent. The agricultural exporting countries also grew relatively slowly, but the rate is slightly higher at 0.8 per cent.

These results appear to be robust in the face of variations in both the time period and the classification criteria. For example, Table 4.1 confirms the weak performance of the mineral economies using data for per capita GDP over the years 1970–93 and a different set of resource endowment classification criteria, based upon domestic market size in 1970 (World Bank, 1995a) and per capita cropland in 1970 (World Resources Institute, 1994; Auty, 1996a).[1] This produces four basic categories, and the one with the most countries in it (the small resource-rich category) can be further subdivided by taking account of the mineral dependence of the countries (Table 4.1).

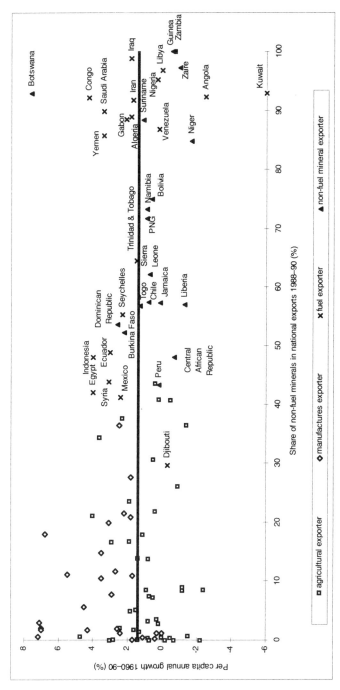

Notes: The horizontal line indicates the median growth rate of this sample of 105 developing countries. PNG = Papua New Guinea.

Source: Traeger (1993).

Figure 4.1 Economic growth and mineral dependence

Table 4.1 Resource endowment and per capita GDP growth, 1970–93
(per cent per annum)

	No. of countries	1970–3	1974–9	1980–5	1986–93	1970–93
Resource-poor [a]						
Large	7	2.8	4.9	3.1	3.5	3.7
Small	13	3.1	4.1	0.7	1.7	2.1
Resource-rich [b]						
Large	10	0.1	–0.2	0.1	0.0	0.0
Small, non-mineral	31	2.0	1.7	–0.7	0.2	0.5
Small, hard mineral [c]	16	2.2	0.2	–1.8	–0.8	–0.4
Small, oil exporter [c]	8	6.5	1.4	–1.7	–0.6	–1.0
All countries	85	2.7	2.0	–0.5	0.6	0.8

Notes:

[a] Large country defined as GDP > US$ 7 billion in 1970.
[b] Resource-rich defined as > 0.3 ha cropland per capita in 1970.
[c] More than 40 per cent of export revenues from minerals.

Source: UNCTAD (1995).

The overall pattern from Table 4.1 is clear: first, both groups of resource-deficient countries achieved growth rates superior to all four resource-rich groups. Second, among the resource-rich countries, the mineral economies recorded the slowest growth. Third, that position is unchanged if the *large* mineral economies are reassigned from the large resource-rich category to the oil-exporters and hard mineral economy groups (but the mean GDP growth rate of the six remaining large resource-rich countries rises to 1.6 per cent). The two main conclusions are, however, that the resource-deficient countries outperformed the resource-rich ones and that among the latter group the mineral economies recorded the most disappointing performance.

The underperformance of the resource-rich countries has received increasing attention (Ranis, 1991; Mahon, 1992; Ranis and Mahmood, 1993; Sachs and Warner, 1995; Lal and Myint, 1996).[2] Sachs and Warner (1995) find a strong positive relationship between inward orientation and dependence on primary product exports. The relationship weakens above the level at which primary product exports reach one-third of GDP (which they attribute to the oil exporters' reduced concern for the protection of their non-mining tradables). Consistent with this view, Ranis and Mahmood (1993) find liberalization and depoliticization of the economy to be beneficial for resource-deficient countries, while Auty (1994) and Lal and Myint (1996) show the tendency of states in the resource-rich countries to leapfrog the labour-absorbing stage of the East Asian model and to intervene excessively in order to upgrade skills and boost employment as the relative size of the resource rents shrinks.

To summarize, the mineral economies are an important subgroup of a larger body of resource-rich countries which have underperformed, probably as a result of policy failure. But the underperformance of resource-rich countries is not inevitable, as countries as diverse as Botswana, Indonesia, Chile and Malaysia show. This chapter evaluates the lessons of Indonesia's successful transition through all three stages of the mineral cycle and then compares it with the experience of mid-income mineral economies – two smaller ones (Trinidad and Tobago, and Botswana) and two larger ones (Chile and Peru) – as they adjusted to the mature stage of the mineral-led cycle (Table 4.2).

Table 4.2   Stage of mineral-led cycle: nine countries in the late 1980s

	Youthful		Early-mature		Late-mature	
	Start	End	Start	End	Start	End
Oil exporters	Colombia		Trinidad & Tobago			Indonesia
Copper exporters		Papua New Guinea	Chile		Peru	
Other hard minerals		Botswana	Jamaica		Namibia	

POLICIES THROUGH THE MINERAL-DRIVEN CYCLE

Economic reform to reduce the distortions created by earlier, ill-judged policies and thereby ensure sound macro management is a prerequisite for the successful management of a mineral economy. Within a soundly managed economy, policies to harness the mineral resource to advantage must be adjusted to each of the three main stages of the mineral cycle (youth, early maturity and late maturity). If the stages of the cycle occurred smoothly, policy would indeed be relatively easy to pursue, as Davis (1995) argues. But, as the examples in this chapter show, the transition may be anything but smooth: countries may find themselves moving abruptly through the entire sequence; locked in a particular stage; or undergoing some regression. With these reservations in mind, the ideal sequence through the mineral cycle is now briefly outlined.

The first (youthful) stage sees the rapid expansion of the mining sector, a real appreciation of the exchange rate and strong Dutch disease effects (a weakening in the competitiveness of non-mining tradables, notably agriculture and manufacturing). The second stage, early maturity, is marked by a sustained slow-down in mining expansion, although the mineral sector still exerts a major economic influence. Policies during this stage need to encourage diversification into alternative sources of taxation and foreign exchange, and also to manage cyclical fluctuations in mineral revenues caused by mineral price swings and output fluctuations. The third stage spans the long-term relative decline of mining, which may be due to flagging competitiveness, depleting reserves and/ or a slower rate of mineral expansion compared with other sectors.

All three stages pose policy challenges, but the successful transition to maturity has proved especially problematic. The remainder of this chapter analyses that transition with reference to case studies, beginning with Indonesia.

THE LESSONS FROM INDONESIA'S SUCCESSFUL TRANSITION

Indonesia is particularly interesting because it successfully managed all three stages of the mineral-led cycle, which were compressed into the period 1973–93. This is because the 1973 and 1979 oil shocks reignited the youthful phase (1973–83), but the subsequent price decline then precipitated an abrupt adjustment through both mature stages. By the early 1990s, Indonesia had technically ceased to be a mineral economy.

Windfall Deployment through the 1974–8 and 1979–81 Oil Booms

During the youthful phase of the mineral cycle, measures are required to capture the windfall and to sterilize it so as to avoid overstraining domestic absorptive capacity and amplifying the Dutch disease effects. Also, care is needed in deploying the windfall to avoid establishing patterns of consumption and investment which cannot be sustained if the windfall declines. Given the uncertainty concerning the scale and duration of the mineral revenue stream, the empirical evidence suggests that mineral revenues are soundly managed by erring on the side of caution (Gelb, 1988; Hill, 1991). This is because less economic damage is done by underestimating the scale of the windfall than by being over-optimistic.

The Indonesian windfall from the first oil shock was around 16 per cent of non-oil GDP annually over the period 1974–8, while that from the second shock was larger (but briefer) at 22 per cent of non-oil GDP for the period 1979–81 (Gelb, 1988). Thereafter, a negative shock occurred that was equivalent to the loss of 15 per cent of GDP over the period 1986–8, having intensified from a loss of 3 per cent of GDP for the period 1982–5 (Ahmed, 1989). Gelb (1988) estimate that one-third of the first oil windfall was saved, and during the second oil windfall more than 40 per cent was prudently sterilized by being saved abroad.

During the first boom, one-sixth of the windfall went into higher domestic consumption, but the largest fraction (around half) went into increased investment which boosted the rate of capital formation by 4.5 per cent of non-oil GDP compared with the pre-shock trend. One-quarter of the domestic windfall investment went on infrastructure, much of it in rural areas through irrigation improvements whose impact was compounded by higher subsidies for fertilizer. This deployment pattern helped to diffuse the windfall benefits throughout the economy and maintain the country's relatively equitable income distribution. A further two-fifths was sensibly invested to prolong oil production and also to diversify into liquefied natural gas. Finally, industrial diversification accounted for the remaining one-third of development investment, roughly evenly divided between the metal sector and the non-metals sectors (Auty, 1990).

During the second oil boom, domestic absorption proved too rapid, even in a cautiously managed economy such as that of Indonesia. Private consumption, public consumption and investment all rose sharply so that inflation accelerated and eliminated the effects of a 1979 exchange rate devaluation. An expansion of subsidized consumption threatened the competitiveness of the previously efficient food grain sector. But when oil prices faltered after 1981 and returned the country to the mature stage of its mineral-driven cycle, taxes were restructured and alternative sources of foreign exchange were stimulated.

Timely and Prudent Adjustment to Maturity

The Indonesian government made prompt cuts in public spending while broadening the tax base, the net effect of which was to boost the non-oil tax share from 8.3 per cent of GDP to 13.2 per cent over the decade 1981–91 (Bhattacharya and Pangestu, 1992). The reserves that were accumulated over the period 1974–81 provided some scope for easing adjustment, but Indonesia also made liberal use of foreign borrowing to restructure its economy. This pushed total foreign debt above 50 per cent of GDP and increased debt service to 36 per cent of export earnings, which required a rapid expansion of non-hydrocarbon exports.

After an initial intensification of industrial protection from 1982 to 1985, trade liberalization began, dismantling the protective system that had been built up since the 1960s. Non-tariff barriers were reduced from 43 per cent of imports to 13 per cent between 1986 and 1991. The number of tariff bands was halved to 11, and average levels of nominal protection were lowered from 37 per cent to 20 per cent. Meanwhile, exporters were allowed to import inputs duty-free and were given assistance with credit and insurance. Effective macroeconomic stabilization enabled two exchange rate depreciations to hold, in 1983 and in 1986 (to 60 per cent of the 1983 value), when oil prices plummeted. Also, domestic competition was boosted by reducing licensing and easing restrictions on foreign direct investment.

The deceleration of agricultural growth in the mid-1980s shifted the burden of diversification on to competitive manufacturing. The legacy of the state-led industrial policy of 1975–85 was a dualistic manufacturing structure (Flatters and Jenkins, 1986) of large, relatively efficient companies which captured size-able rents, alongside a mixture of small, high-cost private firms and large, capital-intensive state-owned resource-based industry (RBI) such as steel and petro-chemicals which were relatively inefficient (Auty, 1990; Hill, 1995). From this mix of firms, the trade reforms triggered a surge in non-oil exports, which rose to 66 per cent of total exports over the period 1990–3 (Table 4.3), with manufactured exports accounting for two-thirds.

Indonesian investment, investment efficiency and GDP growth all recovered during the period 1986–93 (Table 4.4). Meanwhile, the benefits of the oil wind-falls had been widely diffused as a result of the earlier preoccupation of the government with farming. That helped to reduce those below the poverty line from 39 per cent in 1976 to 15 per cent in 1990. The income ratio of the richest quintile to the poorest quintile fell from 6.2 to 4.9 between 1970 and 1990 (Woo *et al.*, 1995; World Bank, 1995a).

Some Qualifications of the Indonesian Lessons

The trade policy reforms went some way towards returning Indonesia to the East Asian development model and were associated with a tripling in industrial output during the 1980s (UNIDO, 1995). But the lessons of Indonesia for other countries require four qualifications. First, favourable conditions already existed in Indonesia for successful mineral windfall deployment – in terms of a relatively egalitarian income distribution and the timely diffusion of green revolution techniques. More-over, the perceived maturity of the hydrocarbon-based mineral sector had encour-aged the government to begin to diversify through liberalization.

Table 4.3 *Export composition of eight mineral economies, 1990–3 (per cent)*

	Botswana[a]	Chile	Indonesia	Jamaica[b]	Namibia[c]	Papua New Guinea[d]	Peru[e]	Trinidad & Tobago
Minerals	87.0	49.5	38.4	57.5	57.9	64.2	49.5	66.7
Fuels	0.0	0.4	34.5	2.6	0.0	0.2	10.3	66.4
Other primary	3.5	34.8	17.9	11.2	20.4	20.4	32.5	2.3
Manufactures	9.5	15.7	43.7	31.3	20.6	15.4	18.0	31.0
Textiles	2.8	1.4	3.1	9.8	n.a.	0.1	3.8	1.8
Machinery	–	1.8	12.5	3.4	n.a.	11.6	1.1	0.6

Note: n.a. = not available.

Sources: World Bank (1995a), except:

[a] Botswana = Central Statistical Office (1994)
[b] Jamaica = Planning Institute of Jamaica (1994). Data cover manufactures during the period 1990–1 and include sugar, coffee and cocoa in the manufactures category
[c] Namibia = World Bank (1994)
[d] Papua New Guinea = 1990–2 only
[e] Peru = 1990, 1991 and 1993 only.

Table 4.4 GDP growth, investment rate and investment efficiency, eight countries, 1970–93

	1970–3	1974–9	1980–5	1986–93	1970–93
GDP growth (per cent per annum)					
Botswana	19.3	11.9	10.9	8.3	11.7
Chile	1.5	3.2	2.3	7.1	4.0
Indonesia	7.4	7.1	5.5	6.3	6.5
Jamaica	6.7	–2.2	–0.8	2.5	1.2
Namibia	1.0[a]	1.0[a]	–0.8	3.5	1.4
Papua New Guinea	7.3	1.6	0.8	5.7	3.7
Peru	4.8	3.5	0.9	0.1	1.9
Trinidad and Tobago	3.2	6.6	0.1	–1.5	1.7
All developing countries	6.4	5.1	2.7	2.3	3.8
Investment (per cent of GDP)					
Botswana	48.1	38.9	34.8	25.5[b]	34.9
Chile	15.4	19.5	17.2	24.5	19.9
Indonesia	19.2	23.5	27.4	30.4	26.1
Jamaica	30.6	19.1	21.3	26.7	24.1
Namibia	n.a.	n.a.	22.1	14.2	n.a.
Papua New Guinea	31.9	20.6	26.8	23.3	24.9
Peru	17.2	21.9	26.7	19.4	21.5
Trinidad and Tobago	29.3	26.6	26.6	16.7	23.7
All developing countries	n.a.	n.a.	24.9	26.1	n.a.
Incremental capital output ratios					
Botswana	2.5	3.3	3.2	3.1	3.0
Chile	10.2	6.1	7.5	3.5	5.0
Indonesia	2.6	3.3	5.0	4.8	4.0
Jamaica	4.6	–[c]	–[c]	10.7	20.1
Namibia	n.a.	n.a.	–[c]	4.1	n.a.
Papua New Guinea	4.4	12.9	33.5	4.1	6.7
Peru	3.6	6.3	29.7	194.0	11.3
Trinidad and Tobago	9.2	4.9	264.0	–[c]	13.9
All developing countries	n.a.	n.a.	9.2	11.3	n.a.

Note: n.a. = not available.

Sources: World Bank (1993), except:
[a] Hartman (1986)
[b] Central Statistical Office (1994) for financial years 1986/87 to 1993/94
[c] Statistic negative.

Second, Indonesia benefited from the emergence of a developmental-state government (Leftwich, 1995) which possessed high autonomy and sought to maximize long-term social welfare. The government provided continuity of policy that was committed to macroeconomic orthodoxy and the prompt correction of fiscal and external deficits. A third favourable factor was the presence of sizeable and diverse non-hydrocarbon resources and a large domestic market. This resource configuration facilitated diversification, compared with the smaller mineral economies with more limited non-mineral resources. Finally, the per capita income of Indonesia was still relatively low when the oil windfalls ended, and this made industrial diversification easier by assisting Indonesia's return to the successful growth path pioneered by the resource-deficient East Asian countries. Those mineral economies which reached maturity with a mid-level per capita income face a more difficult task as a result of having leapfrogged the labour-intensive stage of industrialization.

TRANSITION TO MATURITY IN SMALL, MIDDLE-INCOME MINERAL ECONOMIES

Protracted Adjustment in Trinidad and Tobago

Through the 1970s and 1980s, small mid-income mineral economies as diverse as Trinidad and Tobago, Jamaica and Namibia had difficulty in adjusting to the lost dynamism in their mineral sector (Table 4.4). The case of Trinidad and Tobago is especially interesting because this occurred despite a bias towards cautious macroeconomic management and the accumulation of relatively large financial reserves with which to make the transition. Such caution did not prevent the emergence of sizeable Dutch disease effects, a highly protective trade regime and an overexpanded public sector.

Briefly, the oil windfalls conferred on Trinidad and Tobago the equivalent of an extra 39 per cent of non-mining GDP annually during the period 1974–8 and 35 per cent during the period 1979–81, but then fell sharply. The initial policy response was prudent: the government taxed away five-sixths of the first windfall, established a long-term development fund and managed to save almost 70 per cent of the first windfall (half was invested abroad). Of the remainder, 12 per cent was invested domestically, mostly in relieving a backlog of projects in infrastructure, while, less wisely, 18 per cent was consumed as subsidies on food, fuel and utilities, which expanded to 7 per cent of GDP by 1978. During the second oil boom, around half the windfall was saved, and by 1981 the country's financial reserves had accumulated to 50 per cent of GDP. But a further quarter of the windfall was misguidedly invested in loss-making steel and petrochemicals, as well as in nationalizing the sugar mills and oil refineries. Also, the government further boosted consumption via subsidies which proved unsustainable and quickly drained the financial reserve when oil prices weakened.

During the booms, the share of oil in taxes rose from one-fifth to three-fifths, while the government's share of GDP reached 30 per cent and its share of formal employment reached 50 per cent (World Bank, 1996). The legacy of the Dutch disease effects meant that agriculture was less than two-fifths of the norm (Table 4.5), and although manufacturing was only 4 per cent below the norm, it was dominated by capital-intensive hydrocarbon processing (which generated little employment) and highly inefficient import substitution industry. Yet instead of taking prompt measures to stimulate economic diversification, the Trinidad and Tobago government allowed the exchange rate to appreciate further, to 170 per cent of its 1970–2 level by 1984, and exhausted the financial reserves. Nor was progress made in expanding non-oil revenues, which contracted by one-third in real terms through the 1980s, amplifying the compression arising out of the oil revenue collapse.

The tardy downswing adjustment tripled the external debt of Trinidad and Tobago to 50 per cent of GDP by 1989, and an agreement with the International Monetary Fund was implemented. Public spending was further reduced and expenditure taxes were expanded. Meanwhile, non-tariff barriers were phased out and the maximum tariff was reduced to 11 per cent. But although hydrocarbon processing expanded, the response from the more employment-intensive agriculture and other manufacturing was weak. More employment-intensive growth was therefore needed to reduce unemployment (which doubled to 20 per cent of the workforce during the 1980s) at a time when efforts to enhance the flexibility of the public sector were cutting its contribution to employment. The economy contracted by 1.5 per cent per annum during the period 1983–93, and real per capita income almost halved to drop below its 1973 level, leaving one-fifth of the population in poverty and one-tenth in absolute poverty (World Bank, 1995b).

Yet economic diversification was impeded by the pursuit of a tight monetary policy which kept interest rates high and slowed the depreciation of the real exchange rate (Brewster, 1994). The rate of investment averaged only 16 per cent of GDP during the period 1985–93, compared with 27 per cent during the period 1974–85, and, worse, fell in real terms in both education and public infrastructure. A similarly limited diversification of the economy was seen in Jamaica (Table 4.3), which attempted with little success for 20 years to restore sustained rapid growth (Table 4.4), after misjudgement of its bauxite rents had abruptly propelled the country from the youthful to the mature stage of the mineral-led cycle in the mid-1970s. Like Trinidad and Tobago, Jamaica was slow in adjusting its macroeconomic policies and postponed trade reform for more than a decade. The subsequent establishment of a labour-intensive export processing zone failed to emulate the success of Mauritius as a catalyst for the expansion of

Table 4.5 Structural change in 1972–90, seven mineral economies

Country	Year	Index	Per capita GNP (1980 US$)	Non-mining GDP (%)				Mining (per cent of GDP)
				Agri-culture	Manu-facturing	Con-struction & utilities	Services	
Botswana	1972	Comparator	400	37.0	11.7	10.9	40.4	5.5
		Actual	420	36.9	6.6	12.4	44.1	10.8
	1990	Actual	2308	10.3	8.2	4.4	67.2	46.4
		Comparator	2300	20.1	15.7	14.7	49.7	9.1
Chile	1972	Comparator	2500	14.9	20.2	14.9	50.0	9.4
		Actual	2460	8.3	23.4	14.4	53.8	6.2
	1990	Actual	2600	8.9	17.5	18.3	55.3	7.4
		Comparator	2500	14.9	20.2	14.9	50.0	9.4
Indonesia	1972	Comparator	300	40.1	13.0	10.4	36.5	5.5
		Actual	260	43.0	12.1	4.0	40.8	10.8
	1990	Actual	660	24.9	23.0	7.1	45.1	13.4
		Comparator	650	32.5	17.2	12.4	37.9	7.4
Jamaica	1972	Comparator	1600	19.9	18.6	13.7	47.7	9.1
		Actual	1630	7.4	16.8	10.1	55.5	10.1
	1990	Actual	1280	6.4	19.2	15.0	49.8	9.5
		Comparator	1300	22.0	18.0	13.5	46.5	8.9
Papua New Guinea	1972	Comparator	750	29.6	15.2	12.5	42.6	7.8
		Actual	770	33.2	5.8	20.6	40.4	2.5
	1990	Actual	610	34.0	10.6	7.9	47.6	14.7
		Comparator	600	33.7	14.0	11.9	40.4	6.7
Peru	1972	Comparator	1000	25.3	16.2	13.4	45.0	8.5
		Actual	1040	18.4	22.2	3.4	55.9	10.8
	1990	Actual	814	15.6	24.4	7.4	52.6	11.8
		Comparator	800	29.2	15.5	12.5	42.9	8.0
Trinidad & Tobago	1972	Comparator	1800	18.2	18.7	14.5	48.7	10.6
		Actual	1850	6.0	27.1	12.9	53.9	8.8
	1990	Actual	1430	3.3	11.1	22.6	63.0	21.3
		Comparator	1400	21.1	18.0	13.8	46.7	9.1

Note: The 'norms' discussed in the text are based on data for over 100 countries covering the period 1950–83, and they provide a comparator group against whose norms the performance of an individual country can be compared.

Sources: World Bank (1989, 1995a); Syrquin and Chenery (1989).

competitive manufacturing. Bauxite and tourism remain the key sectors in a still sluggish economy, as they were a generation earlier during the youthful stage of the Jamaican mineral cycle.

Botswana's Uncertain Prospects in Early Maturity

Figure 4.2 traces the growth of diamond production in Botswana since the mid-1970s. Diamond prices conferred sizeable rents estimated at around 60 per cent of export revenues in the mid-1980s (Harvey and Lewis, 1990) and early 1990s (Auty, 1996b). The extrapolation of such a ratio implies that the rents were equivalent to 14 per cent of GNP per year over the period 1976–82 and rose to 36 per cent during the period 1983–9 before declining to 25 per cent of GNP between 1990 and 1993. Rents on such a scale give Botswana the character much more of an oil-producer than of a hard-mineral exporter, but with the added advantage of a more consistent revenue flow.

As in Trinidad and Tobago, the contribution of mining to Botswana government revenues rose sharply, in this case from barely 20 per cent in 1976/7 to more than 50 per cent between 1985 and 1990. Prudently, the government erred consistently towards underestimating its mineral revenue. It set up stabilization funds, sterilizing a substantial fraction in offshore investments (mainly bonds), and also increased its claims on the domestic banking system. By the mid-1990s, financial reserves had reached 125 per cent of the country's GDP (Bank of Botswana, 1994), or US$ 3000 per capita (Harvey and Jefferis, 1995). In real terms, the reserves constitute around two-fifths of the rents.

The domestic absorption of more than three-fifths of the diamond rents underpinned an expansion of public expenditure at a rate which doubled in real terms every six years (Jefferis, 1996) to 45 per cent of GDP by the early 1990s. But the state's capacity effectively to deploy funds on such a scale declined, as shown by the government's disappointing investment efforts designed to force the pace of economic growth in the late 1980s and also by the deteriorating quality of education and health services. But in contrast to Trinidad and Tobago, generally the Government of Botswana wisely avoided large-scale public investment in directly productive activity.

When diamond revenues levelled off in the early 1990s, minerals (mainly diamonds) still dominated exports (Table 4.3). Yet the legacy of the Dutch disease effects was very pronounced, contrary to the view of some observers which is based on the fact that the real exchange rate had been relatively stable (Harvey, 1993; Norberg and Blomstrom, 1993; Bank of Botswana, 1994). Agriculture, which in 1972 had been close to the Syrquin and Chenery (1989) norm at 37 per cent of GDP, had shrunk to 9 per cent of non-mining GDP by 1990, while manufacturing in 1990 was only two-fifths of the norm (Table 4.5). The com-

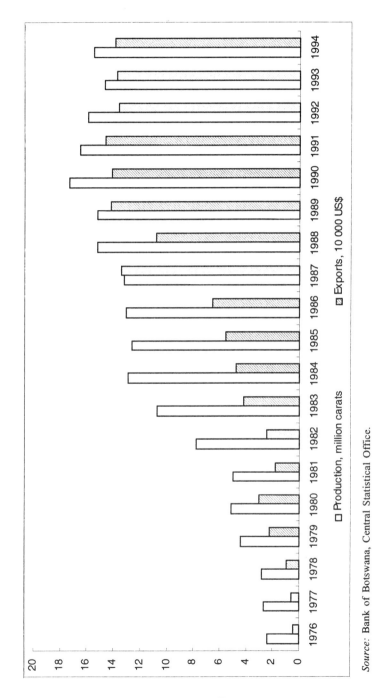

Source: Bank of Botswana, Central Statistical Office.

Figure 4.2 Botswana: production and exports of diamonds, 1976–94

bined shortfall in non-mining tradables was 21.7 per cent of non-mining GDP compared with the comparator countries.

As it entered the mature phase, Botswana had outstripped its agricultural sector's capacity either to absorb more workers or maintain food self-sufficiency. Higher private investment, much of it from overseas in the first instance, may provide a catalyst for growth in skill-intensive manufacturing and financial services to serve the liberalizing southern African market, while tourism offers a wider range of employment potential.

But these sectors are unlikely to meet half the required increase in total employment, and the expansion of low-income urban groups poses a threat to the conservative coalition whose prudent economic management has earned the accolade of development state (Leftwich, 1995). Some prospect of pricing more workers into formal employment is afforded by the real depreciation of the South African rand in the mid-1990s. But the informal sector needs to play a vital role in maximizing the flow of benefits from skill-driven growth to the lagging rural and urban areas. Consequently, this neglected incubator of human capital may merit greater financial support than it has received hitherto.

Nevertheless, economic diversification seems likely to proceed too slowly, as in the case of the two other small mineral economies, Jamaica and Trinidad and Tobago. It is not yet clear whether Botswana can avoid depleting its financial reserves or avert falling living standards without a renewed expansion of diamond mining. The experience of Trinidad and Tobago shows how quickly a large financial reserve can be run down without rapid diversification of tax revenues and exports.

TRANSITION TO MATURITY IN LARGER, MIDDLE-INCOME MINERAL ECONOMIES

Retarded Recovery in Chile

In 1973, Chile was a relatively large, mature, mid-income mineral exporter whose economy was highly distorted. Although its subsequent reform efforts and the eventual renewal of rapid economic growth were protracted, this was due to a serious policy error during the period 1978–82. Prior to the first reform effort of 1975–82, Chilean governments had focused upon increasing domestic control of, and revenue retention from, mining. They responded to Dutch disease effects by protectionist measures. The average tariff exceeded 100 per cent, and both imports and exports had extensive non-tariff barriers (Bosworth *et al.*, 1994). In the early 1970s, the Allende government went further and nationalized the mines, as well as some industry and banks. It also sanctioned a sharp increase in real wages as part of a populist boom which destabilized the Chilean economy (Sachs,

1989). The symptoms of economic repression in Chile included chronic inflation, a relatively low rate of economic growth and frequent crises.

The military government in late 1973 faced an economy in deep recession and
disrupted by civil disorder, with inflation above 100 per cent. But the government was, for Latin America, uniquely independent of either working groups or
industrial interests, so that it came to function as a developmental state. Economic technocrats were insulated from political pressures and given scope for
bold policies. But the failure of a 'big bang' reform in 1982 appeared to make the
case for phased reform in which capital market opening followed trade liberalization which, in turn, followed successful stabilization. Its advocates argued that
a gradual reform strategy of this sort might have rekindled sustained rapid growth
of the Chilean economy from the late 1970s, instead of delaying it by one decade.

As it was, consistent with a mature mineral economy undergoing deteriorating terms of trade, policies were adopted in the mid-1970s to broaden taxes and
diversify exports. A stabilization programme shrank public spending from 45
per cent of GDP to 24 per cent during the period 1973–8, while tax reforms
imposed a 20 per cent value added tax, a 10 per cent tariff on most imports and a
standard 49 per cent corporate tax. The fiscal deficit was cut from 25 per cent of
GDP to 0.8 per cent during the period 1973–8 (Ministry of Finance, 1989). The
current account deficit was tackled in 1974 by a real depreciation of the exchange rate by two-thirds. But the retention of indexation caused inflation to
remain stubbornly high, while the simultaneous pursuit of stabilization, trade
liberalization and capital market reform created policy conflict.

The policy error was to allow the exchange rate to appreciate in the late 1970s,
even as trade liberalization exposed the manufacturing sector to increasing competition. The intention was to use an exchange rate appreciation to suppress
the inflationary tendencies which were expected to accompany a projected rise
in copper prices. The higher exchange rate triggered an inflow of foreign capital
which Chilean policy makers relied on, along with public saving, to finance
investment in the face of the country's remarkably low domestic private saving
rate (3 per cent of GDP). But the capital inflows were not adequately supervised,
and they triggered a balance of payments crisis and the near-collapse of the
domestic financial system. Domestic interest rates rose sharply in response to
capital flight, and GDP plummeted by 14 per cent in 1982. Foreign debt reached
78 per cent of GDP, and debt service approached two-thirds of export earnings,
forcing the Chilean government to approach the International Monetary Fund.
Corbo and de Melo (1987) conclude that it was a mistake to liberalize trade
before stabilization was complete (that is, before inflation fell below 25 per cent).

The military government pursued a less doctrinaire policy after 1982 which
initially stressed stabilization and temporarily reversed the liberalization measures, boosting the average tariff to 35 per cent during the period 1982–4. Sharp

public expenditure cuts were made, and the exchange rate was devalued to two-thirds of its 1982 level, a rate which held into the early 1990s. Institutional changes were belatedly made in order to mute the future disruptive impact of mineral price shifts. The changes included the establishment of a mineral revenue stabilization fund (MRSF) and greater autonomy for the central bank. But the adoption of an MRSF during a period of falling copper prices meant that foreign debt rose to 140 per cent of GDP in 1985 (when debt service absorbed 48 per cent of export earnings). Real per capita incomes had fallen back to their mid-1960s level.

After successful stabilization, Chilean policy emphasized export-led growth from 1985. Short-term capital inflows were restrained by the requirement of a 12-month residency period. A potentially destabilizing upswing in copper prices in late 1987 yielded a fiscal windfall which averaged 3.8 per cent of GDP per annum during the period 1988–9 and 1.2 per cent during the period 1990–2 (Marfan and Bosworth, 1994). But it was successfully managed by a combination of restrictions on short-term capital flows and the MRSF. With stabilization achieved, attention returned to liberalization: import tariffs were cut again to 15 per cent in 1988 and to a uniform 11 per cent by the early 1990s.

The Dutch disease legacy meant that the Chilean agricultural sector was much smaller than the norms and, by 1990, the once protected manufacturing sector was also smaller, having shrunk by one-quarter relative to total GDP since 1972 (Table 4.5). Economic reform reoriented agriculture away from protected food crop production and towards high-value export crops such as fruit. Exports also diversified into non-mineral resources, notably fish and forest products, so that non-mineral primary products increased their share of total exports from 3 per cent to 35 per cent, while manufactured exports doubled to 16 per cent. As a result, minerals, which had comprised 85 per cent of total exports in 1970, fell to just under 50 per cent in the period 1990–3 (Table 4.3). Unlike in the smaller mineral economies, per capita GNP growth in Chile averaged 5.5 per cent during the period 1986–93 and unemployment dropped to 5 per cent. At this propitious stage, however, sizeable capital inflows, in part associated with renewed vigour in copper mining, cast doubt on the continuation of economic diversification and the competitive exchange rate policy.

Peruvian Recovery under 'Big Bang' Reforms

Despite the collapse of Chile's first ('big bang') reform, controversy remains as to whether reform is most effectively achieved by a careful sequencing of stabilization, trade liberalization and capital market reform (Corbo and Fischer, 1994) or by a 'big bang' (Sheahan, 1994). The government of Peru's President Fujimori opted for the latter, drawing upon a national consensus for radical reform which emerged from a generation of policy failure that saw real per capita incomes fall by 10 per cent in real terms over the period 1965–89 (see Figure 4.3).

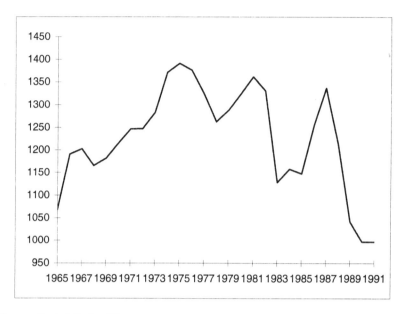

Source: Central Bank of Peru

Figure 4.3 Peru: GDP per capita, 1965–91 (1989 US dollars)

Webb (1991) sees the policies of successive Peruvian governments prior to 1990 as doomed efforts to maintain a predatory state that had thrived by extracting rents from the populace at large, with inadequate regard for either the economic or the social consequences. Lago (1991) concurs: such policies intensified the inward orientation of the economy, curbed foreign investment and failed to reignite economic growth in the face of adverse trends in the terms of trade. By 1990, the Peruvian agricultural sector was barely half the Syrquin and Chenery (1989) norm, while the size of the competitive manufacturing sector is grossly overstated in Table 4.5. This overstatement arises from very high levels of effective protection, which averaged 69 per cent in 1989. Meanwhile, effective protection was negative for exports, where Peru's comparative advantage lay in primary products, pharmaceuticals and textiles (Rossini and Paredes, 1991).

Drawing upon Chilean experience, Paredes and Sachs (1991) urged a phased programme of stabilization, trade liberalization and capital reform which could proceed fairly rapidly, however, because the economy had imploded and had little inflationary potential within it. Nevertheless, the new government opted to move even faster by not only boosting taxation and curbing public spending, but also lifting price controls and liberalizing the capital market (Sheahan, 1994). The exchange rate was unified and allowed to float, while non-tariff barriers were removed and the average tariff was swiftly reduced from 66 per cent in 1990 to 16 per cent by 1994.

Within five years, a primary fiscal surplus of 0.25 per cent of GDP was recorded and inflation dropped to 10 per cent. The rate of investment increased from 16 per cent of GDP in 1990 to 25 per cent in 1995 as the domestic savings rate rose by almost one-half to 17.5 per cent of GDP. The rate of domestic saving was approaching the 22 per cent level which Paredes and Sachs (1991) estimated was needed in order to sustain sufficient investment to lift GDP growth above 5.5 per cent. This would, in turn, pull the fraction of the workforce in full employment up from an estimated 25 per cent in 1990 to 75 per cent.

The restructuring of the Peruvian economy is favouring primary products: it will rejuvenate the rundown mining and fishing sectors (which together earned three-fifths of exports), as well as export agriculture (after reversal of the 1968–73 land reforms). Peru's weak manufacturing sector generated only 18 per cent of exports during the period 1990–3 (Table 4.3), mostly textiles, and much import substitution capacity shut down. Overall, GDP growth rebounded to an average of 5.5 per cent during the period 1991–5, after faltering during the period 1990–2 (Banco Central, 1996). But although ongoing investment (with US$ 10 billion in the pipeline for mining alone) is expected to drive the economy after the year 2000, the prospects until then remain fragile.

Sheahan (1994) summarizes the risks of a 'big bang' reform: it intensifies poverty as export (and employment) potentials are further compressed because of the appreciation of the real exchange rate, and as government revenues are cut because tariffs fall. Half the Peruvian population remained in poverty in 1995, and one-sixth of it, mainly Andean peasant farmers, was in absolute poverty. As in the case of the smaller mineral economies pursuing stabilization and reform, a tight fiscal policy combined with the return of flight capital to cause an appreciation of the Peruvian real exchange rate. The current account deficit was 8 per cent of GDP in 1995, yet exports were still a mere 9.8 per cent of GDP, of which the debt service ratio absorbed one-fifth (the rescheduled foreign debt was 43 per cent of GDP).

The Peruvian Central Bank responds to criticism of the 'big bang' policy by pointing out that in 1995 only 2 per cent of the current account deficit was financed by short-term funds, the remainder being bridged by privatization proceeds (2 per cent of GDP), refinancing of interest payments (2 per cent) and coca proceeds (some 1 per cent of GDP). The Central Bank also notes that the informal sector has ameliorated the adjustment for low-income groups and that poverty appears to be decreasing, albeit slowly. It does not expect manufacturing to be a major contributor to economic growth over the next decade, but it is confident that the rejuvenation of mining, export agriculture and tourism will bridge the gap.

CONCLUSIONS

Many mineral economies have a disappointing economic growth record, like most resource-rich countries. Their governments are prone to distort the economy by restricting trade and misjudging mineral revenue deployment. In theory, prudent macro policies need to be adjusted in line with a country's passage through each stage of the cycle (youthful, early-mature and late-mature).

During a mineral boom, especially during the youthful stage, a mineral revenue stabilization fund can help limit the Dutch disease effects and also smooth the impact of unexpected revenue fluctuations. The transition to maturity, when the mineral sector loses its dynamism, calls for new sources of tax revenues and exports while still managing revenue fluctuations.

The adjustment to maturity has been complicated for most mineral economies by the need to reform a distorted economy. The reform of the 1970s' legacy of a highly distorted economy has faced formidable political obstacles, and differences in the skill with which these obstacles were surmounted may explain variations in the mineral economies' economic growth. A 'big bang' reform may be more effective than sequenced reform, especially if the latter is taken to signal inadequate political resolve.

But structural differences offer an additional explanation for the varied success of the mineral economies. Diversification of the economy is easier not only the less distorted the economy, but also the broader the non-mining resource endowment, the larger the domestic market and the lower the real wage. These factors may explain the superior performance of Indonesia, which enjoyed all three structural advantages. Post-Allende Chile and post-García Peru benefited from the strong growth potential of non-mining resource-based activity, as well as from unusually determined governments. The transition to maturity has been especially difficult for the smaller, less well endowed economies, whose large mineral revenue streams have propelled them to a mid-income level from which they must diversify into industry, having leapfrogged the cheap labour stage of manufacturing-led growth.

NOTES

1. The market size criterion moves six of the largest mineral economies, that is, four oil exporters (Indonesia, Egypt, Nigeria and Venezuela) along with two hard-mineral exporters (Chile and South Africa), into the two large country categories. Reclassification of these countries makes little difference to the relative ranking of the six groups in

terms of GDP growth (the average GDP growth rate of each category is altered by only 0.1–0.2 per cent, except for the large resource-rich group where the exclusion of four large mineral economies significantly raises the mean growth rate of the remaining large countries to 16 per cent). Second, there is evidence that the small mineral economy has experienced more severe adjustment problems than those with larger domestic markets and a more diversified natural resource base.

2. Ranis's six effects are: first, rents may distract governments from the development of human resources; second, the rents on natural resources may divert attention from the process of wealth creation and into rent-seeking activity; third, resource rents sustain the process of import substitution industrialization long after its contribution to development has waned; fourth, international trade in natural resources can worsen income distribution so that society equates trade with the interests of the rich; fifth, the prices of natural resource exports tend to be more variable than the prices of manufactured goods, creating growth collapses in the absence of primary product export diversification; finally, Dutch disease effects may seriously weaken the competitiveness of the non-mining tradables (Krause, 1995).

REFERENCES

Ahmed, S. (1989), 'Indonesia: external shocks, policy response and adjustment performance', Discussion Paper, Washington, DC: World Bank.

Auty, R.M. (1990), *Resource-based Industrialisation: Sowing the Oil in Eight Developing Countries*, Oxford: Clarendon Press.

Auty, R.M. (1994), 'Industrial policy reform in six newly industrializing countries: the resource curse thesis', *World Development*, **22**, 11–26.

Auty, R.M. (1996a), 'A developing country typology by natural resource endowment and political economy', Working Paper 96/04, Lancaster: Lancaster University.

Auty, R.M. (1996b), 'Sustainable development in a mature mineral economy: Botswana in the 1990s', Working Paper 96/01, Lancaster: Lancaster University.

Banco Central (1996), *Memoria 1995*, Lima: Banco Central de Reserva del Peru.

Bank of Botswana (1994), *Annual Report 1993*, Gaborone: Bank of Botswana.

Bank of Botswana (1995), *Annual Report 1994*, Gaborone: Bank of Botswana.

Bhattacharya, A. and M. Pangestu (1992), *Indonesia: Development Transformation and Public Policy*, Washington, DC: World Bank.

Bosworth, B., R. Dornbusch and R. Larain (eds) (1994), *The Chilean Economy: Policy Lessons and Challenges*, Washington, DC: Brookings Institution.

Brewster, H. (1994), 'Dutch disease in the age of adjustment', paper presented to the Conference on Development, Environment and Mining, sponsored by UNCTAD, UNEP, the World Bank and the International Council on Metals and the Environment, Washington, DC, mimeo.

Central Statistical Office (1994), *Statistics Bulletin*, **19** (2), Gaborone: Central Statistical Office.

Corbo, V. and J. de Melo (1987), 'Lessons from the southern cone policy reforms', *World Bank Research Observer*, **2**, 111–42.

Corbo, V. and S. Fischer (1994), 'Lessons from the Chilean stabilization and recovery', in B. Bosworth, R. Dornbusch and R. Larain (eds), *The Chilean Economy: Policy Lessons and Challenges*, Washington, DC: Brookings Institution.

Davis, G. (1995), 'Learning to love the Dutch disease: evidence from the mineral economies', *World Development,* **23** (10), 1765–79.

Flatters, F. and G. Jenkins (1986), 'Trade policy in Indonesia', Cambridge (Mass.): Harvard Institute for International Development, mimeo.

Gelb, A.H. (1988), *Oil Windfalls: Blessing or Curse?*, New York: Oxford University Press.

Hartman, P. (1986), 'The role of diamond mining in the economy of South West Africa/ Namibia 1950–85', unpublished MSc dissertation, Department of Economics, University of Stellenbosch.

Harvey, C. (1993), 'The role of government in the finance of business in Botswana', Discussion Paper 337, Brighton: Institute of Development Studies.

Harvey, C. and K. Jefferis (1995), 'Botswana's exchange controls: abolition or liberalization?', Discussion Paper 348, Brighton: Institute of Development Studies.

Harvey, C. and S. Lewis (1990), *Policy Choice and Development Performance in Botswana*, Basingstoke: Macmillan.

Harvey, R. (1980), 'Chile's counter-revolution: a survey', *The Economist*, Centre Supplement, 2 February.

Hill, C.B. (1991), 'Managing commodity booms in Botswana', *World Development,* **7**, 775–89.

Hill, H. (1995), 'Indonesia: from "chronic dropout" to "miracle"?', *Journal of International Development,* **7**, 775–89.

Jefferis, K.R. (1996), 'Botswana's public expenditure', Gaborone, mimeo.

Krause, L.B. (1995), 'Social capability and long-term economic growth', in B.H. Koo and D.H. Perkins (eds), *Social Capability and Long-term Economic Growth*, Basingstoke: Macmillan.

Lago, R. (1991), 'The illusion of pursuing redistribution through macropolicy: Peru's heterodox experience 1985–90', in R. Dornbusch and S. Edwards (eds), *The Macroeconomics of Populism in Latin America*, London: University of Chicago Press.

Lal, D. and H. Myint (1996), *The Political Economy of Poverty, Equity and Growth: A Comparative Study*, Oxford: Clarendon Press.

Leftwich, A. (1995), 'Bringing politics back in: towards a model of the developmental state', *Journal of Development Studies,* **31**, 400–27.

Mahon, J.E. (1992), 'Was Latin America too rich to prosper? Structural and political obstacles to export-led growth', *Journal of Development Studies,* **28**, 241–63.

Marfan, M. and B.P. Bosworth (1994), 'Saving, investment and economic growth', in B.P. Bosworth, R. Dornbusch and R. Laban (eds), *The Chilean Economy*, Washington, DC: Brookings Institution.

Ministry of Finance (1989), *Gastos, Ingresos y Deficit Fiscal 1970–88*, Santiago: Ministry of Finance, Budget Office.

Norberg, H. and M. Blomstrom (1993), 'Dutch disease and management of windfall gains in Botswana', in M. Blomstrom and M. Lundahl (eds), *Economic Crisis in Africa: Perspectives on Policy Responses*, London: Routledge.

Paredes, C.E. and J.D. Sachs (1991), *Peru's Path to Recovery*, Washington, DC: Brookings Institution.

Planning Institute of Jamaica (1994), *Economic and Social Survey of Jamaica 1993*, Kingston: Government of Jamaica.

Ranis, G. (1991), 'Towards a model of development', in L.B. Krause and K. Kim (eds), *Liberalization in the Process of Economic Development*, Berkeley: University of California Press.

Ranis, G. and S. Mahmood (1993), *The Political Economy of Development and Change*, Oxford: Basil Blackwell.

Rossini, R.G. and C.E. Paredes (1991), 'Foreign trade policy', in C.E. Paredes and J.D. Sachs (eds), *Peru's Path to Recovery: A Plan for Economic Stabilization and Growth*, Washington, DC: Brookings Institution.

Sachs, J.D. (1989), 'Social conflict and populist policies in Latin America', Working Paper 2897, Cambridge (Mass.): National Bureau of Economic Research.

Sachs, J.D. and A.M. Warner (1995), 'Natural resources and economic growth', Cambridge (Mass.): Harvard Institute for International Development, mimeo.

Sheahan, J. (1994), 'Peru returns towards an open economy', *World Development, 22*, 911–23.

Syrquin, M. and H.B. Chenery (1989), 'Patterns of development, 1950 to 1983', Discussion Paper 41, Washington, DC: World Bank.

Traeger, R. (1993), 'A note on the relationship between mineral dependence and economic growth', Geneva: UNCTAD, mimeo.

UNCTAD (1995), *UNCTAD Database*, Geneva: United Nations Conference on Trade and Development.

UNIDO (1995), *Industrial Development: Global Report 1995*, Oxford: Oxford University Press.

Webb, R. (1991), 'Prologue', in C.E. Paredes and J.D. Sachs (eds), *Peru's Path to Recovery: A Plan for Economic Stabilization and Growth*, Washington, DC: Brookings Institution.

Woo, W.T., B. Glassburner and A. Nasution (1995), *Macroeconomic Policies, Crises, and Long-term Economic Growth in Indonesia, 1965-90*, Washington, DC: World Bank.

World Bank (1989), *World Tables 1989*, Baltimore (Md): Johns Hopkins University Press.

World Bank (1993), *World Tables 1993*, Baltimore (Md): Johns Hopkins University Press.

World Bank (1994), *Namibia: Public Spending Review*, Washington, DC: World Bank.

World Bank (1995a), *World Tables 1995*, Baltimore (Md): Johns Hopkins University Press.

World Bank (1995b), *Trinidad and Tobago: Poverty and Unemployment in an Oil-based Economy*, Washington, DC: World Bank.

World Bank (1996), *Trinidad and Tobago: Macroeconomic Assessment and Review of Public Sector Reform and Expenditures: The Changing Role of the State*, Washington, DC: World Bank.

World Resources Institute (1994), *World Resources 1994–95*, Oxford: Oxford University Press.

5. Managing Mineral Revenues in Botswana

Modise D. Modise[1]

INTRODUCTION

It is important to highlight from the outset the economic conditions prevailing when Botswana achieved political independence in 1966. This may partly explain the economic evolution that was to follow. Botswana is a country about the size of France or the state of Texas. In 1966, the population was estimated at 540 000; this meant that the country had a very low population density. It was one of the poorest countries in the world, with an economy based on subsistence agriculture. Estimated per capita income was about US$ 70; life expectancy at birth was 48 years and other social indicators reflected the low level of development of amenities; only half the children of primary school age were at school; the country had about 40 university graduates and 100 people with secondary school leaving certificates; and physical infrastructure was poorly developed. Indeed, Botswana was poor by whatever yardstick one chose to employ. The only economic activity of note was the raising of cattle and the export of beef. Another notable feature, until 1972, was the government's dependence on grants-in-aid from the United Kingdom to support recurrent expenditure. All capital expenditure was financed through foreign aid. It should also be mentioned that the frequent recurrence of drought in Botswana over the years has affected agricultural production and resulted in the government's reallocating resources to provide drought relief. Fortunately, however, even with such difficult development challenges, Botswana has proved to be an enduring and stable multi-party democracy.

MINERAL DEVELOPMENT

It is often believed that minerals have been a feature of Botswana's develop-ment right from independence in 1966. This is not true, however. Mineral development was in fact phased over a number of years, the first few years being largely insignificant. In 1966, agriculture accounted for 39 per cent of gross domestic product (GDP) and by 1976 it accounted for 24 per cent. Since the late 1980s, it has remained at under 5 per cent of GDP. Mining, on the other hand, accounted for 0 per cent in 1966, 12 per cent in 1976, 47 per cent in 1986 and 37 per cent in 1995. Manufacturing accounted for 8 per cent in 1966, 8 per cent in 1976, 6 per cent in 1986 and 6 per cent in 1995 (see Table 5.1). The share of mineral revenue in total government revenues rose from zero at independence to 47 per cent in 1995. This reached a high of 59 per cent in 1988/9 because of the sale of an accumulated stock of diamonds.

A copper-nickel mine in the north-eastern town of Selibe-Phikwe started operations in the early 1970s. It has not been a commercial success because of initial technical problems with the plant, depressed copper-nickel prices over the years and the heavy external debt overhang of the project. While the mine remains an important employer, employing about 5000 people, revenues are negligible, coming mainly from royalties in the recent past. Of late, even royal-ties have been deferred in order to help the mine's cash flow. The export value of copper-nickel in 1995 was 310 million pula. Botswana's other major mineral is soda ash, whose exploitation started in 1991. The export value of soda ash was 86 million pula in 1995. Like the copper-nickel mining venture, the soda ash project has not been a commercial success and has so far contributed practically no revenue to the government, although both projects have made important contributions to national economic development.

Botswana is a significant world producer of diamonds, accounting for roughly 15 per cent of total production, which probably represents about 25 per cent of value. Exploitation of diamonds began in 1970/1 with the Orapa kimberlite mine, which contains some of the largest reserves known in the world. Orapa's pro-duction reached 5.4 million carats in 1995. The Letlhakane mine began produc-tion in 1977 and produced 0.9 million carats in 1995. In 1982 the Jwaneng mine – the third and last mine to be developed – came on stream, and by 1995 it had produced 10.5 million carats. All the diamond mines, employing about 5000 people, are operated by the Debswana Mining Company, which is owned equally by the Government of Botswana and De Beers Centenary AG of Switzerland. The mines operate like private entities, with the government exercising its authority through its representation on the board of directors, whose mandate is similar to that of any other private agency. Diamonds accounted for 14.8 per cent of total exports in 1970/1 and by 1995 accounted for 67.2 per cent. In 1987, they accounted for 84.5 per cent of exports, partly as a result of the sale of a

Table 5.1 Botswana: gross domestic product by type of economic activity in current prices (millions of pula)

	1975/6	1981/2	1985/6	1990/1	1991/2	1992/3	1993/4	1994/5 Prov. rev.
ECONOMIC ACTIVITY								
1. Agriculture	75.0	113.0	132.4	332.9	366.2	443.9	495.2	20.6
2. Mining	37.1	201.6	1133.9	3012.0	3125.9	3042.3	3932.3	4086.3
3. Manufacturing	20.4	69.9	124.2	361.9	411.5	448.6	499.5	593.9
4. Water and electricity	11.1	21.8	57.7	152.1	169.0	206.6	239.4	269.5
5. Construction	26.3	53.0	96.0	551.6	645.4	609.5	694.5	757.1
6. Trade, hotels & restaurants	43.1	182.1	319.9	1059.8	1286.6	1441.0	1706.7	2093.7
7. Transport	14.6	25.0	66.5	207.8	255.1	319.8	363.1	437.4
8. Banks, insurance & business services	18.8	63.4	145.2	557.0	645.4	860.9	1148.6	1397.8
9. General government	43.7	156.3	325.7	1113.7	1307.6	1565.3	1846.7	2159.0
10. Social and personal services	13.1	32.7	66.7	285.7	342.9	410.5	479.3	550.9
Dummy sector	-2.7	-18.9	-47.6	-159.2	-183.1	-222.4	-290.3	-335.0
GDP at current market prices	300.5	899.9	2420.6	7475.2	8372.5	9126.0	11115.0	12530.3
GDP excluding mining	263.4	698.3	1286.7	4463.3	5246.6	6083.7	7182.7	8444.0
GDP per capita (pula)								
Total	412.8	943.3	2194.6	5671.7	6137.1	6462.8	7605.9	8286.8
Excluding mining	361.8	732.0	1166.5	3386.4	3846.1	4308.3	4915.1	5584.4
PERCENTAGE OF TOTAL								
1. Agriculture	25.0	12.6	5.5	4.5	4.4	4.9	4.5	4.2
2. Mining	12.3	22.4	46.8	40.3	37.3	33.3	35.4	32.6
3. Manufacturing	6.8	7.8	5.1	4.8	4.9	4.9	4.5	4.7
4. Water and electricity	3.7	2.4	2.4	2.0	2.0	2.3	2.2	2.2
5. Construction	8.8	5.9	4.0	7.4	7.7	6.7	6.2	6.0

(cont.)

80

6. Trade, hotels & restaurants	14.3	20.2	13.2	14.2	15.4	15.8	15.4	16.7
7. Transport	4.9	2.8	2.7	2.8	3.0	3.5	3.3	3.5
8. Banks, insurance & business services	6.3	7.0	6.0	7.5	7.7	9.4	10.3	11.2
9. General government	14.5	17.4	13.5	14.9	15.6	17.2	16.6	17.2
10. Social and personal services	4.4	3.6	2.8	3.8	4.1	4.5	4.3	4.4
Dummy sector	-0.9	-2.1	-2.0	-2.1	-2.2	-2.4	-2.6	-2.7
GDP excluding mining	87.7	77.6	53.2	59.7	62.7	66.7	64.6	67.4
Banking etc. including dummy sector	5.4	4.9	4.0	5.3	5.5	7.0	7.7	8.5

ANNUAL PERCENTAGE CHANGE

1. Agriculture	7.3	3.6	11.4	8.0	10.0	21.2	11.6	5.1
2. Mining	106.1	-16.5	50.6	4.0	3.8	-2.7	29.3	3.9
3. Manufacturing	36.0	44.7	43.4	11.7	13.7	9.0	11.3	18.9
4. Water and electricity	60.9	13.0	34.5	17.8	11.1	22.2	15.9	12.6
5. Construction	30.8	-23.2	-1.4	16.7	17.0	-5.6	13.9	9.0
6. Trade, hotels & restaurants	25.7	8.2	19.1	26.9	21.4	12.0	18.4	22.7
7. Transport	94.7	14.7	33.8	28.2	22.8	25.4	13.5	20.5
8. Banks, insurance & business services	23.8	17.8	29.6	23.0	15.9	33.4	33.4	21.7
9. General government	48.6	15.8	18.6	28.6	17.4	19.7	18.0	16.9
10. Social and personal services	48.9	20.2	20.6	21.0	20.0	19.7	16.8	14.9
Dummy sector	-18.2	7.4	55.6	10.0	15.0	21.5	30.5	15.7
GDP at current market prices	35.8	2.8	32.4	14.3	12.0	9.0	21.8	12.7
GDP excluding mining	29.6	10.1	19.6	22.6	17.6	16.0	18.1	17.6
Banking etc. including dummy sector	42.5	22.9	19.9	29.0	16.2	38.1	34.4	23.7
GDP per capita								
Total	29.9	-1.4	27.6	10.4	8.2	5.3	17.7	9.0
Excluding mining	23.9	5.6	15.3	18.3	13.6	12.0	14.1	13.6

Note: Series after 1988/9 have been revised on the basis of the actual 1992/3 National Accounts.

Source: Central Statistics Office of Botswana.

stockpile that had been accumulated from 1982 to 1986 (see Table 5.2). It was after 1982 that Botswana's economic landscape changed significantly. Diamonds now contribute virtually all the mineral revenue to the government. Some background information on diamonds is provided below.

Table 5.2   Botswana's diamond exports: relative importance in Botswana and world markets

Year	Total exports (pula million)	Diamond exports (pula million)	Diamonds as percentage of total Botswana exports	Diamond exports (US$ million)	CSO[a] diamond sales (US$ million)	Botswana exports as percentage of CSO sales
1970	18	3	14.8	4	530	0.7
1971	30	5	17.5	7	625	1.2
1972	45	20	43.6	25	849	3.0
1973	59	20	33.9	29	1332	2.2
1974	82	30	36.8	44	1254	3.5
1975	105	32	30.6	44	1066	4.1
1976	153	37	24.5	43	1544	2.8
1977	149	46	30.9	55	2073	2.6
1978	184	75	41.1	91	2552	3.6
1979	360	186	51.6	228	2598	8.8
1980	391	238	60.7	306	2723	11.2
1981	332	135	40.6	162	1472	11.0
1982	467	243	52.0	238	1257	18.9
1983	697	464	66.6	423	1600	26.4
1984	857	616	71.9	480	1613	29.7
1985	1385	1049	75.7	556	1823	30.5
1986	1576	1226	77.8	654	2557	25.6
1987	2656	2253[b]	84.8	1342[b]	3070	43.7
1988	2678	1979	73.9	1071	4172	25.7
1989	3743	2861	76.4	1420	4086	34.8
1990	3319	2614	78.8	1412	4167	33.9
1991	3738	2941	78.7	1465	3927	37.3
1992	3674	2899	78.9	1362	3417	39.8
1993	4312	3340	77.5	1379	4366	31.6
1994	4965	3718	74.9	1393	4250	32.8
1995	5931	3984	67.2	1442	4531	31.8

Notes:
[a] CSO = Central Selling Organization.
[b] Includes sale of accumulated stocks.

Sources: Export figures in pula from *Statistical Bulletins*; CSO sales from *Annual Reports* of the Department of Mines.

SOME FACTS ABOUT DIAMONDS

It is estimated that Botswana's proven diamond reserves will last in excess of 60 years at present rates of extraction. Also, there is ample evidence to suggest that significantly more reserves are available in the country. This has led some independent commentators to suggest that to consider Botswana's diamonds as depleting assets is largely irrelevant. The author does not support this view because, however long the reserves may last, the fact of the matter is that they are finite.

Botswana's diamond mines currently operate as open pits with the cost of production very low relative to the value of output, which gives rise to high economic rents. Some estimates put the level of these rents at 60 per cent of the export value. As the mines age, it may eventually be necessary to sink shafts, which will increase the cost of production and bring down the level of rents.

All of Botswana's diamonds are marketed through the Central Selling Organization (CSO), which is generally thought to supply about 70 per cent, by value, of the world demand for rough diamonds. Although the CSO is often referred to as a cartel, in fact it is not, because there is no collective decision making by producers to influence the market, unlike in the case, for example, of OPEC. In 1995, Botswana diamond sales were equivalent to over 30 per cent of the total value of CSO sales. Diamonds are a heterogeneous good and can be classified into industrial, near-gem and gem. The value of a diamond depends on its size, colour, shape and clarity. There are known to be several thousand categories of gem diamonds. Most of the value is in the latter, and it is this market that is the most crucial. It is generally accepted that the aggregate annual value of Botswana diamonds is one of the largest in the world. The world diamond market has been fairly stable except between 1982 and 1986 and from 1992 to the present, when sales quotas were imposed because of unfavourable market conditions.

MINERAL REVENUES

Revenues from diamonds accrue to the government of Botswana from its shareholding, with corporate tax at 25 per cent, 15 per cent tax on dividends paid abroad and royalties at 10 per cent of sales. Although the terms and conditions governing the profit-sharing agreements are kept secret, it is thought that the government receives about 75 per cent of the total profits. While the profit enjoyed by the private shareholder may appear insignificant, it represents quite a high rate of return on investment, which the private investor finds satisfactory. Diamond earnings are in United States dollars, and pula earnings are affected by exchange rate movements.

Table 5.3 Botswana: government budget, actual (millions of pula)

	1982/3	1983/4	1984/5	1985/6	1986/7	1987/8
REVENUE AND GRANTS	393.7	563.1	802.9	1 133.4	1 547.5	1 825.0
Mineral	99.5	193.8	376.5	581.2	844.9	1 034.5
Customs pool	114.3	156.8	155.8	149.2	192.3	234.1
Non-mineral income tax	58.3	78.9	87.2	93.6	121.1	129.6
Interest	13.5	14.4	25.5	30.6	43.3	47.2
Other taxes	7.1	11.2	9.3	11.2	18.5	25.4
Other revenue	19.0	22.7	89.1	191.5	63.5	46.9
Bank of Botswana profits	35.0	37.0	20.0	35.0	196.4	201.4
Grants	47.2	48.2	39.5	41.1	67.6	105.9
EXPENDITURES AND						
NET LENDING	414.8	460.1	614.7	719.2	1 008.2	1 312.0
Recurrent	226.3	270.6	342.3	427.0	573.0	686.8
Fin. Assistance						
Policy grants	1.0	2.1	2.4	5.2	8.1	8.9
Development expenditure	160.4	140.7	209.7	247.5	405.2	558.1
Net lending	27.0	46.8	60.4	39.4	21.8	58.2
Overall surplus/deficit (−)	−21.0	102.9	188.2	414.2	539.3	513.0
FINANCING OF DEFICIT	21.0	−102.9	−188.2	−414.2	−539.3	−513.0
External loans	58.1	20.0	33.7	13.2	73.1	75.4
Other financing	5.7	−3.9	−0.6	1.0	7.1	3.6
Change in cash balances	−42.8	−119.1	−221.3	−428.4	−619.5	−592.0

Source: Ministry of Finance and Development Planning of Botswana.

1988/9	1989/90	1990/1	1991/2	1992/3	1993/4	1994/5	1995/6	1996/7
2 556.0	2 750.9	3 740.7	4 069.4	4 652.3	5 359.5	4 472.5	5 464.4	5 421.3
1 508.1	1 596.0	2 005.4	1 888.0	1 866.1	2 278.7	2 349.4	2 591.4	2 568.9
292.6	353.1	478.2	761.6	998.4	822.3	711.8	829.4	897.3
164.8	242.8	289.9	357.3	369.9	420.5	386.9	356.9	330.0
94.1	75.4	132.8	66.3	243.8	204.0	200.5	238.4	248.2
23.6	43.3	70.7	84.8	140.1	155.6	184.6	231.6	221.4
43.9	61.0	79.2	79.7	101.9	184.9	112.2	129.1	127.9
319.3	339.2	566.8	761.9	832.1	1 106.8	451.4	1 050.5	959.0
109.7	40.0	117.8	69.8	100.1	186.6	75.7	37.1	68.6
1 787.5	2 214.5	2 942.7	3 372.2	3 771.0	4 481.2	4 276.8	5 195.5	6 057.3
897.0	1 141.8	1 416.6	1 789.8	2 187.0	2 702.4	2 975.1	3 437.6	4 139.7
9.9	13.0	22.0	26.0	28.4	31.2	36.2	72.0	40.0
797.3	827.7	1 090.1	1 098.0	1 207.0	1 558.3	1 377.8	1 672.0	1 847.6
83.3	232.0	414.0	458.5	348.6	189.3	–112.2	13.9	30.0
768.5	536.5	798.0	697.2	881.3	878.3	195.7	268.9	–636.0
–768.5	–536.5	–798.0	–697.2	–881.3	–878.3	–195.7	–268.9	636.0
101.4	55.9	2.9	35.4	91.5	51.2	–21.7	–46.0	–68.5
3.7	45.1	–20.8	189.9	–153.7	39.7	91.2	136.7	12.0
–873.6	–637.4	–780.1	–922.6	–819.1	–969.2	–265.2	–359.6	692.5

In 1982/3, mineral revenues were the second largest source of government revenues after Customs Union revenues. They contributed 99.46 million pula and Customs Union revenues 114.32 million pula, accounting for 25 and 29 per cent respectively. By 1983/4, mineral revenues amounted to 193.80 million pula (34 per cent) and Customs Union revenues to 156.84 million pula (28 per cent), and have surpassed all other revenues since that time. In 1995/6, mineral revenues totalled 2591.41 million pula. Between 1982/3 and 1995/6, therefore, mineral revenues increased by an average annual growth rate of 24.1 per cent in nominal pula (see Tables 5.3 and 5.4). Part of this increase is due to price increases for diamonds and increases in output, but is also a reflection of exchange rate movements. At the end of 1983, the pula was equivalent to US$ 0.8654, whereas by 1995 it was equivalent to US$ 0.3544. This means that during that period pula earnings rose by 144 per cent on account of exchange rate movements alone.

Bank of Botswana profits, representing earnings on foreign reserves, have become an important source of government revenues and have in some years exceeded Customs Union revenues. Foreign exchange reserves rose from 457.3 million pula at the end of 1983 to 13 249 million pula at the end of 1995, an average annual growth rate of 35.8 per cent. During this period, Bank of Botswana profits increased from 34.9 million pula to 1050.53 million pula, an annual average growth rate of 32.8 per cent.

Mineral revenues, Customs Union revenues and Bank of Botswana profits accounted for 63 per cent of total government revenues in 1982/3. This rose to 81 per cent by 1995/6. It is important to realize that mineral revenues have a bearing on both Customs Union revenues and Bank of Botswana profits. They make it possible for the government to finance its state enterprises and various forms of assistance to Botswana entrepreneurs, who may in turn import capital equipment and inputs from outside the Common Customs Area which may be liable for customs duties. Foreign exchange reserves have accumulated largely because of mineral revenues. There can be no question that, everything being equal, both Customs Union revenues and Bank of Botswana profits would have been much lower had there been no mineral revenues. Mineral revenues are therefore much more important than their direct contribution to total government revenues suggests. Similarly, the role of mining GDP is much greater than appears from its direct percentage share of GDP, as much of the GDP of other sectors is 'mineral-driven'.

GOVERNMENT EXPENDITURE

Total expenditure and net lending amounted to 414.76 million pula in 1982/3 and had reached 5195.46 million pula by 1995/6. During that period, total expenditure

Table 5.4 Botswana: government budget (per cent)

	1982/3	1983/4	1984/5	1985/6	1986/7	1987/8	1988/9	1989/90	1990/1	1991/2	1992/3	1993/4	1994/5	1995/6	1996/7
REVENUE AND GRANTS	100	100	100	100	100	100	100	100	100	100	100	100	100	100	100
Mineral	25	34	47	51	55	57	59	58	54	46	40	43	53	47	47
Customs pool	29	28	19	13	12	13	11	13	13	19	21	15	16	15	17
Non-mineral income tax	15	14	11	8	8	7	6	9	8	9	8	8	9	7	6
Interest	3	3	3	3	3	3	4	3	4	2	5	4	4	4	5
Other taxes	2	2	1	1	1	1	1	2	2	2	3	3	4	4	4
Other revenue	5	4	11	17	4	3	2	2	2	2	2	3	3	2	2
Bank of Botswana profits	9	7	2	3	13	11	12	12	15	19	18	21	10	19	18
Grants	12	9	5	4	4	6	4	1	3	2	2	3	2	1	1
EXPENDITURES AND NET LENDING	100	100	100	100	100	100	100	100	100	100	100	100	100	100	100
Recurrent	55	59	56	59	57	52	50	52	48	53	58	60	70	66	68
Fin. Assistance Policy grants	0	0	0	1	1	1	1	1	1	1	1	1	1	1	1
Development expenditure	39	31	34	34	40	43	45	37	37	33	32	35	32	32	31
Net lending	7	10	10	5	2	4	5	10	14	14	9	4	-3	0	0

Source: Ministry of Finance and Development Planning of Botswana.

and net lending grew by an annual average rate of 23.4 per cent. Recurrent expenditure grew from 226.34 million pula to 3437.63 million pula, an annual average growth rate of 25.4 per cent. Development expenditure increased from 160.36 million pula to 1671.97 million pula, an annual average growth rate of 21.6 per cent. In some years the increase in total expenditure and net lending has been as high as 33 per cent, for example between 1989/90 and 1990/1 (see Table 5.3).

MINERAL REVENUES AND ECONOMIC MANAGEMENT

Botswana's approach to the increasing revenues from minerals was relatively simple. Some independent commentators have suggested that it was predetermined by the relatively poor economy and the undeveloped infrastructure and human resources. The approach was to use the returns from mining to develop physical and social infrastructure such as roads, water supplies, power supplies, telecommunications, health facilities, schools and human capital. The development strategy was supported by the people of Botswana. It was recognized that there could be no meaningful economic diversification of the economy without such infrastructure. In the early years, most educated people were in government, and technocrats worked in close coordination with political leaders.

Botswana's National Development Plans (NDPs) were initially five-year plans rolling over after three years, but they are now six-year plans with a mid-term review after three years. NDPs set out the policy framework and the projects and programmes to be implemented over the period in question, given projected resources. In the early years, the NDPs were adhered to and instilled fiscal discipline. There was recognition of the need to do what was practically possible, given the known productive capacity and ready acceptance of saving for the 'day when it does not rain'. The frequent recurrence of drought, at a time when the vast majority of the people of Botswana were engaged in the agricultural sector, must have had something to do with this acceptance. The phenomenon of an export boom and higher government revenues creating euphoric optimism about future revenues, slackening budgetary discipline and allowing investment in projects with little or no serious analysis of likely returns was certainly not prevalent in Botswana. The existence of very few prestige projects attests to this.

Botswana enjoyed high levels of foreign aid and technical assistance because of its multi-party democracy and pursuit of a free-enterprise economic system. In addition, international support for Botswana came from its being surrounded by hostile neighbouring countries, namely Rhodesia (now Zimbabwe), South West Africa (now Namibia) and South Africa, where the struggle for majority rule was in progress.

The Incomes Policy was introduced in 1972 to prevent a widening gap between rural and urban incomes, as well as to prevent competition for scarce skills from exacerbating uneven income distribution among formal sector employees. Also, there was the fear that if mining wages were left unchecked, they could drive average wages in the economy upwards and discourage private investment. Over time, the Incomes Policy has been relaxed as more and more skills have become available and meaningful competition has become possible. Although it may be true that employers who were willing to pay higher wages were in fact made to earn higher returns, it has to be borne in mind that some of this was captured through taxation. To the extent that some of the excess profits were reinvested, thus creating employment, the Incomes Policy served to promote development. In any case, the adverse effects of the policy were considered a reasonable price to pay to prevent excessive income disparities which might have had severe social and economic effects in the early stages of Botswana's economic development. Although there were some real wage increases during the period, the Incomes Policy moderated them.

Botswana is a member of the Southern African Customs Union (SACU), together with South Africa, Namibia, Lesotho and Swaziland. Nearly 80 per cent of Botswana's imports come from South Africa and a significant proportion of non-traditional exports go to the South African market. Exchange rate policy has therefore been managed with a view to maintaining competitiveness in the South African market, which has effectively meant a close link with the South African rand. During the time of economic sanctions against South Africa, the rand declined against most major currencies, and the pula followed. The pula was not allowed to appreciate on account of the large diamond earnings, although it was probably higher than it would have been without diamond revenues.

Another important aspect of SACU is the regime governing industrial protection. Infant industry protection for the smaller member states is permissible for a period of eight years, whereas protection in the entire SACU area is conditional upon an industry's satisfying at least 60 per cent of the market. While it is true that SACU has been used mainly as an instrument to promote industrial development in South Africa, it is equally true that the SACU provisions provided checks against excessive industrial protection. There was very little direct subsidy for industry in Botswana until the Financial Assistance Policy (FAP) was introduced in 1982 and subsequently reviewed three times. Subsidies are provided over a maximum period of five years, mainly on the basis of the unskilled employment level of the industry concerned. An objective evaluation is made of the economic and financial viability of projects.

Was there a Dutch disease problem in Botswana? Did wage increases and the exchange rate policy militate against the development of the manufacturing and agricultural sectors? As Table 5.1 shows, manufacturing accounted for 4.7 per cent of GDP in 1994/5, and the highest it has ever reached was 7.8 per cent in 1981/2. A major point to bear in mind is that, given the large size and relative contribution of the mining sector to GDP as well as its growth, the contribution of comparatively small sectors was somewhat masked. Both manufacturing output and employment have grown since 1975/6. There was also some modest diversification. Between 1982/3 and 1994/5, output in real terms grew by an annual average rate of 7.4 per cent and employment by 6.8 per cent. The main constraints on manufacturing development are lack of skilled human resources, a nascent industrial culture, slow processing of applications for land, work and residence permits, the long distance to seaports in South Africa and a small domestic market. While manufacturing remains relatively small, there have been some positive developments.

With respect to agriculture, it should be borne in mind that up to the present day it has not been subject to minimum wages. Moreover, unlike in other countries, there has been no deliberate government policy to depress prices for agricultural crops in order to subsidize the urban elite. The higher wages paid to manufacturing, mining and other employees are thought to have affected the agricultural sector by attracting able-bodied males into those sectors. The other effect is through inflation arising out of higher expenditures resulting from mining revenues.

While these two factors led to some adverse effects on agricultural production, there were natural factors that worked against the sector. Principal among these are frequent and severe droughts and poor soils. The arable sector is the most affected. To counter these effects, extensive subsidies have been extended to the agricultural sector. The terms-of-trade losses were probably more than compensated for by the subsidies. The implementation of subsidy programmes has given rise to concerns about the level of subsidies, targeting, economic efficiency, disincentive effects, environmental impact and long-term sustainability. It would therefore appear that natural factors adversely affected agricultural development more than any other factor. Furthermore, mineral revenues made it possible to support a scale of subsidies that would otherwise not have been possible.

One of the possible measures of sustainability in the use of mineral revenues is the ratio of non-investment recurrent expenditure (excluding health and education) to non-mineral domestic revenues. Ideally, this ratio should not exceed 1. In 1983/4, it amounted to 0.41; in 1988/9 it was 0.63 and in 1995/6 it was 0.84. However, the planned developments over the period of National Development Plan 8, that is, 1997–2003, involve the ratio rising to 1.35 by the sixth year. This in effect means that 35 per cent of non-investment recurrent expenditure will be financed from mineral revenues. A worrying trend is developing, namely the increasing inclination to use mineral revenues for non-investment activities.

The government will need to consider the privatization of some of its 50 per cent share in the mining companies. As the quantum of funds is likely to be quite large, this would need to be done gradually and in consonance with the development of the nascent stock exchange. The advantages of privatization are many. The main ones are, first, that private investors are likely to want, much more than the government, to enhance their returns and secure improved performance. Second, private investors are likely to reinvest their returns much more productively and sustainably than the government, thus enhancing long-term sustainable development. Furthermore, the government will avoid the ever-increasing temptation to use mineral revenues for consumption through financing recurrent expenditures, although this is not to say that private investors cannot use their returns for consumption. All these, together with the avoidance of financing low-yielding investments, are among critical measures needed to contain the dissipation of mineral revenues. The government's revenue base will not be unduly eroded, as it will continue to earn income through royalties and taxes from mining operations and other lucrative secondary activities. What is beyond question is that, with diminishing returns on some of the public sector investments, much more thought needs to be given to the consideration of other options, including privatization of some of the government's shareholding.

The rising level of education, stronger opposition parties, the relatively large proportion of young people in the population, increasing concern about inequitable income distribution, the increasing role of organized labour, and increasing urbanization mean that future development strategies may not be accepted as readily as in the past. There is a need for public education on the merits of pursuing a strategy in keeping with the sustainable use of mineral revenues.

EVALUATION OF PERFORMANCE

At the macro level there can be no question that Botswana has promoted economic development through prudent management and avoidance of the dissipation of mineral revenues. Per capita income rose from roughly US$ 70 in 1966 to US$ 2800 in 1995. There has been an improvement in social indicators such as school enrolment, access to health, access to clean water, the infant mortality rate and life expectancy. In addition, there has been significant development of infrastructure such as roads, telecommunications and power supplies, which to date are fairly well maintained and reliably operated. Botswana has progressed from being among the least developed countries in the world to a lower-middle-income developing country with a stable and growing economy (see Tables 5.5–5.8).

Botswana has been able to deal adequately with the disruptions to the diamond market in 1982 and the ongoing sales quota on production that has been

Table 5.5   Botswana: selected measures of infrastructure

	1975	1980	1985	1990	1995	Average annual growth rate
Kilometres of tarred roads	219	1121	1885	2565	4177	14.7
Number of registered privately owned motor vehicles ('000)	15.4	27.3	45.7	74.4	101.5	9.4
Domestic electricity generation (millions kWh)	270	387	457	906	1040	7.0
Telephone subscribers connected	n.a.	n.a.	10 079	22 195	50 447	19.6

Note: n.a. = not available.

Source: Central Statistics Office of Botswana.

Table 5.6   Botswana: population and fertility indicators

	1981	1991	Average annual growth rate
Total population ('000)	941.0	1327.0	3.5
Life expectancy at birth	56.2	65.2	1.5
Total fertility rate	7.1	4.2	−5.2
Crude birth rate (per 1000)	48.7	39.3	−2.1
Crude death rate (per 1000)	13.9	11.5	−1.9

Note: Demographic data are for the census years.

Source: Central Statistics Office of Botswana.

Table 5.7 Botswana: education and health indicators

	1975	1980	1985	1990	Most recent estimate	Date	Average annual growth rate
Education							
Primary enrolment ('000)	116.3	171.9	223.6	283.5	319.1	1995	5.2
Secondary enrolment ('000)	12.1	18.3	32.2	56.9	104.7	1995	11.4
University enrolment	465	928	1773	3677	5501	1995	13.1
Primary school net enrolment rate (percentage)	72	92	93	91	89	1993	
Health							
Doctors per 100 000	n.a.	15	17	18	24	1994	3.4
Nurses per 100 000	n.a.	124	156	216	217	1994	4.1
Total hospital beds	n.a.	2060	2554	3211	3245	1994	3.2
Daily calorie supply per capita (number)	2137	2111	2310	2392	2468	1994	0.8
Access to safe water (percentage of population)	n.a.	45	n.a.	54	90	1994	

Notes:

Demographic data are for the census years

n.a. = not available.

Source: Central Statistics Office of Botswana.

in force since September 1992. As diamond revenues are not immediately spent, the impact of lesser revenues on government expenditure and the rest of the economy does not result in sudden severe adjustments.

Furthermore, Botswana has been careful to avoid the external debt trap, with the result that total outstanding external debt in 1995 amounted to US\$ 750 million, representing a debt service (as a percentage of exports of goods and services) of 4.5 per cent. The bulk of the debt is owed to multilateral and bilateral agencies, and there is very little commercial debt.

There is some evidence that the increase in government expenditure did at times cause the economy to overheat and reduce the efficiency of resource use. A case in point is the cost of construction in the mid-1980s, which rose at an

Table 5.8 Comparative economic and social indicators

	Botswana	Averages for	
		Sub-Saharan Africa	High-Income economies
Economic indicators, 1993			
GNP per capita (US$)	2790	520	23 090
Economic structure (percentage contribution to GDP)			
Agriculture	4	20	4
Industry (including manufacturing)	46	33	41
Manufacturing	6	16	30
Services	50	47	55
Average annual growth rate of			
merchandise exports (1980–93)	8	2.5	5.1
merchandise imports (1980–93)	3.9	–2.2	5.8
Average annual rate of inflation			
(1980–93)	12.3	16.1	4.3
Social indicators			
Average annual population growth			
rate (1980–1993)	3.5	2.9	0.6
Average annual labour force			
growth (1980–93)	3.3	2.5	0.7
Crude birth rate per 1000			
people (1993)	39.3	44.0	13.0
Crude death rate per			
1000 people (1993)	11.5	15.0	9.0
Infant mortality rate			
(per 1000 live births)	42.0	93.0	7.0
Life expectancy at birth (1993)	65.2	52.0	77.0
Urban population as a percentage			
of total (1993)	45.7	30.0	78.0

Source: With the exception of GNP per capita, the data for Botswana are from the Central Statistics Office. Demographic data for Botswana are based on the 1991 Population Census. Other data are from the World Bank, *World Development Report, 1995*.

unsustainable rate on account of demand pressures directly emanating from the government sector. The bubble finally burst in the early 1990s when demand normalized. The contraction had effects on employment, the performance of financial institutions and private investment, as many enterprises and people had invested in real estate on account of the artificially high returns. The country is still recovering from the after-effects of the construction boom.

Other evidence of inefficient use of resources has been cost and time overruns on projects as well as substandard workmanship. Quite a number of public enterprises did not perform well, with the result that some have had to be liquidated or capital has had to be substantially restructured and/or employees retrenched. The financial ill-health of the enterprises continued far longer than would have been the case in the absence of mineral revenues.

SUCCESS FACTORS

Botswana has a small and largely homogeneous and cohesive population, which currently stands at 1.5 million. In the early years the political arena was dominated by one political party, which has ruled the country since independence. The politicians worked closely with technocrats, who were allowed a large degree of autonomy. The leaders were dedicated and committed to the economic development of the country. The bureaucracy was fairly small and efficient. Because of the poorly developed educational system, the leadership enjoyed the trust and unquestioning support of the people. The main development challenges of the time were simple and straightforward: development of infrastructure and human capital development.

Adherence to planned developments contained in National Development Plans instilled the required fiscal discipline. Perhaps the housing of the Finance and Development Planning portfolios in one ministry contributed to this. Even though some adjustments were made to resource levels in the light of increasing availability, the general policy thrust remained largely on course.

It is somewhat of a paradox that some of the modest expenditure was in fact due to capacity constraints in the economy, and not so much to acts of deliberate policy. In the last five years, the government has been able to spend only between 70 and 80 per cent of all the funds intended for development. If the financing of drought is factored out, the performance is even worse. The main reasons for this are insufficient skilled human resources, poor coordination by responsible agencies, overoptimistic implementation programmes, frequent changes to design briefs, poor pre-project preparation, lack of water at intended project sites and delayed acquisition of land rights.

In the early years of mineral exploitation, when the economy was growing rapidly (in fact, at some point it was the fastest-growing in the world), and employment and incomes were increasing, there was hardly any cause to question the country's development strategy. For this reason, the accumulation of cash balances and foreign exchange reserves was not seen as impeding development. The above factors may not necessarily be prerequisites for success in all countries, but certainly seem to explain some of the factors responsible for Botswana's performance.

CONCLUSIONS

There are many factors that may influence a country's approach to the use of its resource-based revenues. The main ones include the size of the economic rent, the marketing of the commodity (including the world market share for the country concerned) and the longevity of reserves.

The higher the economic rent and the longer the reserves are expected to last, the less the pressure for the country to adopt viable and sustainable policies for the use of revenues. Also, cartel arrangements for marketing tend to make countries complacent, especially during those periods when the cartel seems to be fully in control of the market. Countries with a larger market share sometimes overestimate their potential to influence the market in the desired direction. A concrete example of this is the withholding of cocoa from the market by Côte d'Ivoire in the late 1980s, which resulted in favourable market conditions for its competitors. Countries also tend to be oblivious to the dynamism of the market and competitive forces, for example new competitors or existing ones producing more competitively or the loss of market share to substitutes.

Countries with non-renewable natural resources face the greatest challenge in the utilization of revenues from such sources. It is critically important for governments to adopt long-term planning horizons and resist the temptation to base expenditure plans on existing and continuously increasing revenues from non-renewable natural resources. Windfall gains that are assumed to continue can cause the plans to go awry. The long-term strategy should provide for the ability to withstand short-term market disruptions without causing severe macroeconomic imbalances and instability. Economic diversification and developing alternative sources of revenue that are sustainable should go hand in hand with the utilization of revenues from non-renewable natural resources. Properly managed, natural resources are great assets and need not be curses.

NOTE

1. The opinions expressed in this chapter are those of the author and do not necessarily reflect the views of the Government of Botswana.

BIBLIOGRAPHY

Cooper, R.N. (1994), *Boom, Crisis and Adjustment: The Macroeconomic Experience of Developing Countries, 1970–90. A Summary*, Washington, DC: World Bank.

Harvey, C. and Lewis, S. (1990), *Policy Choice and Development Performance in Botswana*, Basingstoke: Macmillan.

Ministry of Finance and Development Planning (1991), *National Development Plan 7: 1991– 97*, Gaborone: Government Printer.

Ministry of Finance and Development Planning (1994), *Mid-Term Review of NDP 7*, Gaborone: Government Printer.

Ministry of Finance and Development Planning (1996), *Macroeconomic Outline for National Development Plan 8*, Gaborone: Government Printer.

Tilton, J.E. (ed.) (1992), *Mineral Wealth and Economic Development*, Washington, DC: Resources for the Future.

6. Oil Resources in Iraq: Economic Growth and Development until the Mid-1990s

Abbas Alnasrawi

In 1961, Iraq's real GDP in 1980 prices was US$ 10 billion. In 1979, it peaked at US$ 54 billion before falling to US$ 10 billion by 1993. But those figures tell only part of this unique episode in this natural resource country, since in 1961 the population was 7 million, while in 1993 it was approaching 21 million. This means that per capita GDP, which had increased from US$ 1410 in 1961 to US$ 4219 in 1979, had declined to an estimated US$ 485 by 1993.

This chapter addresses three issues pertaining to the experience of an oil-based economy in an attempt to explain the above features: (a) the contribution of the steady and sudden increases in oil revenue to economic growth of both the non-oil sector and the economy at large; (b) whether the pattern of the deployment of oil revenue was optimal; and (c) the impact of the severe external shocks. The chapter concludes with some observations regarding the future of the Iraqi economy.

DEPLOYMENT OF OIL REVENUE AND DEVELOPMENT: AN ASSESSMENT

The idea that oil is an exhaustible national resource, producing revenue to be used for investment, goes back to 1927 when the Iraqi government decided to earmark this revenue for infrastructure projects. A dual budgeting system of ordinary and capital expenditures continued until 1950, when the era of development planning was formalized by the creation of the Development Board (DB). Initially, all oil revenues were appropriated by the DB. With oil revenue rising and given the need to finance ordinary government expenditure, the share accruing to the DB was reduced first to 70 per cent and then to 50 per cent of oil revenue.

OIL AND DEVELOPMENT UNDER THE MONARCHY

In the period between 1951, when the first five-year general development plan was launched, and 1958, when the monarchy was overthrown, the DB budgeted US$ 874 million but spent only US$ 499 million, or 57 per cent of its spending target and 69.5 per cent of its budgeted revenue. Of the US$ 499 million, 34.5 per cent was spent on agriculture (mainly dams and irrigation); 10.7 per cent on industry; 21.6 per cent on transport and communications; 13.5 per cent on building and housing; and 19.8 per cent on other projects. The development policy of this period was criticized for its neglect of the industrial sector, as evidenced by the low level of spending in that sector, and in particular for its neglect of the agricultural sector.

When development spending was launched, Iraq was an agricultural country in which about 80 per cent of the labour force was employed in agriculture, and in which agriculture contributed between 22 per cent and 36 per cent to non-oil GDP. As in many other developing countries, this sector suffered from chronic underemployment and from seasonal unemployment that reached levels as high as 75–80 per cent. The neglect of this important sector was aggravated by the nature of the prevailing land tenure system, which ensured that the benefits of agricultural development spending were captured by the upper stratum of the landowning class.

The degree of land concentration is revealed by the fact that out of a total land area of 8 million hectares (ha) some 0.356 million ha, or 4.43 per cent of the total area, was held by eight owners. Moreover, the top 33 owners controlled 0.758 million ha, or 9.8 per cent of the total area. At the bottom of the landownership pyramid were 162 000 owners with a total ownership of 0.293 million ha, or 3.67 per cent of the total area. Further scrutiny of the data shows that 1.7 per cent of all owners had 63.1 per cent of the total area, while nearly 84 per cent of owners had 15.3 per cent (Sayigh, 1978, pp. 27–8).

This grim picture of land concentration was made even worse by the fact that the income of farmers corresponded to only between one-fifth and one-fourth of the value of their output. This pattern of relationship was based on a law of 1933 which provided that no labourer could leave the land if he was in debt to the landowner. Given that labourers (*fellahin*) were perpetually in debt, their situation was comparable to that of serfs.

OIL AND ECONOMIC DEVELOPMENT PROBLEMS SINCE 1958

The monarchy was overthrown in July 1958. Two months later, the Republican regime under Qasim adopted the Agrarian Reform Law setting ceilings on agricultural landholdings and introducing mechanisms for the distribution of small parcels of land to previously landless peasants.

During the five years of Qasim's regime, development spending was budgeted to be US$ 1.6 billion, but actual spending amounted to US$ 749 million, with 18.6 per cent going to agriculture, 14.9 per cent to industry, 21.8 per cent to transport and communications, 35.8 per cent to building and housing, and 8.9 per cent to other projects.

One of the major criticisms of development during this period was its failure to provide the necessary resources and inputs to make agrarian reform operative. Another criticism related to the gap between the regime's announced industrial bias and the lack of achievement in the industrial sector. However, spending on infrastructure development was expanded during this period.

During the operation of the Five-Year Plan 1965–9, actual development spending continued to be below the level of appropriations: appropriations amounted to US$ 1.9 billion, while actual spending was US$ 1.023 billion. The distribution of the latter was as follows: agriculture 15.4 per cent; industry 27.2 per cent; transport and communications 18.1 per cent; building and housing 19.4 per cent; and other projects 19.8 per cent. Available data regarding the performance of the economy reveal the following average annual rates of growth (in 1966 prices) for the period 1953–69: GDP 6 per cent; agriculture 5 per cent; the oil sector 4.5 per cent; manufacturing 8.6 per cent; construction 5.2 per cent; water and electricity 15.3 per cent; transportation and communications 5.9 per cent; trade 6.7 per cent; banking and insurance 9 per cent; and public administration and defence 11.4 per cent (Ministry of Planning, 1970, pp. 132–3).

THE 1970s: THE LAST DECADE OF DEVELOPMENT AND GROWTH

The Baath party came to power in 1968; two years later, it produced its National Development Plan (NDP) for the years 1970–4. The NDP has been the first and only plan to have been drafted, implemented and allowed to run its course under the same government. The one guiding principle of the plan was to accelerate the rate of growth of the economy in all its sectors by increasing efficiency, productivity and resource allocation. Diversification of production and export activities away from oil was given priority. Priority was also given to the expansion of the public sector in all sectors of the economy. All economic indicators were projected to increase at unprecedentedly high rates.

The NDP was initially drawn up with a total allocation of US$ 1.8 billion, but because of the sudden and dramatic rise in oil revenue, this amount was revised sharply upwards to US$ 6.5 billion. Because of the unprecedented magnitude of the plan's income and allocation it was labelled the 'explosive plan'. But in reality the revised plan served as a storage facility for the unplanned rise in oil income, since actual spending amounted to US$ 4 billion or 61.4 per cent of planned spending. The sectoral distribution of actual spending was as follows: agriculture 17.5 per cent; industry 27.9 per cent; transportation and communications 15 per cent; building and services 14.5 per cent; and other projects 25.2 per cent.

Ironically, the huge increase in oil income and NDP revenue dashed planners' hope of changing the structure of the economy. Thus, instead of the oil sector's contribution to GDP falling to 26.4 per cent in 1974, its share actually increased to 60.4 per cent. In contrast, the contributions of agriculture and manufacturing, which were projected to contribute 19.7 per cent and 11.4 per cent of GDP in 1974 respectively, amounted in that year to 6.9 and 5.2 per cent (Alnasrawi, 1994, pp. 62–74).

A careful inspection of industrial sector allocations reveals that a strategic decision was taken by the government to invest heavily in the oil sector in order to develop oil reserves, expand production capacity, increase the number of refineries, purchase oil tankers and invest heavily in petrochemicals. In short and contrary to decades of policy pronouncements about lessening the dependence of non-oil GDP on the oil sector, the thinking of the 1970s was driven by higher oil prices to reverse policy and increase dependence on this particular sector.

The 1970–4 NDP was the last published plan. Although technocrats at the Ministry of Planning were thinking of a long-term plan (1975–95), the political authorities decided instead to resort to a series of annual investment programmes. In 1977, a number of planning documents for the years 1976–80 were adopted but not published. Subsequently released data indicate that the 1976–80 plan had a total appropriation of US$ 53.1 billion.

Iraq's development experience has taken unexpected turns since 1980 under the impact of the war with Iran, the invasion of Kuwait and the imposition of economic sanctions, as discussed below.

PLANNED AND ACTUAL DEVELOPMENT SPENDING, 1951–80: A SUMMARY

One of the common and striking features of Iraq's economic development over the period 1950–80 is the failure of planners and implementers to spend the funds allocated in development plans and programmes. Table 6.1 shows that between 1951 and 1980 the government appropriated US$ 67.5 for development spending, while actual spending amounted to US$ 45 billion or 67 per cent of the appropriation. Relative to the oil revenue of the period (that is, US$ 95.8 billion), planned spending was 67 per cent, while actual spending amounted to 47 per cent of oil revenue.

Table 6.1   Iraq: planned and actual development expenditures, 1951–80

	Planned expenditure (US$ billion)	Actual expenditure (US$ billion)	Actual to planned (per cent)
Agriculture	10.2	4.9	48
Industry	18.9	12.4	66
Transport and communications	10.2	6.9	68
Building and services	11.0	6.8	62
Other	17.0	14.1	83
Total	67.3	45.1	67

Sources: Government of Iraq, *Annual Abstracts of Statistics*, and Central Bank of Iraq, *Quarterly Bulletin*, various issues.

One of the most serious flaws in Iraq's development strategy since the creation of the Development Board was that it was driven by the level of oil revenue. Regardless of the nature of the political regime – its orientation, its proclaimed philosophy or rhetoric – development was in reality a function of oil revenue.

This dependence of development expenditure on oil revenue called for accelerated growth in the oil sector and the utilization of the oil income to develop the non-oil sectors. While the first goal was to a considerable extent accomplished – thanks to a combination of factors, including a series of economic/political policy decisions, foreign assistance (especially from the former Soviet Union), the role of OPEC and the changing nature of the international oil market – the second goal was far from being attained.

The inability of development agencies to meet their spending targets and the ever-increasing oil revenue encouraged successive governments to divert increasing portions of oil revenue to finance current spending. Thus the initial formula of 100 per cent allocation of oil revenue to development was changed to 70 per cent, then to 50 per cent and abolished altogether in 1974. However, this change allowed the government to avoid the difficult task of increasing taxes. Thus the share of non-oil revenue in the ordinary budget declined from 63 per cent in 1966 to only 13 per cent in 1980.

The meagre contribution of the personal income tax system is reflected in the small increase in tax collection. Thus between 1966 and 1980 personal income tax receipts rose from US$ 41 million to US$ 186 million, or by 4.5 times. Yet during the same period GDP increased 17.5 times and non-oil GDP increased by 8.6 times.

It is important to point out that development spending was only a part, albeit a major one, of total investment in the economy. There are two other sources of investment. First, there is investment spending by government or state-owned enterprises (SOEs), whose activities were lumped together under what at times was called 'the socialist sector'. The SOEs were engaged in a wide range of economic activities producing a large array of goods and services in all sectors of the economy. They had their own budgets, which were independent of the government's ordinary budget and the budgets of the economic development plans. Available data on SOEs for the period 1969–81 show that their combined annual appropriations exceeded appropriations under the ordinary budget or the annual allocations under development plans.[1]

Second, public sector investment – development plans and SOEs – was augmented by private sector investment, which amounted to 46 per cent of total investment during the period 1957–70. With the three sources taken together, investment spending represented between 15.5 per cent and 27.7 per cent of Iraq's GNP during the period 1957–70 (Hashem, 1975, pp. 122–4). The ratio of private to public sector investment declined in the 1970s as the state expanded the scope of its economic activities and as oil revenue fuelled public sector investment. For the three years 1976–8 the share of the private sector in gross fixed capital formation amounted to 19 per cent, with the remaining 81 per cent supplied by the public sector.

THE DESTRUCTIVE IMPACT OF THE IRAQ–IRAN WAR

When the Iraqi government decided to launch the war against Iran in September 1980 the Iraqi economy was on the threshold of another decade of economic growth. The immense increase in oil revenue enabled the government to increase spending simultaneously on infrastructure, goods-producing sectors, social services, imports and the military. This high level of spending was reflected in significant changes in some key economic indicators, as shown in Tables 6.2 and 6.3.

Table 6.2   Iraq: changing composition of GDP, 1975–88

	1975	1980	1982	1984	1986	1988
GDP by type of expenditure (Iraqi dinar bn)						
GDP in current prices	13.9	53.5	43.6	47.5	47.8	55.9
GDP in 1975 prices	13.5	24.0	19.1	17.0	18.3	20.2
Distribution of GDP (per cent)						
Government consumption	21	15	36	32	30	30
Private consumption	35	23	46	53	53	53
Change in inventories	9	8	13	–8	–1	5
Gross fixed investment	26	22	44	27	23	17
Exports of goods and services	51	63	26	25	19	22
Imports of goods and services	41	31	65	29	31	28
GDP by origin (per cent)						
Agriculture	8	5	10	13	15	16
Industry – total	57	66	32	34	27	33
Manufacturing	7	4	7	8	11	12
Construction	9	7	17	10	9	6
Trade	5	5	12	13	13	11
Transport and communications	5	4	7	5	7	7
Other activities	17	13	24	28	32	29

Sources: United Nations (1991a, 1991b).

The war damage to oil facilities, such as loading terminals, pumping stations, refineries and pipelines, caused oil output to decline sharply from 3.4 million barrels a day (MBD) in August 1980 to 0.9 MBD in 1981. This in turn resulted in Iraq's oil revenue collapsing from US$ 26.1 billion in 1980 to US$ 10.4 billion in 1981, that is, by 60 per cent. Moreover, changes in the international oil industry further depressed Iraq's oil income to US$ 6.4 billion by 1986 and implied that it would not return to its pre-war levels.

Table 6.3 Iraq: average growth rates of selected economic indicators, 1970–89

	1970–80	1980–5	1985–9
GDP	11.7	−8.1	−1.7
Government consumption	13.6	−1.3	−4.4
Private consumption	13.2	−7.6	−4.6
Gross fixed investment	27.6	−0.3	−1.5
Export of goods and services	4.4	−8.8	−1.1
Imports of goods and services	22.5	−8.2	−2.9
Agriculture	1.4	6.3	−6.7
Industry	10.2	−7.3	11.4
Manufacturing	13.4	0.3	−3.1
Construction	28.4	−7.8	−16.2
Domestic trade	16.8	1.3	−10.8
Transport and communications	19.9	−12.4	1.8

Sources: As for Table 6.2.

In a country that had grown so dependent on a single export these external shocks forced the economy to cope with a number of serious problems, including inflation, suspension of or severe reduction in development spending, stagnant agriculture, an increase in the share of military personnel in the labour force, an increase in the number of foreign workers, a reduction in non-military imports, a drastic decline in per capita income and living standards, a contraction in non-military public spending, the issue of the role and size of the public sector and state-owned enterprises, exhaustion of foreign exchange reserves, and the slide for the first time into foreign debt.

MILITARIZATION OF THE ECONOMY AND THE BURDEN OF MILITARY SPENDING

One of the most significant changes to take place in the Iraqi economy in the 1970s and 1980s was the massive shift of labour from the civilian economy to the military and the sharp increase in military spending and military imports. In 1970, 2.9 per cent of Iraq's labour force – or 62 000 persons – was in its armed forces. By 1980, the share of its labour force drafted into the armed forces increased to

13.4 per cent or 430 000. And by the time the war with Iran ended in 1988 the government was employing more than 21 per cent of the labour force – or 1 million persons – in the armed forces.

A very serious effect of this development was its financial claims on Iraq's resources. In 1970 the Iraqi government spent less than US$ 1 billion on its military (or 19.4 per cent of GDP) – a high ratio by world standards. By 1975 it had increased military spending to US$ 3.1 billion or 22.8 per cent of GDP. By 1980 it had increased it by more than six times the 1975 level – to US$ 19.8 billion or 38.8 per cent of GDP. Another way of measuring the burden of military spending is to relate it to the country's oil revenue. In 1980 the government appropriated 75 per cent of oil revenue to military spending. Such spending increased sharply afterwards, absorbing between 117 and 324 per cent of oil revenue between 1981 and 1988. In other words, in the 1980s the government spent several times the country's entire oil revenue on the war effort. In relation to GDP it spent between 23 and 66 per cent of the country's GDP between 1980 and 1988 on the war with Iran.

Similarly, that war changed the composition of imports in favour of military imports. From a share of 17 per cent of total imports in 1980, military imports reached a share of 83 per cent in 1984. In relation to income, arms imports absorbed between 5 and 19 per cent of Iraq's GDP in the 1980s.

Iraq's losses during the eight-year war with Iran were estimated to be US$ 452.6 billion (Mofid, 1990, p. 133). The magnitude of these losses may be appreciated if we remember that the cumulative revenue from oil for the period 1980–8 amounted to US$ 104 billion. It is worth pointing out that during the war years Iraq's total GDP amounted to US$ 433 billion.

THE INVASION OF KUWAIT AND THE IMPOSITION OF SANCTIONS

Iraq entered the post-war period with a smaller and disorganized economy that was overburdened with inflation and foreign debt. To cope with the economic crisis, and also to fund an ambitious programme of military industrialization, it had to rely on a shrinking source of oil revenue which in 1988 generated only US$ 11 billion or 42 per cent of the 1980 level of oil income. In the meantime the population had increased by 33 per cent. The exhausted state of the economy was made worse by the 9 per cent decline in GDP in 1989 over 1988 – a decline that was a severe blow to the government and which forced it to adopt an austerity programme of spending.

The Government of Iraq decided to take the country into another war by invading Kuwait in August 1990. A comprehensive regime of sanctions was imposed on Iraq. Its oil sector was reduced to meet domestic consumption requirements.

In January and February 1991 Iraq was subjected to an intensive bombing campaign that left its economy and society in a state of ruin. The impact of the air war was assessed by a UN special mission to Iraq immediately after the war (United Nations, 1996, pp. 186–8):

> It should, however, be said at once that nothing we had seen or read had quite prepared us for the particular form of devastation which has now befallen the country. The recent conflict had wrought near-apocalyptic results upon what had been, until January 1991, a rather highly urbanized and mechanized society. Now, most means of modern life support have been destroyed or rendered tenuous. Iraq has, for some time to come, been relegated to a pre-industrial age, but with all the disabilities of post-industrial dependency on an intensive use of energy and technology.

This vast scale of destruction should not be surprising given the fact that the initial plan of bombing included 84 targets but was expanded in the course of the war to include 723 targets (United States House Armed Services Committee, 1992, p. 86).

OIL AND THE FUTURE OF THE IRAQI ECONOMY

Although the aims of the Gulf War were secured in March 1991 the sanctions regime against Iraq is still in force. One of the numerous assessments of the impact of the sanctions (Food and Agriculture Organization and World Food Programme, 1993, p. 1) had this to say:

> it is a country whose economy has been devastated by the recent war and subsequent civil strife, but above all by the continued sanctions since August 1990, which have virtually paralyzed the whole economy and guaranteed persistent deprivation, chronic hunger, endemic malnutrition, massive unemployment and widespread human suffering.

Given such abnormal conditions of the economy and society, it is clear that any attempt to speculate about the future is constrained by the reality of the sanctions. In the following paragraphs the future is assumed to be without the sanctions and with Iraqi oil back in the world market.

The return of Iraq's oil to the world market, even at full capacity output and export, will not mean a return of the oil sector to its leading role in driving Iraq's economic growth and structural change. The most obvious reason for this is that oil is not expected to generate in the near future the sort of revenue it once generated in the 1970s and the early part of the 1980s. In the case of Iraq, a combination of past development policies and future financial claims will simultaneously make the oil sector more necessary than it has ever been in the past, yet incapable of generating sufficient foreign exchange earnings to meet the claims.

In addition to the normal needs of the economy for foreign exchange to finance imports of foodstuffs, consumer goods, inputs and capital goods, the oil sector will be called upon to meet the claims for reparations and foreign debt service. Moreover, Iraq will need foreign exchange to rehabilitate and reconstruct its infrastructure.

Current estimates of foreign debt tend to place it at US$ 100 billion. Moreover, current estimates of reparation claims being processed by the United Nations Compensation Fund are placed at US$ 200 billion. It is worth noting that the United Nations Security Council decreed that 30 per cent of Iraq's oil revenue be earmarked to meet those claims. Furthermore, a 1991 Security Council document put at US$ 97 billion the value of Iranian assets destroyed during the Iraq–Iran war. In addition, the value of Iraqi assets destroyed in the course of both the Iraq–Iran war and the Gulf War has been put at US$ 300 billion. In short, the oil sector is called upon to finance claims ranging up to US$ 700 billion. But if one were to focus on external claims only, that is, debt and reparations, the figure would be US$ 400 billion – 15 times the peak oil revenue of US$ 26 billion achieved in 1980.

Even in the absence of these external claims the oil sector's ability to play the role it had played up to 1980 is severely constrained. According to the Iraqi government's 1991 estimates, a five-year investment programme of US$ 92.1 billion (with a foreign exchange component of US$ 55.2 billion) would generate an average growth rate of 3.4 per cent in non-oil GDP. But since the annual population growth rate was estimated to be 2.8 per cent, this means that the annual rise in per capita non-oil GDP would be a mere 0.6 per cent.[2]

Given these constraints, it would be no exaggeration to say that it will take the Iraqi economy and its oil sector several decades to return to previous levels.

NOTES

1. See Law No. 38 of 1969, Law No. 82 of 1971, Law No. 39 of 1974, Law No. 49 of 1976, Law No. 165 of 1977, Law No. 6 of 1978, Law No. 10 of 1979 and Law No. 3 of 1981.
2. *Middle East Economic Survey*, 13 May 1991, pp. D6–D9. Al-Shabibi (1991) projected nine different scenarios for the GDP growth rate up to the year 1995. Depending on the assumptions made, he came up with GDP growth rates ranging from a positive growth rate of 11.2 per cent to a negative growth rate of 5.2 per cent.

REFERENCES

Alnasrawi, A. (1994), *The Economy of Iraq: Oil, Wars, Destruction of Development and Prospects, 1950–2010*, Westport (Conn.): Greenwood Press.

Al-Shabibi, S. (1991), 'Iraq's financial obligations could cripple economic prospects', *Middle East Economic Survey*, 4 November.

Food and Agricultural Organization and World Food Programme (1993), *FAO/WFP Crop and Food Supply Assessment Mission to Iraq*, Rome: Food and Agricultural Organization.

Hashem, J. (1975), *Capital Formation in Iraq 1957–1970*, Beirut: Arab Organization for Studies and Publishing [in Arabic].

Ministry of Planning (1970), *Analysis of the Iraqi Economy to the Base Year 1969*, Baghdad: Ministry of Planning [in Arabic].

Mofid, K. (1990), *The Economic Consequences of the Gulf War*, London: Routledge.

Sayigh, Y.A. (1978), *The Economies of the Arab World: Development since 1945*, New York: St Martin's Press.

United Nations (1991a), *National Accounts Statistics: Main Aggregates and Detailed Tables, 1989, Part I*, New York: United Nations.

United Nations (1991b), *National Accounts Statistics: Analysis of Main Aggregates, 1988–89*, New York: United Nations.

United Nations (1996), *The United Nations and the Iraq–Kuwait Conflict, 1990–96*, New York: United Nations.

United States House Armed Services Committee (1992), *A Defense for a New Era: Lessons of the Persian Gulf War,* Washington, DC: United States House Armed Services Committee.

PART THREE

National Experiences with Renewable Natural
Resources

7. Agricultural Development in Israel

Raanan Katzir

AGRICULTURE IN ISRAEL: CHALLENGES AND RESPONSES

During its short history, agriculture in Israel has gone through different stages: from improved productivity in traditional agriculture, to diversified agriculture, to (at present) specialized agriculture geared towards a market for local consumption and export. Throughout this period, Israel's agriculture has been characterized most by rapid socioeconomic and technological adaptation. This adaptation can be attributed to the introduction and integration of knowledge, modern technology, government support, credit and extension services, a highly skilled workforce, the use of farmers' experience, and most important, the sustainable management of natural resources. Agricultural production in Israel – an industrial country – accounts for only about 3 per cent of GNP. The agricultural workforce in Israel is small: only 2.5 per cent of the population is engaged in agriculture, compared with 20 per cent some 25 years ago. The professional level of farmers is high, and they invest in high-level agricultural inputs and the use of advanced technologies. A third of the fresh and processed agricultural production and a large amount of Israeli-produced inputs are exported. This relatively high share of exports in total agricultural production testifies to the importance of agriculture for the Israeli economy as a whole.

With a total surface area of about 20 000 square kilometres, half of which is desert, the State of Israel is small. Only 20 per cent of its land can be cultivated. Precipitation varies from 50 millimetres a year in the south to 1000 millimetres a year in the north. The geography of the country is such that the north has an abundant water supply, while the central part receives less rain, and the south is a desert-like, very dry area. Similarly, the climate in Israel varies from Mediterranean and tropical to mild European. This gives rise to an enormous variability in water supply within the country and poses a great problem for agriculture. There is a long-standing principle in Israel, based on a national, political consensus, that agricultural settlement should take place in all regions without any exception, even in the marginal ones. This means that in order to facilitate agricultural activities throughout the country, water has to be channelled from the north to the south. Thus, the fact that a large part of the Israeli land area is a desert, the uneven distribution of natural water supplies between regions and the relatively unfavourable climatic conditions constitute the three main limiting factors with regard to agricultural production in Israel.

The challenge of finding ways and means to optimize the use of scarce natural resources has been met in two main ways. The first involves extensive research, which has led to the introduction of new plants and seed varieties along with more productive agricultural techniques which are adapted to Israel's specific climatic, soil and water conditions. The second is the setting up of an institutional framework which involves the government, the private sector and the individual farmers, and consists of national extension services and credit, and export and farmers' organizations. The aim of this framework has been to guide and direct agricultural development with a view to finding region-specific solutions to the above-mentioned problems. This chapter discusses how research and the specific institutional set-up have been used to maximize the contribution of agriculture to the economic development of Israel.

THE DEVELOPMENT OF REGION-SPECIFIC AGRICULTURAL TECHNOLOGY

Research

Agricultural research has been based on long- and short-term requirements. From the long-term perspective, it has been guided by the need to develop crops which are competitive on the potential market, and to solve basic problems in production for export. The short-term aim has been to find solutions for more immediate needs, such as irrigation, plant protection and cultivation machinery. A guiding principle has been to conduct applied research which is integrated into the framework of regional research and development (R&D) schemes. Israel has gained a reputation for its regional R&D system, which has aimed to produce regularly updated knowledge and technology. R&D schemes are dictated by market opportunities. Produce which has a potential for local or export markets and can be produced profitably will enjoy a wide range of research and extension services. Multidisciplinary teams of researchers, economists and planners tackle the problems in accordance with budgetary constraints and economic priorities. Such a concept leads to the development of existing agricultural branches, the creation of new branches and the advancement of technologies and know-how with a view to improving and promoting the final produce. This comprehensive approach ensures rapid adaptation to current circumstances while at the same time being forward-looking.

Water

The drip irrigation system has been widely used as a low-consuming water system for irrigation purposes. It enables precise water application integrated with the application of fertilizers, and has thus become known as 'fertigation'. This system saves on the cost of water to the farmer and allows the efficient use of saline water for irrigation purposes. Saline water, which is found throughout the arid lands, can be used to irrigate tolerant crops such as tomatoes, melons, wheat, cotton, beets, asparagus, Bermuda grass, dates, grapes and olives. Even in arid zones, when it rains, water which is not absorbed by the soil flows in dry river beds towards the sea. Water reservoirs with various capacities have been built along the dry river bed. During the rain the water is pumped from the stream into the reservoirs. The conserved water is used for irrigation purposes for cotton, maize, sorghum and legumes. In arid zones, water from these reservoirs serves as an economic resource, depending on the alternative price of water.

In the southern regions, thermal water has been derived from very deep wells and is used to heat greenhouses. Hot water is pumped into a sealed network of plastic pipelines which are placed close to the plants on the plant bed in order to heat the air surrounding the plants. The water is then channelled to storage tanks, where it is allowed to cool before being used again for irrigation in a separate drip irrigation system. In the north, an old water stream is used for the production of trout, which are considered a delicacy and fetch high prices in the market. The only freshwater lake is used as an economic resource for tourism, recreation, fishing, and water supply for drinking, industry and agriculture. In regions where the use of land and water for agricultural purposes is limited, a special hydroponics system, constructed in greenhouses and based on water and fertilizer supply, is operated in a closed system. The water used is treated by filtration and ultraviolet radiation to prevent contamination of the micro-organisms. Such a system, in which water is circulated permanently through concrete and plastic beds, makes possible the growing of ornamental pot plants.

The intensive use of water has contributed to water shortages in many areas. As a result, large water-supply projects needed to be constructed; they have allowed water to be carried over great distances, sometimes hundreds of kilometres, but they have also made water more expensive. Taking into account the fact that water has an economic value, there is a need to set the price of water and simultaneously to create a mechanism for controlling and limiting its use through the establishment of consumption quotas.

Israel follows a specific policy for water, which is determined by the Ministry of National Infrastructure. The regulations are controlled by the 'Water Commissioner'. All producers have a quota for irrigation water which can be reduced during periods of water shortage. The price of water ranges between US$

0.2 and US$ 0.4 per cubic metre, that is, within the margin of economically profitable agricultural production; the price is lowest for the first third of the quota and highest for the last third. Those exceeding their quota have to pay substantial fines.

Sewage water which finds its way into natural waterways is considered a serious ecological threat. Hence, wherever possible, the use of high-value potable water has been replaced by the use of recycled sewage water, to the benefit of both urban and rural communities. This water can also be used for the cultivation of algae, which are then used as raw material for industrial products. Another solution for saving water is to ensure more efficient management of water-conveying installations in order to avoid losses due to deteriorating water-supply systems. Lastly, the process of desalinization of sea water for drinking purposes is an expensive option which can be exercised when no other alternative exists. However, technological advances such as reverse osmosis indicate that the price of desalinization is declining.

Soil and Plants

Because of the use of fertigation, sand dunes are being used to produce crops such as citrus, avocado, mango, vegetables and flowers. Under desert conditions, in which marginal land and lack of water are dominant, specially adapted crops can be grown successfully. The desert is characterized by high heat radiation and adequate temperatures during the winter for intensive greenhouse production of off-season crops, mainly vegetables, fruit and flowers for export to the European market. Water supply, radiation, temperature, air humidity, nutrition and carbon dioxide levels are fully controlled. Two commercial crops were introduced into the desert area of Israel almost two decades ago: the jojoba, which produces oil seeds used in cosmetic production; and a thornless cactus called tuna (*opuntia*), whose leaves serve as animal feed and whose fruit has a valuable market.

Israel's agriculture is well known for the intensive introduction of botanical species from various parts of the world. Plant geneticists in Israel produce varieties of wheat adapted to drought conditions, which is a practical solution to growing wheat in arid regions. Furthermore, they have discovered a long list of species which are tolerant of saline water irrigation, and have produced varieties of melon and tomato resistant to soil pathogens and virus diseases. The long shelf-life of the Israeli tomato is well known in most European countries. To deal with pest and disease problems, which are recognized as the main limiting factor affecting irrigated agriculture, the Integrated Pest Management (IPM) system was introduced and has been commonly applied. Regional IPM services are based on the monitoring of pests, threshold levels and selective pesticides.

Biological control methods are applied to reduce as much as possible the use of chemical pesticides with a view to reducing threats to human health.

Animal Husbandry

The heat stress caused by raising dairy cattle under the extreme temperatures of the desert negatively affects milk production. Various measures such as ventilation and humidifiers were developed and successfully introduced into the milk production industry to alleviate heat stress and increase milk production. The technology of using chicken manure for cattle nutrition is also widely utilized. Artificial insemination is common in dairy herd management, and the use of genetic technology can be considered a primary reason for the high level of milk production in Israel.

THE INSTITUTIONAL FRAMEWORK

Farmers and policy makers, in particular those of the Ministry of Agriculture, have established an institutional mechanism with a view to guiding and directing agricultural development under changing circumstances, continually taking into consideration the local socioeconomic and foreign market situations. It is important to understand the socioeconomic, professional and organizational criteria that have made this adaptation possible.

The National Extension Service

The most important requirement for export crops is quality, which in turn requires a high production standard. Farmers cultivating such crops must have the capacity and ability to use advanced agro-technology in the production process. Traditional farmers therefore have to adapt, which means that they must learn how to use advanced agro-technologies. The duty of the extension service is to help farmers advance through the introduction of more knowledge and better agro-technologies. Extension support is provided by the government via the Ministry of Agriculture and by the private sector through companies selling pesticides, fertilizers, machinery and auxiliary tools. Farming Branch Technical Committees (FBTCs) are headed by an Extension Officer, within the framework of the Ministry, and integrate all aspects of research, extension and other technical activities.

Sustainable agriculture geared towards market-oriented agriculture and exports can take place if parallel efforts are devoted to promoting economic development, culture and health. The tasks involved include improving community functions, supporting the role of women, improving education, generating knowledge by (mainly applied) research, solving local problems and overcoming barriers to agricultural production.

Israel's farmers are highly skilled (a large number of them even have an academic background), make extensive use of capital and orient their largely mechanized production towards both the domestic and export markets. Research findings and innovations are readily implemented.

Government and Private Organizations

Agricultural and commercial banks transfer money to farmers in the form of credits, loans or grants for development or working capital in the form of advance payments and so on. In addition, production and marketing boards provide farmers with advance credits for cultivating export crops on the basis of binding contracts. A government company covers export risks such as a price collapse on foreign markets.

The main organization in charge of all export activities in Israel is AGREXO. It was set up jointly by the government and the production and marketing boards, and operates on a fully commercial basis for both producers and potential buyers. It takes care of all the logistical requirements of its export activities: planning, providing guidelines for quality, credit allocations, sales, marketing, and organizational and financial management.

The Insurance Fund for Natural Damages belongs jointly to the government and the farmers, and guarantees the reimbursement of lost inputs in the case of damage caused by natural disasters. Only the actual costs of production are covered in order to avoid discontinuation of the production process. The production and marketing boards are joint boards of the government and the producers; they aim to organize the commercialization of production, to oversee the price system in order to ensure stable incomes for farmers, to assist the producer in purchasing inputs at reduced cost, and to encourage the establishment of transportation systems. Another important function of these boards is to plan agricultural output in the form of quotas in accordance with the needs of local and export markets in order to avoid supply surpluses and losses for farmers. The boards also give financial support to research whose outcome can be exploited as a decision-making tool in planning and export policies.

The national and regional farmers' organization represents farmers in the Agricultural Branch Committee, the production and marketing boards, AGREXO, and so on. Its task is to encourage the publication of professional material, to maintain contacts with similar foreign organizations, and to promote direct research and extension in accordance with farmers' needs.

The Agricultural Branch Committee, a directing committee, forms a national infrastructure for directing and coordinating the above-mentioned activities. All elements relating to the agricultural production process are represented in it, including government offices, negotiating export targets, and distribution of resources for research, extension and planning.

THE EXAMPLE OF COTTON IN ISRAEL

Cotton is a relatively new crop in Israel, introduced in the early 1950s. Continuous research and development was essential for reducing production costs and increasing yield and quality. Cotton is grown in Israel in the dry season (April to October) and has therefore to be cultivated as an irrigated crop. Growing is fully mechanized. It is an intensive crop with high input costs: water, fertilizers, pesticides and cultivation machinery. The input costs in Israel are about US$ 0.70 for one pound of fibre. The profits are marginal, and there is a high financial risk factor. The government recently guaranteed a minimum price for local cotton of US$ 0.75 per pound in order to tackle the problem of the decreasing area under cotton cultivation. Yield is high and can reach 6200 kg per hectare.

Israel has a highly developed research and extension system for cotton growing which is well coordinated at both national and regional levels. A National Cotton Committee, composed of researchers, extension specialists and cotton growers, is in charge of distributing the available financial resources among research, development and extension. Intensive research led to the development of local varieties which respond well to irrigation, are disease-resistant and have a high yield of good quality. Cotton farmers are assisted by a well-developed extension service, laboratory facilities for defining soil, water and fertilizer relationships, national and regional services for pest control, a reliable air spraying service, and a dependable supply of fertilizers and pesticides. Other important technological innovations originating in Israel for the development of cotton growing include computer programs for the control of cotton cultivation, regional gin and grading systems and quality control of the produce, together with the introduction of drip irrigation. Through regional service centres, farmers are the owners of gins for the separation of cotton fibre. The Cotton Production and Marketing Board, run by cotton growers, is responsible for growing and marketing cotton, negotiating minimum prices, defining quality (grading) and providing storage facilities for cotton stocks. It also provides collective insurance to all cotton growers against damage resulting from natural disasters. A special insurance fund exists in Israel which provides insurance against damage by rain, extreme temperatures, storms and flooding, in which the Ministry of Agriculture, the Ministry of Finance and the farmers participate.

Cotton picked selectively by hand is of higher quality than that harvested mechanically. Despite this fact, cotton in Israel is harvested exclusively by mechanical equipment, given that the supply of manual workers in agriculture is very small. Harvesting machines are used for cotton picking. Raw cotton is compacted into modules of 8–9 tons each. Special attention is paid to post-harvest handling. Modules are left in the field, wrapped in plastic sheets to avoid damp from dew or rain and from the soil below. They are placed a few metres apart from each other in order to minimize damage in case of fire.

The quality level of raw cotton is assessed by a regional control system. The raw material is supplied to the gin at a uniform quality level. This enables the gin to work uninterrupted, increasing efficiency and reducing costs. Development of cotton varieties is guided by the following quality requirements: yield, length of fibre, colour, resistance to diseases and pests, amount of impurities and flexibility. The criteria for the quality of the fibre are determined by the needs of the textile industries.

NEW CHALLENGES AND DEVELOPMENTS

In recent years, new aspects of agricultural development procedures have been focused on agro-industry, agro-tourism, peri-urban agriculture and small-farmer entrepreneurship. All of these are based on the principle of making sustainable use of natural resources.

Most of the immigrants in developing countries settle in neighbourhoods of large capital cities. These neighbourhoods are usually poor and have a low level of economic activity. Consequently, living conditions are hard and sanitary facilities are inadequate for the number of people. The continuing urbanization process and its confrontation with the peri-urban area cause many social, economic and environmental problems. Intensive urbanization also creates extreme ecological disturbances. Proper agro-ecological solutions as well as some changes in the peri-urban rural sector can offer mutual benefit to both farmers and the city population. The 'family farm', for example, producing in the neighbourhood of a big city, allows young farmers to provide food for the city and improve their income. Small farms tend to produce specialized crops for the city. These usually command high prices, and on those farms the production process becomes capital-intensive, based on advanced technologies. A further step in the development process and one step ahead of specialized farming is agro-industrialization. In this case, the farmer becomes an entrepreneur and establishes an industrialized business based on high-value agricultural farm products. The advantages of an agricultural farm being near the city, such as cheap labour and proximity to an international airport, can be exploited for improving export performance.

The transition from family farming to agro-business began many years ago. The United States was one of the first countries in which family farms were converted into large commercial farms, managed like any industry in the agricultural sector. These commercial and business-like farms are characterized by their entrepreneurial approach, the intensive and high production level for both the local and export markets, advanced technologies, their operating independently of central authority, their high level of management capacity and their flexibility for rapid adjustment to changing conditions.

CONCLUSIONS

The Israeli model of agricultural development can be characterized as one which did not stem purely from privatized agriculture but was strongly influenced by the state. Israel may have enjoyed some advantages over other developing countries in the form of high levels of external financial support and skilled labour facilitating the transition to a specialized agricultural economy. None the less, the mechanisms of market systems coordinated jointly by government, private entities and producer organizations, the provision of an effective organizational structure, export promotion, the integrated approach of research and extension services, and the sustainable use of natural resources may serve as a model of agricultural development for other developing countries.

8. From Primary Production to Resource-based Industrialization in Malaysia

Rabbi Poobal Royan[1]

INTRODUCTION

Malaysia is one of the few developing countries which in recent years has mastered the transition from an economy based on the exploitation of natural resources to an industrialized economy. This transition, based on the belief that the joint development of the primary sector and of resource-based manufacturing offers dynamic complementarities, relied essentially on technological innovation in the natural resource sector and a flexible adjustment of economic policies to changing circumstances and needs. The development of commercially applicable innovations in the natural resource sectors and their subsequent use substantially increased productivity in those sectors and, hence, the surplus which could be transferred from the primary sector and used productively for investment in industrialization. While the Malaysian economy's production structure has changed and the natural resource sector's direct contribution to economic growth has declined over the past three decades, the importance of this sector has not diminished. A wide range of policies were implemented in order to diversify the economy, with the public sector playing a lead support role. The large-scale production of palm oil, cocoa and rubber created economies of scale, particularly in terms of management and supervision, marketing, and research and development. This chapter reviews some of the important government efforts that were undertaken to ensure that activities in the renewable natural resource sector continue to contribute to economic growth and development.

BACKGROUND PERSPECTIVE

The main development goal in Malaysia since independence has been the improvement of the quality of life of the people through the achievement of growth with equity. Malaysia's economic policy is strongly influenced by the government's objectives of eradicating poverty and eliminating the identification of race with economic function. These goals, set in the aftermath of the ethnic riots of 1969, were translated into affirmative action in favour of the indigenous Malays (Bumiputras). Since most indigenous Malays live in rural areas, strengthening agricultural development was a logical objective of government strategy. While the philosophy of growth with equity continues to underpin the government's efforts, the strategy was broadened in 1990 to include the concept of balanced development. This concept comprises: balanced development between sectors, strata and regions; balance between growth and environment (sustainable development); balance between material well-being and social and spiritual development; and the promotion of human resource development and science and technology. The main aim of this wider strategy of balanced growth is to make Malaysia a fully industrialized country by the year 2020, a target known as 'vision 2020'.

However, in 1957, at the time of independence, the Malaysian economy was based predominantly on the primary sector, particularly agriculture. The country was then the world's largest producer and exporter of natural rubber and tin, and the economy was largely dependent on these commodities, which accounted for 70 per cent of total export earnings and 36 per cent of total employment. During the 1970s the economy began to diversify as growth was propelled by large-scale production of palm oil, as well as by increased economic activity in the timber and cocoa sectors. By 1971, timber and palm oil had already emerged as significant export commodities, accounting for 17 per cent and 5 per cent of gross export earnings respectively. Following the discovery and exploration of new oil and gas fields, crude petroleum and gas also gained significance. Industrial development, however, remained in its infancy, and was concentrated in resource-based industries such as the processing of rubber and wood products, as well as basic import-substitution industries. Only since the mid-1980s has the growth momentum been successfully supported by the expansion of more broad-based manufacturing activities. This momentum is expected to propel the country towards industrial nation status.

Malaysian economic diversification strategy can thus be characterized by three main transition stages. The first stage was aimed at horizontal diversification from a narrow to a wider range of primary products, that is, from rubber and tin to palm oil, cocoa and timber. The second stage was marked by vertical diversification into downstream agro-processing for the purposes of import substitution. The third stage was based on export-led, resource-based manufacturing. The success of these transitions is evident: whereas in 1970 three largely unprocessed primary commodities (rubber, tin and sawn logs) accounted for about 70 per cent of Malaysia's export earnings, during the early 1990s about three-quarters of the country's export earnings came from manufactures, as illustrated in Figures 8.1 and 8.2.

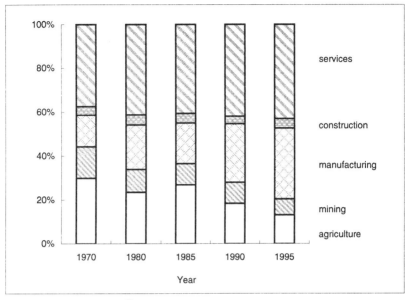

Source: Government of Malaysia.

Figure 8.1 Malaysia: structure of production, 1970–95 (per cent of GDP)

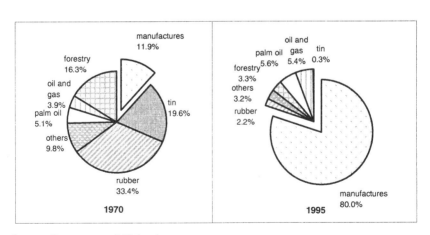

Source: Government of Malaysia.

Figure 8.2 Malaysia: diversification of exports (per cent of total exports)

HORIZONTAL AND VERTICAL DIVERSIFICATION

The heavy dependence on rubber and tin set the stage for the diversification policy which was to be the basis for Malaysia's structural transformation towards a resource-based industrial economy. This dependence meant that the economy was highly susceptible to the vicissitudes of international trade. It prompted the government to embark on an export diversification drive in order to widen the country's production and export base, thereby widening income options for those dependent on agricultural commodities. Palm oil production was particularly emphasized. This was due to Malaysia's favourable climatic conditions for oil palm plantations, expected higher profits from palm oil compared with rubber production, and the fact that existing infrastructure in rubber estates could be used for palm oil production.

The implementation of new land development and resettlement schemes by the Federal Land Development Authority (FELDA) had a major impact on the growth of oil palm cultivation in the 1960s. FELDA was established in 1962 to offer previously landless peasants the opportunity to become smallholder farmers in an effort to alleviate rural poverty. The settlers received a FELDA loan for income support for the first three years, and in return a certain amount was deducted from the sales of the settlers' crop for a period of 15 years. Firm managerial control was exerted by FELDA in order to exploit the scheme's economies of scale. In October 1988, it was decided that settlers involved in all FELDA schemes would be granted individual land titles once their debts had been repaid. FELDA's approach of increasing the area under production was later complemented by the use of more intensive methods of production leading to a larger export base. The government also supported the extension of oil palm cultivation by allowing replanting grants for rubber to be used to plant oil palms and through a special tax policy for rubber and palm oil. Replanting grants which were funded by duties levied on palm oil exports and by taxes imposed on rubber exports allowed both the smallholder producers and estates to bridge financial losses during the switch from rubber to palm oil production. Moreover, the differential tax rate for palm oil exports (4 to 8 per cent), as compared with that for rubber exports (17 to 24 per cent), further boosted the attractiveness of palm oil exports.

The government actively encouraged downstream processing and refining of palm oil with a view to fostering vertical diversification. For example, the government's export duty structure exempted palm oil products from some or all duties, depending on the degree of processing. In addition, the government provided specific support for a limited period of time to allow companies to adjust to new conditions, but the companies were eventually expected to withstand competition.

The Palm Oil Registration and Licensing Authority (PORLA) was created in 1980 in order to facilitate palm oil marketing. PORLA, funded by a tax on palm oil production, is responsible for establishing quality standards and grading systems and for overseeing the quality of palm oil exports. The Malaysian Palm Oil Promotion Council was established in 1990 to initiate and coordinate market development programmes, public relations and promotion, as well as scientific and technical services, with a view to promoting effectively the marketing of Malaysian palm oil.

Starting from a very low level of production in the mid-1970s, cocoa production increased sharply during the period of high cocoa prices on the world market at the end of the 1970s. The rate of growth slowed during the 1980s in the face of lower cocoa prices. None the less, by the end of the 1980s, Malaysia had become the world's fourth largest cocoa producer, accounting for about 8 per cent of total world cocoa production, the world's third largest exporter of cocoa beans, and the third largest developing country exporter of cocoa products. This expansion was largely the result of new land development similar to the expansion of palm oil exports in the 1960s. However, the price responsiveness of farmers also played a crucial role. Farmers started to grow cocoa as an insurance against low rubber and falling pepper prices. The high productivity of cocoa growing was the main reason for the steep increase in production during the 1980s. Productivity in the cocoa sector grew by 6 per cent per annum during the 1980s as a result of, for example, improvements in drainage and irrigation facilities, the use of improved plant seed varieties, and the adoption of improved technologies.

The production of cocoa beans was given further impetus by the development of highly productive domestic cocoa-processing facilities. A striking feature of this evolution is that, in 1993, export earnings from processed cocoa products actually exceeded those from cocoa beans, and that vertical diversification was achieved despite the presence of tariff escalation in the markets of industrialized countries. Apart from quality improvements due to research, Malaysia's favourable climate made the country a reliable source of cocoa beans in a world market subject to large oscillations caused by cocoa trees' susceptibility to rainfall. This supply stability attracted foreign investors to Malaysia to form joint ventures in cocoa processing. Investors were also attracted by the fact that the Malaysian government had reduced the duty on high-quality cocoa imports from 35 per cent to 5 per cent in order to facilitate cocoa blending in Malaysia.

With respect to petroleum resources, the Malaysian government introduced the National Depletion Policy in June 1980 to ensure that the nation's limited oil resources were not exhausted too quickly. This policy was aimed at limiting production of crude oil from major oil fields to 3 per cent of its original oil in place and deferring development by about three to five years to ensure that the oil reserves last longer. During the period 1990–5, the government embarked on a strategic move to reduce dependence on oil as an energy resource. This resulted in the development and wider utilization of environment-friendlier natural gas.

Forest resources constitute an invaluable part of Malaysia's natural resources. About 72 per cent of Malaysia's land area is under forest and tree plantations. The key elements of the government's policy of sustainable forest management include (a) reduction of the annual logging rate in Peninsular Malaysia and Sabah, and planned reduction of log production in Sarawak to an annual rate of 9.2 million cubic metres; (b) increasing the capacity of the federal and state forest services to manage forests better; (c) making greater use of remote sensing to monitor logging; (d) strengthening the research and development capacity of the Forest Research Institute of Malaysia; and (e) repairing the damage done by shifting cultivation, particularly in the state of Sarawak.

Timber processing was encouraged by the government's phased approach, that is, imposing a gradual ban on log exports while providing a variety of incentives for processing. In November 1972, the government introduced a ban on the export of the ten most popular species from Peninsular Malaysia, with the result that the share of exports in production dropped to 7 per cent within one year. In September 1976, a quota for the export of logs with a diameter greater than 16 inches was introduced for all species. The eastern state of Sarawak has followed a policy of granting 25-year licences which stipulate that 34 per cent of log production can be exported, 40 per cent has to be used in local saw milling, and 26 per cent must go into plywood and veneer production. In the other eastern state – Sabah – the government decided in 1977 to reduce exports of logs and encourage downstream processing of timber.

The role of tin, which used to be a mainstay of the Malaysian economy, has gradually declined over the years. The most recent major setback was market-driven, caused by the breakdown of price support under the International Tin Agreement and the collapse of the tin market in October 1985. Before 1985, in contrast, the declining importance of tin was the consequence of a deliberate strategy by the government to support the development of palm oil, a renewable resource, rather than tin, a depletable resource.

RESOURCE-BASED MANUFACTURING

During the 1960s early inroads were made into light manufacturing in agro-based industries such as rubber, food, wood and rattan products, beverages and tobacco. These industries were, however, marked by a low level of technology and small-scale production. The major momentum into agro-based industries developed in the 1970s and 1980s. In 1972 the Rubber Task Force Committee was created to assess the growth potential of rubber-based processing activities and to identify market potential and marketing channels for such products. A technology centre was established at the Rubber Research Institute of Malaysia in order to provide training and facilitate the transfer of technology. The government emphasized rubber-processing activities among the leading resource-based manufacturing sectors in order to encourage greater domestic utilization of natural rubber, so as to increase domestic value added and foreign exchange earnings. A main objective of the Industrial Master Plan, which was implemented in 1985, was to develop high value added downstream processing of agricultural commodities, particularly rubber products. Purchasers of natural rubber as inputs for manufactured export products were given discounts on the price of rubber. In addition, manufacturers of rubber-based products were allowed a discount on their electricity bills, depending on the share of exports in their company's production, and any company exporting its entire production enjoyed an allowance of 20 per cent. Both these schemes operated between 1985 and 1990, when the government abolished them, considering that Malaysian exporters could compete successfully in the world market without specific support. As a result of these support measures and a substantial increase in the demand for latex products, Malaysia became the world's largest exporter of household gloves, examination gloves, surgical gloves, catheters and latex thread.

The increasing transformation of the Malaysian economy towards resource-based manufacturing necessitated a change in strategy for agricultural development. Thus, *in situ* consolidation and rehabilitation programmes became prominent tools for agricultural development from the mid-1980s. By this time new land for development was scarce and labour shortages were occurring in rural areas. These shortages led to upward pressure on wages for resident agricultural workers, tempered by inflows of semi-legal immigrant workers. Wages in Indonesia – which has emerged as a major competitor for rubber, palm oil and cocoa exports – are well below those in Malaysia, and the continuous upward pressure is threatening to erode Malaysia's price competitiveness for these products unless cost increases can be offset (at least partly) by increases in labour productivity and the adoption of more productive technologies. Research has been intensified to address the productivity aspects. Moreover, attempts have been made to develop opportunities for a second source of income for rural households from non-agricultural activities, for example by locating industrial estates within the reach of rural household members and by encouraging farmers to undertake off-farm activities such as handicrafts and other home-based, simple manufacturing activities.

RESEARCH AND DEVELOPMENT ACTIVITIES

Research and development (R&D) activities have been central in the overall efforts to increase the competitiveness of natural resource products. During the Sixth Malaysia Plan period (1991–5), M$ 274 million – nearly half of the total amount approved under the Intensification of Research in Priority Areas programme – was allocated for research and development in agriculture. Government agencies charged with the task of research and development, such as the Palm Oil Research Institute (PORIM), the Rubber Research Institute of Malaysia (RRIM), the Forest Research Institute of Malaysia (FRIM) and the Malaysian Cocoa Board, have consistently worked towards developing high-yielding varieties and clones, as well as improving agronomic practices, developing more efficient farm management methods, promoting better processing technology and diversifying end-products.

The imposition of a levy on rubber and palm oil producers was instrumental in the funding of R&D activities in these sectors by the agencies concerned, particularly research into high-yielding varieties and methods, new uses, and productivity-enhancing methods. Moreover, levies on palm oil producers also financed the marketing efforts of the government agencies in charge of promoting palm oil exports. In effect, through this levy, the palm oil sector to a large extent financed its own development. PORIM, for example, which was established in 1979 to increase the quantity and quality of palm oil production while keeping costs at a minimum, was funded mainly by the industry itself, with a production levy of M$ 5 per ton, bringing in over M$ 12 million a year for palm oil related research.

The focus of R&D activities has evolved, depending on the needs of each sector and economic circumstances. During the period 1991–5, for instance, PORIM intensified its R&D efforts, particularly in breeding new high-yielding varieties, enhancing and diversifying palm oil utilization, improving production efficiency and promoting non-food applications of palm oil. In addition, R&D activities in the area of mechanization, especially regarding the use of infield transporters and fresh fruit bunch cutters, were undertaken. The development of a technique which allowed manually assisted pollination to be replaced by weevil pollination helped to alleviate the labour constraint. Demand for palm oil exports was bolstered by research results showing that palm oil was superior to other oils in terms of oxidation stability and performance during frying applications. New end-uses were created, for example by developing processing technologies that produced 'Golden Palm Oil' – the only known inexpensively produced, refined vegetable oil that is rich in carotenoid. During the mid-1980s, research studies partly sponsored by the Malaysian government provided a better understanding of the nutritional and health attributes of palm oil consumption; this countered a controversial allegation made by the American

Soybean Association that palm oil was partly responsible for the high incidence of coronary heart disease in the United States.

In the case of natural rubber, RRIM concentrated its efforts on the production of new forms of natural rubber and new applications of rubber. R&D activities were also directed towards increasing productivity through the improvement of labour-saving techniques such as the low-intensity tapping system. New high-yielding clones of rubber from the RRIM 900 and RRIM 2000 series, which have shorter maturity periods and higher-quality latex and rubber wood, were also propagated.

FRIM's R&D activities focused on forest plantations, energy from biomass, wood-processing technology, new end-products, genetic diversity and a breeding system for different tree species for conservation purposes. In future, the activities of FRIM will notably include research into the management of natural forests, the management and development of forest plantations, minimizing adverse impacts on the environment, improved wood-processing technologies, and the establishment of a database for forest and wood-based industries.

Close collaboration between the government and the private sector has been a determining factor in the development of commercially applicable results by the various research institutes. The governing boards of the latter include representatives of both the public and the private sector, and meetings are chaired alternately by a representative of the Ministry of Primary Industries and of the private sector. Such arrangements have helped not only to balance different sectoral interests but also to identify diversification potential, as well as the R&D and market penetration activities required to realize that end.

INNOVATIVE SUPPORT MEASURES

In order to cope with land and labour shortages, the primary commodity sector, particularly rubber and oil palm, is increasingly adopting a transnational outlook. In effect, the government encourages plantation companies to invest overseas and open up plantations in countries which have both land and labour resources. This strategy, followed in the palm oil sector for example, is known as reverse investment and is aimed at exporting Malaysian technology and managerial skills with a view to maximizing the returns on investment in research and development, as well as obtaining additional market outlets. Combined with market intelligence and marketing expertise, this strategy has allowed new markets to be penetrated, despite the presence of tariff escalation in the industrialized countries.

With regard to export-related financial facilities and incentives, the Malaysian central bank (Bank Negara) has bilateral payment arrangements with the central banks of several other countries in order to help diversify Malaysia's export structure. These arrangements convert commercial trade-related risk into sovereign risk. Other arrangements guarantee payments for imports undertaken by companies or individual residents in the respective countries. Such arrangements, which help strengthen Malaysia's trade with other developing countries, operate under several different forms. The 'Iranian model' provides guarantees for payment default by importers, that is, the central bank pays the exporter if the importer fails to pay for goods received. This system is usually applied with countries that do not have a modern banking system but have little constraint in their use of external reserves. In the 'Aladi model', exporters receive payments in domestic currency from the central bank, while central banks periodically settle among themselves the amount due in United States dollars, thus shifting the exchange rate risk to the central banks. Operating this system requires the country of the partner central bank to have both sufficient external reserves and a modern banking system. The 'revolving credit model' is based on the Aladi model with the difference that Bank Negara grants a credit limit in United States dollars to the other central bank, while the debtor central bank issues a list of eligible goods and persons entitled to trade under this arrangement. Finally, the 'palm oil credits and payments model' is equivalent to the revolving credit model, but palm oil exports from Malaysia are the only eligible products and the period of deferred payment is set at a maximum of two years.

CONCLUSIONS

Malaysia is making the transition from primary producer to industrial nation, and this transition is already evident in the country's economic structure. The primary sector now accounts for 21 per cent of GDP, as compared with 43 per cent in 1970. The share of manufacturing has increased from under 4 per cent to 33 per cent during the same period. However, despite the much reduced share of the primary sector, its importance remains central because the manufacturing sector is to a great extent resource-based. This evolution is the outcome of careful and purposeful planning by the government. Also, Malaysia enjoyed a relatively favourable external environment in terms of the positive evolution of world demand for those commodities into which the country was diversifying. Nevertheless, without government action, in particular in the area of research and development, and a flexible adjustment of economic policies to the changing environment, it is difficult to imagine that Malaysian exporters could have taken advantage of the new market opportunities to such a great extent.

Today, in spite of increasing land and labour scarcity, the natural resource sector can continue to contribute to the growth of the economy. In effect, the government attaches great importance to industries which are based on rubber, palm oil, timber, cocoa and oil. The expansion of this industrial activity will contribute to expanded output of downstream products, such as advanced ceramics, furniture and oleochemicals. This will entail improving intersectoral linkages and widening the industrial base, as well as improving off-farm income opportunities. Looking for new opportunities with a competitive edge, and where returns can still be high, will also mean intensifying research and development activities and a continuing emphasis on the participation of the private sector. In this regard, large companies with access to capital are already venturing into downstream manufacturing utilizing biotechnology and other environment-friendly technologies. For smaller firms, the government will implement credit and assistance policies for upgrading and modernization, and public sector research institutions will also provide support through contract research and the commercialization of research and development findings.

NOTE

1. The opinions expressed in this chapter are those of the author and do not necessarily reflect the views of the Government of Malaysia.

9. Horticulture Development Policy in Kenya

F. Phillip Muema

Horticultural products, that is, fruits, vegetables, nuts and cut flowers, have been one of the few product categories in the natural resource sector to have experienced dynamic demand on world markets over the past few years. A number of developing countries have gained growth momentum from a sustained increase in such exports. Kenya has been among this wider group of developing countries but has remained virtually the only country in sub-Saharan Africa which has been able to take advantage of market opportunities arising in this area. Figure 9.1 shows that the country achieved a very substantial increase in its exports of fruit and vegetables, both fresh and processed, and, more recently, in exports of cut flowers in particular. It demonstrates that the value of horticultural exports from Kenya has more than doubled since the late 1970s. This product category has increased its share in Kenya's total export earnings from about 8 per cent in 1979 to about 11 per cent in 1994, after reaching a peak of about 14 per cent in the late 1980s. Thus, it has emerged as Kenya's most important foreign exchange earner after tourism and tea. Cut flowers, canned pineapples, french beans, strawberries and a wide range of so-called Asian vegetables (such as chillies, okra and karela) have been the most successful individual products. Horticulture crops, excluding cut flowers, currently cover an area of about 250 000 hectares, delivering a total annual production of about 3.2 million tons of fruits and vegetables. The bulk of these crops are produced for immediate local consumption, while 160 000 tons are processed for the local market and for export, and 84 000 tons are exported unprocessed.

Part of this successful evolution is undoubtedly due to favourable demand conditions. Rising income levels and health consciousness on the part of consumers, combined with the emergence of large immigrant communities whose diet includes 'Asian type' vegetables, have created an export potential particularly in the European Union, which has been the main destination of Kenya's horticultural exports. Increased availability of air-freight facilities, such as between Nairobi and London, has provided the required transport facilities for horticulture exports.

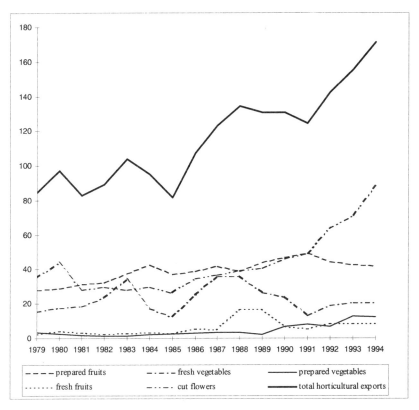

Source: UNCTAD database.

Figure 9.1 Kenya: exports of horticultural products, 1979–94 (US$ millions)

However, there would probably not have been a commensurate supply response if the Kenyan government had not pursued a deliberate development
strategy in this sector. This strategy has been expressed, for example, in a
partnership between the government and the domestic and foreign private sectors. The partnership has been characterized by the fact that production and
marketing are controlled by the private sector, with the government playing a
supervisory role. The government exercises this role through the Horticultural
Crop Development Authority (HCDA), the Fresh Produce Exporters Association of Kenya, the Flower Council of Kenya and the horticultural crops division
of the Ministry of Agriculture, Livestock Development and Marketing, which
provide technical and marketing information to both exporters and producers,
as well as production advice to farmers and market intelligence for the sector as

a whole. The interests of producers and exporters of fresh produce are represented by the Fresh Produce Exporters Association of Kenya. The four organizations work closely together, and the HCDA and the Ministry of Agriculture, Livestock Development and Marketing have a representative in the Fresh Produce Exporters Association of Kenya and the Flower Council of Kenya. This institutional structure shows that, unlike in most other agricultural sectors in Kenya, there has never been a parastatal centralized marketing board with major trading functions in the horticultural sector.

In the early 1980s, the Kenyan government adopted policies to encourage economic activities in the horticulture sector, mainly for the following reasons: first, horticultural products are relatively high value and suitable for intensive farming; second, the crops are labour-intensive; and third, they are suited to smallholder farming in a wide range of agro-ecological zones, which allows Kenya to supply products during off-season periods in temperate climate zones.

This chapter discusses some of the characteristics of Kenya's horticultural sector, as well as policies which have been put in place by the Kenyan government since the early 1980s to ensure the sector's continued growth and which have been adjusted continuously to guide infrastructure development and encourage private investment.

THE OWNERSHIP STRUCTURE IN THE KENYAN HORTICULTURAL SECTOR

The government's strategy of developing horticultural exports has led to a substantial increase in the coverage of areas used for production and in the number of smallholder farmers producing for export. It has thus provided a valuable new source of income and employment to a large number of people in rural areas. This marks a significant change from the production structure of both more traditional export crops and horticulture production up to the early 1970s, characterized by the domination of a few medium- to large-scale farmers operating in a few centralized areas close to urban settlements. However, in spite of the government's efforts to increase the number of smallholder farmers active in horticulture, the bulk of economic activities in this sector has continued to be concentrated within a few companies. These companies have had an advantage in producing and particularly in exporting horticultural products because of their long experience in this sector, and because they have been able to draw on family ties abroad for both investment funds and marketing outlets. Moreover, the relatively small output of smallholder farmers has often made it difficult for them to secure scarce air-freight space on a continuous basis, and to develop a brand name for their produce which would have enabled market outlets to be secured. These factors have allowed the larger companies to operate with considerably lower risk and transaction costs than the small market entrants with no prior experience in horticultural production and trade.

In an effort to overcome these problems, some smallholder farmers have formed grower associations the main functions of which are to assist individual farmers in grading their produce and in negotiating prices with buyers. However, they have had difficulty in competing with the larger farmers, for example because of problems with guaranteeing timely supplies of the right volume and quality. Moreover, exporters of horticultural produce have encouraged production in different regions in order to reduce their supply risk through geographical diversification of procurement. This has led to situations where smallholder farmers have produced more than the exporters can purchase. Given that there are no formal contractual agreements between these farmers and exporters, smallholder farmers have occasionally been unable to sell substantial amounts of their perishable produce.

Whereas the development of fresh horticultural exports has relied on domestic actors, the adoption of a liberal regime for foreign investment has given a boost to exports of cut flowers, as well as of processed fruit and vegetables. Foreign investors brought the technical skills and marketing expertise which were not available in Kenya. The major investments in fruit and vegetable processing have entailed joint ventures between the government and transnational corporations, while the cut-flower sector has been dominated by medium- to large-sized companies, about 40 per cent of which are foreign-owned. Local smallholder farmers have not had the means for substantial capital investment, such as drip irrigation and on-farm pre-cooling facilities, or access to patented and proprietary planting material, which is indispensable for the development of cut-flower exports.

TRAINING AND EXTENSION

Given the government's objective of ensuring the presence of a multiplicity of producers and exporters in the area of horticulture, the provision of appropriate training and extension services has been a crucial measure. It has been applied with a view to meeting the high quality standards of export markets. To this end, the government has adopted a policy of intensively training the population in agricultural issues at all levels. Agriculture is taught as a compulsory subject for the first 12 years of education, both at primary and secondary school level. Post-secondary education in agriculture and horticulture is provided at three (out of the five existing) public universities and at one private university, both at undergraduate and postgraduate level, to make professionally competent staff available locally. Middle-grade training up to certificate and diploma level is undertaken at three public institutions. A staff training college – the Embu

Agricultural Staff Training College – is used to update serving extension staff on the various technologies and policies.

This trained pool of officers is deployed by the Ministry of Agriculture, Livestock Development and Marketing at several levels, including the villages, to advise farmers on modern farming methods and initiate and develop development programmes. The general approach has been to involve farmers at all levels of activities in order to teach them how to carry out activities at each level. Regarding direct training of farmers, the extension staff make farm visits and conduct group training sessions at demonstration plots, where they hold field days to familiarize the farmers with new technologies and their application in planting, crop care, crop protection, harvesting, and so forth. The government has established in each district Farmers' Training Centres, where farmers can be accommodated and given intensive training as and when necessary. The general objective of these training activities has been to demonstrate to farmers the beneficial effects of applying new methods.

The government has adopted policies to conserve soil and water with a view to ensuring that correct farming practices are in place: farmers have been trained in terracing to avoid soil erosion, as well as in the proper use of pesticides to avoid produce containing pesticide residues and to prevent the poisoning of persons applying pesticides. A number of crops, such as mangoes, are grown without the use of any pesticides, while for others the environmentally safest pesticides are used.

POLICY ON TECHNOLOGY DEVELOPMENT

The fact that technology imports in the horticultural area are neither dutiable nor taxable has facilitated access to improved technologies such as modern irrigation equipment, shade netting, PVC-covered protected production, tissue culture, and lighting for daylight lengthening, as well as the introduction of new varieties that are high-yielding and quality-competitive in international markets. It has also increased the availability of cheap and high-quality inputs such as fertilizers and pesticides for pest and disease control.

The biggest obstacle to the adoption of modern technologies by farmers has been the lack of funding to acquire the recommended inputs. The fact that the Kenyan government has systematically widened the area where land can be acquired by individuals has facilitated farmers' access to credit since the land-owning farmers are able to use their land as collateral for commercial loans. It has also allowed a relatively smooth change from the traditional slash-and-burn system of cultivation to intensive production methods. This is in sharp contrast to the legislation in many other developing countries, particularly in Africa, where customary land tenure systems are still in place. In such systems, the right of landownership does not extend to individuals or households; rather, individuals enjoy secure and transferable rights to use the land within the tribe or kinship group. The managerial capacity of the tribe or kinship group determines whether the land is used appropriately. However, these customary land tenure systems have lost much of their original utility because of increasing population pressure on scarce arable land, increased labour mobility, and the failure of many governments to adapt the land system to the changing economic and social environment. As a result, landownership has become insecure in many African countries and put a brake on investment and technological development in agriculture.

The Kenyan government has put in place policies that encourage the private banks to lend to smallholder farmers. These include a standing instruction to the commercial banks to ensure that 17 per cent of their lending goes to the agricultural sector. This instruction has not met with much success, however, since lending to agriculture appears to be not very attractive for banks, perhaps because land is often considered a difficult collateral to manage. The Agricultural Finance Corporation, a government agency, has been encouraged to provide cheap credit to farmers by lending at interest rates below those of commercial banks, granting longer grace periods and allowing repayments to be spread over a longer period of time. However, its activities have been limited owing to lack of funds.

MARKETING

Export marketing has been encouraged through the liberal issue of licences to investors and exporters, who have been able, for example, to lease aircraft charters for their exports. The shortage of air-freight capacity has limited exports, and the government has tried to encourage more aircraft into Jomo Kenyatta International Airport in Nairobi through the provision of efficient airport services and a reduction in fuel taxation. Given that cargo planes usually go to the Middle East, Kenyan exporters need these planes to stop on their way back to Europe. In addition, exporters need to ensure rapid loading, as well as improved ground service facilities for the planes and competitive regulations regarding landing fees and documentation requirements in order to minimize the amount of time the planes spend on the ground.

Marketing requirements in Europe have been changing from central wholesale marketing to high-quality, pre-packaged produce delivered direct to supermarkets. Consumers appear increasingly to prefer ready-for-consumption products. Kenyan exporters, therefore, have changed the way in which they present their supplies to buyers on export markets, for example by supplying pre-packaged prepared products with the price tags already on, so that supermarkets can display the products on their shelves straight from the export cartons. The adoption of this new way of presentation has offered Kenyan exporters additional employment and value added. A related action has been to improve inspection services and product standards in order to offer high-quality products to the consumer.

PROCESSING

Exporting processed horticultural products is an attractive alternative since these products have a longer shelf-life than fresh products, and because farmers who produce both fresh and processed products increase the market potential for their products. Moreover, processed products can be transported by sea to Europe, and this avoids the problem of limited air-freight capacity. The government has encouraged processing by lowering the tax levied on imported equipment and by the creation of tax-free export-processing zones. As there have sometimes been shortages in the supply of raw material for processing activities, the government has supported production planning at the farm level. Also, it has made it possible for large processing companies which want to engage in production activities to lease land for this purpose.

Some processing companies have established contractual relationships with growers, whereby the companies provide inputs, such as seeds, fertilizers and sometimes credits, as well as services such as grading; in exchange, the growers deliver the produce at a pre-established time, the quantity, quality and price also being pre-established. Such arrangements are designed to ensure a continuous flow of raw material to the processors, as well as to guarantee a minimum level of quality. However, they have sometimes been abused by processors' entering into arrangements with more growers than are necessary to ensure their supply of raw material. This has put growers into competition with one another and has driven prices below pre-established levels. Both the actual occurrence of such a situation and growers' fear that it may occur have led some growers to renege on their contractual obligations and to sell their produce to buyers other than those with whom they had signed the contract. In response to this situation, the government has made it a requirement that produce-growing contracts be signed between growers and buyers and countersigned by the Horticultural Crops Development Authority. It has been made a regulation that the price of the product must be agreed before it is collected from the farmer and, once collected, cannot be returned to the farmer, but has to be paid for at the agreed price. Payment is to be made immediately unless credit arrangements have been made, which should not involve a period of more than 30 days.

THE EFFECTS OF A LIBERAL INVESTMENT CLIMATE

The government's adoption of a liberal climate for foreign investors has triggered a substantial inflow of foreign investment. Import licences or restrictions have been abolished, except for goods of a national security nature. As of May 1993, exporters have been permitted to retain 100 per cent of their foreign exchange earnings, whereas previously they were obliged to surrender all their export proceeds to the Central Bank. Moreover, capital controls have been abolished so that now the import and export of foreign currency is unrestricted. This has enabled foreign investors to invest without fear that their profits will be held in the country. The abolition of capital controls has also led to offshore borrowing at lower interest rates than would be possible for domestic borrowing. Finally, the adoption of a unified floating exchange-rate system has led to several episodes of depreciation of the domestic currency with respect to the dollar over the past few years, and this has improved the price competitiveness of exports from Kenya.

An immediate tangible effect of this liberalization policy has been the emergence of Kenya as one of the main world exporters of cut flowers, including roses, carnations, statice and alstroemeria. Apart from making offshore borrowing possible, the government has allowed planting materials and equipment to be imported without duty and cut flowers to be exported without restrictions except those relating to quality standards, which have been deliberately kept high to ensure international competitiveness. The combination of these policy measures, Kenya's favourable climate and the availability of clean water and good soils has made Kenya one of the best sites for cut-flower growing. In fact, the flower industry has just started to boom, and the future is bright. Initially, exports went mainly to industrialized countries, but it is now expected that Central and Eastern European countries will become increasingly important export destinations.

THE FUTURE

The future of horticultural exports from Kenya is bright, but the government needs to adapt its policies flexibly as new challenges arise. The focus of Kenya's future policy in the horticultural area will be on increased quality through intensive supervision and advice to farmers, use of high-quality seed, and inspection of fields and produce to ensure that high quality is maintained at favourable prices for an increased market share. The problems which Kenyan exporters face and which the government will need to address include the following:

1. Since Kenya is not a destination for air cargo, the availability of cargo planes has been limited. This situation has worsened with the lifting of the trade embargo against South Africa; during the embargo, cargo planes sometimes went to Kenya in order to beat the trade restrictions on South Africa. Now exporters need to develop their own air cargo capacity or hire charters flying between Europe and the Middle East. In addition, the possibility of sea freight is being explored. With the new controlled atmosphere technology being implemented, sea freight could become an important method of transportation.

2. Flower exports have faced problems in the United States, where Kenyan exporters have been taken to court for alleged dumping, that is, selling a high-quality product below market price, with that price being calculated on the basis of production costs in the United States. The government will need to assist these exporters to find means to deal with anti-dumping measures effectively. In Europe, the situation has been somewhat more favourable, in spite of the fact that Kenyan flowers have not been admitted to Dutch auctions during the summer period. Kenyan exporters have already started to tackle this problem by selling directly to retail sales outlets rather than to wholesalers.

3. The shortage of domestic investment requires easier access to offshore borrowing. The government has encouraged such borrowing through (a) the liberalization of the economy so that investors are not required to declare their foreign exchange, exporters can retain their foreign exchange earnings to service any offshore loans, and companies can operate foreign accounts without restriction; and (b) the determination by market forces of both interest rates and the exchange rate.

10. The Forestry Sector in Ghana

Samuel K. Appiah

Ghana is one of the few countries in sub-Saharan Africa whose economy has virtually turned around from stagnation and near-collapse to satisfactory economic performance. The adjustment programme which started in 1983 has yielded stronger export growth and led to a favourable evolution of other socioeconomic indicators. There has been growth in agricultural sectors, particularly cocoa and timber, and also in the mining sector, where the investment response has been encouraging. Cocoa production grew by 77 per cent during the adjustment period. Also gold production increased from 200 000 ounces to about 1 million ounces in 1995. The economy has been growing at 5 per cent per annum since 1983, with per capita income rising at 2 per cent per annum. The adoption of sound macroeconomic policies, liberalization of the exchange rate regime, removal of controls, adoption of trade reforms and the achievement of political stability have been responsible for this turnaround. Economic growth is still fragile and further reforms are needed, but substantial progress has been made since the start of economic adjustment.

Table 10.1 shows the structure of production and reveals that the manufacturing sector is very small, while services are relatively large and have been an important source of growth. Growth in the agricultural sector has been low by world standards, and this has limited the potential for the accelerated growth of the economy as a whole. Following these general remarks on Ghana's economy, the remainder of this chapter will discuss issues relating to the development of the forestry sector in Ghana.

GHANA'S FORESTRY SECTOR

The forestry sector had virtually collapsed before the initiation of economic reforms in 1983. The utilization capacity of processing mills was 25 per cent and export receipts had dropped to US$ 15 million. Since then, the supply response of the forestry sector to the reform process has been tremendous. The industry's utilization capacity has increased to about 60 per cent and foreign ex-

Table 10.1 Ghana: structure of production

Sectors	Share in GDP, 1990 (%)	Growth, 1983–90 (%)
Agriculture (including forestry)	43	2.7
Industry	14	7.5
Manufacturing	9	9.5
Services	43	7.5

Source: Ghana Statistical Service.

change receipts from forestry products in 1994 were about US$ 230 million (that is, 18 per cent of total export earnings), ranking third after earnings from gold and cocoa exports. This development is at least partly due to the fact that the government removed an export tax of 20 per cent and introduced a foreign exchange retention scheme through which exporters of logs, sawn timber and veneer sheets could retain offshore 20 per cent of their foreign exchange earnings, while exporters of tertiary products could retain 35 per cent. These measures were designed to enable exporters to have access to foreign exchange to import needed spare parts and equipment, as well as to acquire expertise for production. The scheme is still operational for sawn timber, veneer sheets and tertiary products, but has been abolished for log exports.

The contribution of the forestry sector to gross national product is about 8 per cent, including 2 per cent from non-timber forestry products such as fuel wood and charcoal. The forestry sector employs some 75 000 people, providing a livelihood for about 2 million Ghanaians. The forest industry comprises some 250 logging firms and 130 saw milling, veneering and ply milling companies. In addition, there are more than 200 small-scale furniture and woodworking enterprises. The industry has traditionally concentrated on unprocessed logs and lumber, with tertiary products constituting a small proportion of total exports from the sector. In response to the imposition of export levies on raw lumber, exports of processed wood goods are increasing. This positive trend sets the stage for growth in further value-added production and marketing. Table 10.2 shows timber export trends by products.

Given the magnitude of capital investment, employment and value of production, the forestry sector is a significant contributor to the economy. However, the strong supply response has exacerbated the demand for forestry products, which has been threatening both the sustainability of exploiting timber resources and the sector's ability to contribute to the country's socioeconomic development and to maintain environmental stability. The present condition of the

Table 10.2 Ghana: exports of timber and timber products, 1972–95

Years	Logs		Lumber		Veneers	
	Volume	Value	Volume	Value	Volume	Value
1972	1 020.9	40 217.9	188.4	15 684.8	–	–
1973	1 006.8	86 549.1	234.8	40 148.8	6.5	1 481.2
1974	471.7	47 791.1	215.4	27 754.1	5.8	1 782.7
1975	602.3	49 982.5	174.0	27 445.1	3.7	1 105.9
1976	531.0	58 995.4	149.3	31 868.0	4.4	1 245.5
1977	454.3	52 851.1	73.1	20 042.9	5.5	1 460.0
1978	311.6	40 021.8	77.2	21 774.1	7.8	2 282.1
1979	198.4	19 758.8	77.6	21 817.1	5.5	2 502.3
1980	105.0	13 189.7	69.4	24 694.4	7.5	3 123.1
1981	54.2	4 671.0	52.9	12 738.4	7.1	2 366.9
1982	53.2	3 690.8	39.7	8 973.5	5.3	1 383.1
1983	61.5	4 572.9	44.8	8 306.3	8.9	1 821.3
1984	70.0	5 139.9	56.4	10 050.9	11.5	2 534.4
1985	129.5	8 710.2	76.4	14 553.4	13.5	2 875.2
1986	195.8	25 392.7	83.6	18 839.6	14.1	4 088.0
1987	298.3	32 176.0	162.5	35 720.1	19.8	5 991.1
1988	338.9	43 254.9	170.3	43 406.7	21.0	8 398.2
1989	200.7	23 626.2	154.0	43 426.7	15.0	8 933.2
1990	197.6	29 429.2	202.3	75 071.1	17.4	13 090.1
1991	218.0	32 310.8	182.6	59 674.2	19.6	13 774.3
1992	181.5	24 857.5	235.7	73 843.8	23.9	17 038.5
1993	519.9	59 367.1	250.9	74 706.5	25.7	15 449.6
1994	614.3	76 643.0	297.6	115 520.9	35.5	24 479.4
1995	149.9	23 907.9	330.5	122 986.7	46.2	34 482.8

Note: Volumes are expressed in thousands of cubic metres, and values in thousands of United States dollars.

Source: Ghana Timber Export Development Board.

Years	Plywood		Processed wood		Total	
	Volume	Value	Volume	Value	Volume	Value
1972	28.1	4 198.4	–	–	1 237.5	60 101.1
1973	32.6	9 623.8	2.0	369.9	1 282.7	138 172.7
1974	13.1	5 506.5	4.1	714.9	710.0	83 549.3
1975	13.1	4 724.9	2.6	534.9	795.8	83 793.4
1976	12.9	4 773.0	0.9	217.8	698.6	97 099.6
1977	1.9	701.8	4.9	2 167.1	539.7	77 222.8
1978	1.8	823.2	5.2	2 005.0	403.5	66 906.2
1979	1.8	618.5	5.5	2 551.6	288.9	47 248.3
1980	1.5	40.5	5.2	2 861.7	188.6	43 909.3
1981	0.2	46.4	3.3	1 903.4	117.6	21 726.0
1982	0.3	54.3	1.8	1 194.1	100.3	15 295.7
1983	0.2	33.6	1.9	1 043.0	117.3	15 777.0
1984	0.2	54.0	2.2	967.8	140.2	18 747.0
1985	0.1	23.8	2.0	787.9	221.5	26 950.5
1986	0.2	33.1	2.3	1 410.5	296.0	49 764.0
1987	0.8	259.7	4.1	2 691.3	485.6	76 838.2
1988	1.1	279.5	4.9	3 536.6	536.2	98 875.9
1989	1.0	300.8	5.0	4 023.2	375.8	80 310.1
1990	1.8	661.1	8.3	7 037.4	427.4	125 288.9
1991	1.4	643.5	6.2	7 454.3	427.9	113 857.1
1992	1.5	717.6	9.2	9 534.6	451.8	125 992.0
1993	2.4	856.2	9.8	9 270.6	808.7	159 650.0
1994	4.5	2 994.8	11.8	10 626.9	963.7	230 265.0
1995	7.5	4 582.3	13.6	12 293.5	547.6	198 253.2

forest resource base is such that the annual sustainable harvest must be restricted to a maximum of 1 million cubic metres for the foreseeable future. However, the annual cut has to satisfy a timber industry that is characterized by excessive capacity and low recovery rates. As discussed below, efforts are already being made to address the overexploitation of resources through institutional reforms, training, legislation, rationalizing the structure of the industry, developing improved infrastructure, fiscal interventions and a log export ban.

TOWARDS SUSTAINABLE FOREST RESOURCE MANAGEMENT

Growing interest and concerns about the rate of tropical forest degradation and depletion with consequent environmental damage have led to a number of initiatives. Some of these are based on the assumption that trade in tropical timber products has contributed in a substantial way to the tropical forest depletion which has occurred. In this context, one proposal has been the introduction of certification and eco-labelling of timber and timber products with a view to providing consumers with information on the environmental effects of forest production processes and promoting the consumption and production of environmentally more friendly forestry products.

A key problem in this area is to find a definition of sustainability and express it in measurable criteria. This is because, for example, the multiple uses of forests and the wide variety of conditions under which timber is grown make it difficult to set down a clear and simple set of globally applicable standards for the sustainable management of forests. The International Tropical Timber Organization has worked out a guideline definition of sustainable forest management: it should provide a continuous flow of forest products and services, without undue reduction of the forests' inherent value and future productivity and without undue undesirable effects on the physical and social environment. However, no universally applicable concept of forest management sustainability has so far been adopted, and individual countries and certifying bodies use their own sets of criteria.

Another part of the problem is that only about one-fifth to one-fourth of the production of wood products actually enters world trade. Hence, the bulk of forestry products is consumed in the producing countries; and thus the real reasons for forestry depletion must lie elsewhere, not in international trade. In fact, the direct causes of tropical forest depletion may be identified as being, in order of importance, land clearing for agricultural production and cattle ranching, use of forests to extract fuel wood, and unsustainable commercial logging. While these causes are closely related to issues of economic development in general, there are some measures which can specifically address the domestic use of forest resources in producing countries.

Policies regarding the granting of logging concessions are an example of such measures. Assuming that natural regeneration will allow a sustained yield of wood products from the forest from one harvesting cycle to another, such a policy may entail the introduction of selective logging requirements, including the stipulation of a sufficiently long harvesting cycle, an annual allowable cut for each concessionaire, a selection of stems with a minimum diameter, and a concession period at least as long as the stipulated harvesting cycle. The fee for obtaining a concession should reflect the concession's real economic value, and concessions should be allocated through bidding rather than arbitrarily. Although these elements are valid from an analytical point of view, their implementation may face difficulties since for them to be effective the government must be able to monitor the concessionaire's performance and to cancel the arrangement if necessary.

In any case, measures designed to increase the sustainability of forest resource management are likely to raise production costs both directly through increased selectivity in logging, and indirectly through the information, inspection and management costs which are caused, for instance, by running a reliable certification and labelling scheme. However, a precise assessment of this cost increase is difficult because, for example, certified products may fetch higher prices or obtain higher market shares and thus cover part of the increased production costs.

The best policy for sustainable forestry management would be to reinforce the positive incentives for sustainable management, rather than to penalize or restrict production of and trade in timber not meeting certain standards. Increased international cooperation and consensus between producing and consuming countries would seem to be an important mechanism in this regard. Certification and eco-labelling may also contribute to sustainable forestry management. However, the following principles should be kept in mind while developing certification or eco-labelling systems for forestry products: (a) labels should be based on an international consensus between producers and consumers, rather than on national initiatives; (b) due account needs to be taken of different national environmental priorities and objectives, and methods of achieving them, with priority being given to the concerns of developing countries; and (c) appropriate training in the testing and verification of products needs to be ensured for developing countries.

FOSTERING WOOD PROCESSING

The overall objective of the government with regard to the forestry sector is to promote and develop viable and efficient forest-based industries, particularly in secondary and tertiary processing. The production and export of value-added semi-finished and finished products, for example wood-based panels such as veneers and plywood, and of furniture have been encouraged with a view to replacing traditional exports of lumber. To achieve this objective, as well as to conserve natural resources, the government started in the late 1980s to gradually introduce restrictions on exports of unprocessed timber, such as logs. Bans on exports of round logs now cover 18 species. Export levies of between 10 and 30 per cent of the free-on-board (f.o.b.) price have been introduced in respect of nine species of green and air-dried lumber to encourage downstream processing, as drying is the first and necessary requirement for the production of tertiary products. These export restrictions are seen as a means of increasing foreign currency earnings, generating greater employment, increasing export receipts and assisting in establishing sustainable forest management programmes. Even though some progress has been made, as shown in Table 10.2, the full potential of the industry has yet to be realized.

There is disagreement about the effects on the economy of the ban on exporting logs. There are those who have argued that by diverting export sales of the resource on to the home market, export restrictions have lowered the resource's domestic price. Even though this lowered price has benefited processors, the government has run the risk of encouraging inefficient industries which might become permanently dependent on its support. Moreover, the effect of the decline in the domestic price could be divided into a gain accruing to processors and a deadweight loss; the latter consists of the difference between the amount of foreign exchange earnings which could have been obtained with the export of logs and the amount actually earned from plywood exports. This loss could easily accumulate to millions of dollars.

It has also been argued that the objective of using export restrictions to promote domestic value-added has conflicted with the goal of forest conservation, since those restrictions were likely to encourage the felling of more trees to feed wood-processing industries. For example, lowering domestic log prices by restricting lumber exports but not the exports of processed timber products has not only encouraged processors to expand production, but also reduced the financial incentives for processors to adopt efficient, less wasteful technology and processing practices. Similarly, the incentives for owners of natural resources to engage in conservation and reforestation practices have been diminished. Overall, export restrictions were likely to be environmentally counterproductive since they led to an undervaluation of logs and, hence, reduced market incentives for both owners and processors to conserve natural resources. The most effective method of conserving natural resources is not through trade-distorting measures, but rather by controlling their depletion with policies that do not discriminate between domestic and export markets, such as a logging quota or royalty payments on trees felled. While some of these arguments may be valid from an analytical point of view, it is not always clear whether they refer to actual market conditions, as discussed below.

MAIN CONSTRAINTS FACING THE GHANAIAN FOREST SECTOR

The main constraint on the development of the forestry sector may be considered to be the relatively low price of logging rights, which in principle should signal resource scarcity. This, combined with the ban on log exports, has led to an enormous growth in wood-processing industries, although the processing facilities cannot compete internationally without protection and subsidies. Inefficient wood-processing plants not only underutilize forest resources, which in turn reduces rents from forest resources, but also reduce government revenues and economic growth.

The low level of education and skills of the labour force and the lack of appropriate infrastructure (in particular, well-developed support services to provide inputs, research and development, management and so on) have not allowed the potential of the tertiary processing sector to be fully realized. Furthermore, the underdevelopment of the financial sector, combined with the high cost of capital, has prevented companies from recapitalizing their activities and, hence, improving their efficiency. Private foreign investment in joint ventures and strategic alliances, which would have alleviated the situation by injecting fresh capital and know-how, have not been forthcoming as expected, in spite of the adoption of a liberal investment code. The share of private investment in GDP is less than 8 per cent, which is far below the level required for self-sustained growth.

Moreover, the lack of appropriate marketing know-how has hampered the ability of companies to innovate in product development, design, pricing strategies, production processes, marketing and distribution. Also, the fact that institutional capacities are weak and that private trade associations have been unable to fill this void completely has led to a regulatory marketing regime which has distorted prices and marketing mechanisms. Finally, the neglect of the local market has hampered the growth of local industry processing for export. It is noteworthy that a strong and expanding domestic market has been largely responsible for the growth in the tertiary wood-processing industry in the Republic of Korea.

MEASURES ADOPTED TO ADDRESS CONSTRAINTS

In 1994, a new Forest and Wildlife Policy was adopted with the aim of 'conservation and sustainable development of forest and wildlife resources for maintenance of environmental quality and perpetual flow of optimum benefits to all segments of society'. The government is currently preparing a 20-year Master Plan. The elements of this Master Plan reflect the main national development principles of the government, particularly with respect to ongoing macroeconomic reforms, acceptance of the private sector as the engine of growth and the need to encourage industries based on local raw materials while paying close attention to international trade trends. At the same time, various proposals have had to take into account the need to improve the state of the forests and the environment.

The following policies have been adopted to further develop the forestry sector and improve its competitiveness. First, the allocation of logging concessions and the level of stumpage fees will be reviewed with a view to allocating logging rights competitively and making fees reflect scarcity and product values. This will eliminate inefficient plants, while surviving mills will be stimulated through fiscal incentives and access to concessionary credit to overhaul and modernize equipment and move into downstream production. Concrete measures to be taken are currently under study.

Second, local market demand will be supported through data surveys and fiscal incentives to encourage processing for local needs. In addition, export levies on air-dried lumber are being introduced as an incentive to companies to dry their timber as a precursor to further processing. Moreover, feasibility studies will be conducted to identify marketing opportunities and promote targeted investment options, and to facilitate the upgrading of technical skills and productivity through support for wood processing and value-added wood villages. This concept has worked effectively in Malaysia.

Fifth, an essential activity will be to encourage free-zone processing by pursuing investments for production of re-export items based on imported raw material. All the usual free-zone incentives will apply here. Also, the dialogue between the government and the private sector will be strengthened, and the role of the institutions involved in timber marketing will be redefined with the aim of deregulating marketing completely and allowing the private sector to take a leading role in marketing. Furthermore, the export of logs will be discouraged by free-market forces and fiscal means with a view to maximizing value added and the sector's contribution to socioeconomic growth. Measures for capacity-building in both the public and private sectors will be taken, emphasizing the development of entrepreneurial skills and the contributions from the private sector to policy formulation. These measures, together with the ongoing macroeconomic and trade reforms, are expected to boost economic activities and growth in the forestry sector. Some success is already visible. For example, the relationship between the public sector and the private sector has greatly improved, and the latter is enjoying a programme of skill upgrading provided by the Wood Industries Training Centre which the government has set up.

CONCLUSIONS

East Asian countries, both those abundantly and those poorly endowed with natural resources, have based much of the strong economic growth which they have experienced over the past few years on their competitive advantage in technology, skilled labour, infrastructure, capital and marketing know-how. Their governments have catalysed this advantage by providing an environment conducive to growth through adopting sound macroeconomic policies, working closely with the private sector, providing incentives for basic research and applied technology transfer, upgrading education, enabling relations between labour and industry, adopting policies for raw materials to be sourced easily, extending credit on concessionary terms, and, most important of all, providing political stability and incentives to attract foreign capital and business. Sub-Saharan African countries – both those with and those without natural resource abundance – can over time move in the same direction as these countries, provided that they adopt similar measures. The principle of comparative advantage in resource abundance should be seen as a necessary but not a sufficient condition for growth.

In conclusion, there are two issues which need to be taken into account when development issues relating to renewable natural resources are being addressed. The first has to do with the impact of environmental issues on trade, especially with regard to trade in forest products from developing tropical regions. Care should be taken that recent developments in the certification of timber do not become a non-tariff barrier to trade, thereby affecting the external competitiveness of the countries in those regions. The other has to do with the interdependence of deforestation and agricultural productivity. Certain agricultural policies may cause excessive conversion of tropical forest lands for agricultural use, which would threaten the sustainability of the forest resource. This proposition can be generalized by stating that the relative profitability of forest investment depends not only on forest policies and forest investment, but also, and crucially, on agricultural policies and incentives. This interdependence should be examined critically so that forestry and agriculture can coexist for balanced development.

PART FOUR

Natural Resource Policy from a Local and
Regional Perspective

11. Mining in Goa: the Need to Integrate Local, Regional and National Interests

Ligia Noronha

INTRODUCTION

The policy discourse regarding the development of mineral resources has been primarily in terms of the factors that are of concern to national governments. These include factors such as the quantum of revenues to be earned from developing the resource, the foreign exchange implications of exporting the mineral, the employment imperative and strategic considerations. The focus of attention has always been the implications of resource development for the national economy and the relations between the host government and the mining companies. This has often resulted in mineral development policy being inattentive to local and regional concerns and in the regional/local tiers of government abdicating their responsibility for safeguarding regional concerns. This has occurred in part because the more micro-level impact that the development of the resource has on the region immediately around it, for example through mining activity, has been inadequately considered in mineral policy. Perhaps what is needed is a tiered mineral policy whereby the concerns and interests of each level are worked into the aggregate picture. This would result in a more holistic and perhaps a more sustainable policy of development of resources. This chapter, based on a case study of iron ore mining in Goa, India, highlights the need to have a regional dimension to mineral policy to remedy this imbalance. It does this by studying mining activity, its structure and its impacts within its spatial context.[1]

In July 1991, the Indian government introduced a new economic policy which departed significantly from that of previous decades. This policy introduced major changes in industrial and trade policy, moving from an earlier preoccupation with statism and protectionism towards a more open and market-oriented approach to development. The underlying objective of both industrial and trade policies is to increase the operational efficiencies within the system through increased productivity, reduced costs and improved quality of goods and services, with a view to making Indian industry internationally competitive.

New policy measures to liberalize the economy sought to simplify procedures and make them transparent, remove restrictions on trade and industry and open up to the private sector, both Indian and foreign, areas of industry hitherto reserved exclusively for the public sector. One of the main objectives of this policy is to globalize the Indian economy by increasing trade and investment flows. Successive budgets have added to these reforms through a number of changes in tax, price structures, subsidies and incentive structures.

The new mineral policy launched in 1993 was intended to streamline mineral development and bring the sector into the new liberalized paradigm, as set out in the appendix to this chapter. The policy continues to emphasize the strategic and scarcity aspects of mineral resources that have dominated Indian thinking on resources since 1947. It does, however, stress certain other aspects, such as sea-bed mining, development of proper inventories, the linkage between mineral exploitation and the development of the mineral industry, environmental protection in the context of mining activity, and the need to export metals in their value-added form. Attracting investment into mining has become important with both the national government and local governments. There have been significant attempts to woo foreign and Indian capital through the removal of some of the major deterrents that have existed in Indian industry, namely excessive bureaucratic red tape, restrictions on foreign equity shares and foreign technology agreements.[2]

At the level of the federating states, however, there is a certain apprehension among the public that the thrust of the new economic policy may result in negative local effects, as the central and local government authorities may tend to be lenient towards industry in the interest of attracting and competing for investment funds. More specifically, there may be a tendency to accept inadequate, shoddy, generalist environmental studies just to fulfil a procedural requirement. The new mineral policy highlights the need to protect the environment from mining activity. However, despite a number of environmental management plans being submitted under earlier regulations, it is evident that there has been considerable degradation as a result of mining operations all over the country. More importantly, what is observed is that there has not been a careful study of the costs and benefits of mineral development for the region in which it is located. A certain *ad hoc*ism – in Lindblom's terms a 'muddling through' – characterizes local government policy.

The concern with regional implications also raises a political question because of competitive politics within a democratic society. This competition is intense not only between interests but also between regions and between the federating states and the centre. Small states such as Goa do not have adequate representation at the centre, and what representation there is often speaks on behalf of the dominant interests.[3] It is important, therefore, that in an era of globalization, one aspect of which is the opening up of the country for the development of its mineral resources, the regional dimension seen in terms of the environmental impacts of the development of the resource, the competing agricultural sector and local linkages, and so on, be integrated into the policy.

THE IRON ORE MINING INDUSTRY IN GOA

This section will discuss, first, the structure of the iron ore industry in Goa, with emphasis on its position in the international market, and second, its economic and environmental impacts on the local economy.

The mining belt in Goa extends over an area of 500 square kilometres. The main minerals found are iron ore, manganese ore, bauxite and silica sand. Iron ore is the main mineral found here, as can be seen in Table 11.1. The iron ore of Goa is low-grade, with over 60 per cent of the reserves below 62 per cent iron (Fe) and less than 2 per cent over 65 per cent Fe. Lumps are in the 58–61 per cent range, and a limited quantity of fines have an Fe content of 65 per cent, but on average the Fe content is below 60 per cent.

Table 11.1 Goa: reserves of important minerals (million tonnes)

Mineral	Recoverable reserves as at April 1990			
	Proved	Probable	Possible	Total
Bauxite	8.43	9.88	9.78	28.09
Iron ore				
Hematite	362.56	200.26	199.41	762.23
Magnetite	64.86	3.88		164.55
Manganese ore	2.15	11.43	95.81	23.55
Quartz and silica sand	0.02	1.68	9.97	17.02

Source: Indian Bureau of Mines, *Indian Minerals Yearbook 1993.*

Of the 108 mineral leases currently in operation, 75 are for iron ore and are being worked at present by 15 mining companies, all in the private sector. Leases are on average less than 100 hectares in size.[4] Most of the mining activity is concentrated in just four of the administrative units of the state, known as talukas, namely Bicholim, Sanguem, Satari and Quepem.[5]

Structure of the Iron Ore Mining Industry

The industry has two types of mining companies: (a) those that only extract ore; and (b) those that extract and export the ore. The five largest companies are of the second type and between them control 75 per cent of production and 80 per cent of exports of mineral ore. Of the five large mining companies, the largest controlled 30 per cent of production and 25 per cent of exports of ore as of 1994/5. The second largest has about 17 per cent of total production and 13 per cent of exports; the next two are approximately the same size, with average production and export shares of about 13–15 per cent. The fifth firm has 10 per cent of exports and 5 per cent of production. Table 11.2 provides a breakdown of the production and exports of iron ore for these five companies for 1994/5.

Table 11.2 Goa: production and exports of iron ore, 1994/5 (million tonnes)

Company	Production	Exports
Sesa Goa (SG)	3.9	3.7
Dempo (VSD)	1.9	2.2
V.M. Salgaonkar (VMS)	1.3	2.2
Chowgule & Co (CCL)	2.2	1.9
Fomento (FO)	0.7	0.9
Others	3.2	3.2
Total	13.2	14.1

Source: Goa Mineral Ore Exporters' Association.

Annual production of iron ore in Goa over the last ten years has averaged around 12–13 million tonnes per year. However, production was stepped up in 1994, and in 1995/6 it was about 15 million tonnes.[6] This constitutes over 22 per cent of the country's iron ore production. All of Goa's production is exported, since there is no local market for its low-grade ore. In terms of exports, Goan ore represents over 60 per cent of India's ore exports, and in value terms the iron ore exported from India constitutes around 5 per cent of all its exports. Iron ore has been identified as one of the key thrust areas for export promotion.

In order to comply with export specifications, the ore from Goa is beneficiated and is used for blending by foreign steel mills with higher-grade ore imported from other countries. The destinations of exports are given in Table 11.3, and the high dependence on the Japanese market is evident. Individual companies' dependence on Japan is shown in Table 11.4. The share of the main non-Goan exports to Japan is as follows: Australia, 47 per cent; Brazil, 24 per cent; and other Indian mining areas, 5 per cent. The balance is made up by several other countries.

Table 11.3 Goa: destination of iron ore

Country	Japan	Europe	Rep. of Korea	China	Others[a]	Total
Percentage of ore exports	56	21	9.5	9.4	4.1	100

Note: [a] 'Others' includes Taiwan Province of China, Malaysia, the United Arab Emirates and Saudi Arabia.

Source: Goa Mineral Ore Exporters' Association, *Mineral and Export Intelligence*, June 1996.

Table 11.4 Goa: share of company exports to Japan

Company[a]	SG	VSD	VMS	CCL	FO	Others
Percentage exported to Japan	22	74	43	86	90	68

Note: [a] Abbreviations of company names are explained in Table 11.2.

Source: As in Table 11.3.

The companies in Goa have individual contracts with trading houses in Japan, which in turn supply the ore to seven integrated steel mills. This is done through annual tonnage contracts. Within Japan, 47 per cent of Goan ore is sold to Nippon Steel Corporation and 21 per cent to NKK (Table 11.5). An analysis of the supplies to Japan reveals that most of the exporting companies are heavily dependent on sales to only one steel company, with five of the eight main exporting firms exporting over 80 per cent of their ore to Nippon Steel Company. Two companies are 100 per cent dependent on Sumitomo and Kawasaki. Diversification of clients is evident only in the case of the largest company, Sesa Goa, and to some extent in the case of Fomento. This highlights the dependence of the exporting companies, and therefore their vulnerability to the decisions of the buyers.

*Table 11.5 Goan iron ore exports to Japan: consumption by individual
Japanese steel mills*

Steel mill	NSC	NKK	KSC	SMI	KSL	NSC	NSW
Percentage share	46.5	21.2	10.1	12.6	3.3	2.1	4.2

Note: NSC: Nippon Steel Corporation; NKK: Nippon Kokan Kaisha Corporation; KSC: Kawasaki Steel Corporation Ltd; SMI: Sumitomo Metal Industries Ltd; KSL: Kobe Steel Ltd; NSC: Nisshin Steel Corporation Ltd; NSW: Nakayama Steel Works Ltd.

Source: Goa Mineral Ore Exporters' Association, *Mineral and Export Intelligence*, June 1966.

For the last 20 years, the Goan ore exporters have operated totally in a buyer's market:

1.   The price for them is fixed, as they are very small operators with only 5 per cent of the Japanese market.
2.   The steel mills, operating through the trading houses, enter into direct quantity contracts with the producers with a clause that provides for reduced or expanded offtake by the buyer. No such option is given to the seller. Moreover, the sellers have to meet the stringent specifications of the buyer, as the ore is used to blend with the high-quality ores imported from other parts of the world.

Prices have not hitherto been a determining factor in the supply responses of the local producers, as they plan their production on the basis of the long-term commitments entered into with the buyers. These commitments in turn have been dependent on the stocks available at the steel mills and their supply contracts with other producers. An analysis of price movements for iron ore indicates that price movements follow a five-year cycle. The international prices for iron ore have been rising over the last two years after a continuous decline over the five-year period after 1991/2. According to industry observers, prices are expected to firm up over the next five years, as the demand for steel in the newly developing countries is increasing.

The average operating costs of Goan iron ore production compare favourably with those of the industry internationally. The average operating costs of the main iron ore exporters are set out in Table 11.6; the average operating cost of Goan iron ore production is around US$ 11 per tonne. The inland waterways enable the ore to be carried very economically by barges over an average distance of 46 kilometres. If the Indian railways were used to transport this low-value bulk commodity, the economics of the industry would be badly affected, as railway freight costs are high. Also, the industry is faced with high port charges. In Goa, pit-to-market operations are more integrated than in the rest of India, since the producer enters into direct negotiations with the buyer, markets the ore and ships directly to the country of destination. However, there are many producers, and all are relatively small. The industry as a whole does not have an integrated system of export operations from mining to transportation, shipment and marketing. This results in many ore handling points and has implications for the environment, as will be discussed below.

Table 11.6 Iron ore: relative average operating costs, 1996

Country	Australia	Brazil	India	South Africa
US$/tonne ore	11.0	12.5	13.8	13.9

Source: Goa Mineral Ore Exporters' Association, *Mineral and Export Intelligence*, May 1996, pp. 20–1.

In 1996, the international price for iron ore with 62 per cent Fe content was US$ 13.76 per tonne, making the margin of profit for mining companies very slim. The current trend among major steel producers is to increase the use of low-quality but lower-cost fines. However, the need to upgrade the product mix either by pelletizing or upgrading the lower-value fines will exert considerable pressure on profit margins, thereby further squeezing the small-scale, high-cost producer. This pressure on profit margins may have significant implications for the industry's ability to absorb the costs of environmental regulations. If the producer's costs were initially competitive, the incremental cost of compliance may cause a loss of competitive edge. Both this possibility and the perception, especially in developing countries, that environmental regulations almost always imply higher costs, need to be addressed in order to ensure that this aspect of resource development is not ignored.

Impacts on the Local Economy

Contribution of the mining belt to the local economy

The importance of mining and quarrying to the net state domestic product has been decreasing over the last 25 years. In 1971, the share of income from the mining sector was 11.7 per cent; by 1980/1 it had fallen to 6.3 per cent and by 1990/1 to 4.7 per cent. An attempt has been made to estimate the income of the talukas (administrative units) in which these mines are located, and particularly of the iron ore mining belt.[7] This comprises the villages in which the mining leases are actually located. This assessment of local income is made in order to arrive at an estimate of the relative importance of mining activity to the region.

The analysis reveals a varying picture of the importance of mining activity. The income generated in the iron ore mining belt is very important to the economy of Sanguem and Bicholim talukas, relatively less important to Satari and not important to Quepem. Mining activity has certainly provided the trigger to boost the economies of these talukas and place them at a higher level of economic activity. Over the period 1971–91, the income of the four talukas increased considerably; the average annual growth rate over the 20-year period is given in Table 11.7.

Table 11.7 Goa: average annual rates of growth in the mining talukas, 1970/1 to 1990/1 (%)

Mining talukas	Satari	Quepem	Sanguem	Bicholim
Average annual rates of growth of net domestic product	10	6	7	8

Source: Government of Goa, Department of Planning and Statistics.

Within the mining belt, considerable diversification has occurred, as is evident in the declining share of mining income over the last 20 years (Table 11.8).

Table 11.8 Goa: sectoral shares of total income of the mining belt (%)

Sectors	1971	1991
Agriculture	23.6	25.9
Forestry and fishing	2.9	5.9
Mining and quarrying	54.9	14.5
Secondary	5.7	26.9
Tertiary	12.9	26.8
Total	100.0	100.0

Source: Author's estimates.

It is evident from Table 11.8 that agriculture has maintained its position in total income, despite the fact that there has been a decline in the amount of land under cultivation in the mining region, for reasons which are discussed below. The adoption of high-yielding variety seeds explains in part the unchanged contribution of agriculture to regional income. The steep increase in income from the secondary sector is related to mining activity, as the activity in this sector is linked to mining, especially the servicing and repair of equipment, which are carried out in the household sector. Income from the transport sector has also increased considerably, and this is likewise connected with mining activity, as discussed later in this chapter. Thus, it can be said that mining has been a boost to the economy of the region. What is not clear is how long the mining industry can continue this anchoring role in the region and what will happen to the regional economy if mining activity begins to decline more quickly than anticipated. No set of policy initiatives exists among the different actors in the industry, that is, government, mining companies and local communities, to deal with this eventuality. The industry faces a number of constraints, some due to market conditions, others due to the environmental impact that it is having on the other economic sectors and to the resulting local disaffection, as there is a growing perception now that the industry is beginning to have a negative local effect.[8]

A considerable part of this disaffection is due to the very serious dust problem that mining has created on important public roads in the region.[9] In the late 1970s, the mining companies began the practice of contracting out the transporting of ore to the loading points. Over the last 20 years, a large trucking industry and ancillary shops to service and repair the trucks have sprung up in the villages around the mining areas. Contracting out has had a number of consequences, with mixed benefits to the region and industry.[10] It has:

- reduced the cost to companies of purchasing and maintaining trucks;
- increased transaction costs for companies in terms of negotiating with transporters on rates and tonnages that are to be carried;
- created political and economic pressure groups within the mining region and competition among the groups for a stake in the industry. It has now become very difficult for the mining industry to contemplate a change in the mode of transportation of ore to the loading points, as this would have serious political ramifications;
- given a boost to the rural bank network, as the trucks are purchased with loans from local banks;
- diversified the asset base of the community, from land to capital assets; and
- increased dust pollution in the region, because payment for trucks is made on the basis of tonnages. This creates an incentive to overload and speed in order to make more trips.[11] As a result, ore falls by the wayside.[12] The companies water the roads to reduce the dust; this weakens the surface and has led to accidents due to the slippery conditions of the roads.

The companies have externalized the problem of transporting ore by involving truckers. They now have no direct responsibility for the practices adopted by the truckers and yet have reduced their own costs. Thus, partly for organizational reasons and partly as a result of a lack of policies, undervalued resources such as public roads and the atmosphere have been appropriated by the industry, and the costs of ore transportation have been shifted from the national/regional level to the local region.

The problem faced by the local region is very much the creation of the mining industry but has been compounded by the total absence of government policy to regulate transportation in the region. The stakes that have now been created in transport and allied services make it politically difficult to consider alternative modes of transport. The transportation industry which has grown out of the mining industry has had a dual impact on the region: on the one hand, it has led to a growth in the capital assets of the region; while on the other hand, it is also causing a decline in community assets such as clear air and good roads. Political interests add to the difficulty the mining industry has in trying to mitigate the problem by suggesting dedicated roads for ore transport, but no one wants the new roads to be located in their political constituency. This has added to the constraints to be overcome in arriving at a solution to the problem.

Impact on agricultural lands

The impact that mining has had on agricultural activity in Goa is observed in the change in the area under cultivation around the mining areas, and the loss in productivity of cropland due to dump run-off. The change in area under cultivation has been noted through both satellite imagery and census data. Table 11.9 indicates the changes in cropland over the period 1981–9 in the five main mining clusters in Goa. These clusters are Bicholim, Sanquelim and Pale in the taluka of Bicholim; Pissurlem in the taluka of Satari; and Codli in the taluka of Sanguem. Iron ore mining activity in these three talukas accounts for over 90 per cent of the iron ore mining in Goa.

It is clear from the data that over the eight-year period in question, while mining-related activities increased by 57.83 sq km, the amount of land under thick vegetation, that is with forest covering over 40 per cent of the area, fell by 3.5 sq km, and land under moderate vegetation with forest covering between 20 and 40 per cent fell by 62 sq km. Over this period, 11.16 sq km of agricultural land with standing crops were also lost to mining, while there was an increase of 5 sq km in the amount of fallow land (Table 11.9). Census data for 1991 also indicate that there has been a substantial decrease in the area under cultivation in the mining villages, as in the villages surrounding them, relative to the area under cultivation in 1981. In the taluka of Bicholim, the change has been in the range of 7–50 per cent in relation to the 1981 figures; in Satari taluka, the change has been in the range of 5–90 per cent; and in Sanguem, the change has been in the range of 10–30 per cent.

Table 11.9 Goa: land-use/cover in the main mining areas (sq km)

Data used	Mine areas	Crop-land	Fallow land	Thick vegetation	Moderate vegetation	Sparse vegetation	Scrub land
MSS-81	19.6	101.4	35.8	54.5	277.3	245.0	219.3
MSS-84	36.6	95.0	34.2	51.8	268.0	228.6	231.5
TM-87	54.9	84.8	46.9	52.7	234.7	198.1	226.0
SPOT-89	77.2	90.2	40.8	51.0	215.3	171.6	243.5
Change in 8 years	+57.6	−11.2	+4.9	−3.5	−61.9	−73.4	+24.2

Notes: MSS-81: Multi Spectrum Scanner of Landsat, data collected in 1981; MSS-84: Multi Spectrum Scanner of Landsat, data collected in 1984; TM-87: Thematic Mapper, data collected in 1987; SPOT-89: data collected from the French satellite SPOT in 1989. Figures differ from the original table due to rounding.

Source: Centre for Resources Engineering, *Environmental Impact of Iron-Ore Mining in Goa* (Final Report submitted to the Ministry of Environment), Bombay: Indian Institute of Technology, April 1992.

While in the rest of India the ratio of ore to overburden is on average 1:0.25, in Goa it ranges from 1:2 to 1:3. This implies that an enormous amount of overburden is being generated per tonne of ore mined in Goa, and once generated, it must be put somewhere. Given that most mining leases are about 100 ha or less in size, there is very limited space or none at all within the lease area to dump waste from rejects; this creates a need for land outside the lease area for the purpose.[13] The issue of limited dumping space has thus become a priority for land management, as policy has to focus on ways to reduce the demand for more land through utilization of the waste material, and so on.[14]

Because land is in short supply, dumps are typically steep, with slopes of 50° and heights of 30–40 m over small surface areas, making up in height what they cannot achieve in basal area. Overburden dumps are situated in the upper part of the valley regions. Goa is prone to very strong monsoons for three and a half months of the year, with rainfall of about 3000–4000 mm during that period, and run-off from the dumps blankets agricultural fields and watercourses.

A 1981 survey by the Indian Bureau of Mines revealed that 2.53 sq km of agricultural land close to reject dumps was affected. Estimates by the Department of Agriculture in 1996 indicate that in three of the administrative units 11.50 sq km of crop land has become unproductive because of mining rejects. The fact that damage to agricultural fields in the five main mining clusters is extensive is also evident from the annual compensation payments made by the companies to farmers for the removal of the silt from their land and for loss of production. A rough indication of the magnitude of these payments is obtained from the fact that for one mining company they account for 15 per cent of the total budget for environmental control. In general, these figures do not fully reflect the problem, as most often it is difficult to hold a single mine-owner accountable for damage to a field, because it is the result of the overflow of silted streams, caused by water discharged from distant mines or from dump run-off from a group of mines. Mining companies try to purchase the fields in order to reduce the need for compensation payments, but this is often resisted as the owner of the field is loath to part with the land.

The Khazan lands are a unique estuarine agro-ecosystem which extends over an area of 180 sq km. They lie in the basins of the two main rivers and form the food bowl of the state. During the monsoon period, paddy is grown on these lands, as the rain dilutes the salinity. River water reaching the fields through various waterways has also made the Khazan lands the spawning ground for fish and shrimps. Over the years this system has been used and protected by the community management, which has been responsible for building embankments and sluice gates. While the latter have played an important role in regulating seawater ingress into the fields during tidal ebb and flow and in regulating fishing activities, the former (built of local material) have served to protect the fields from inundation by brackish water. The embankments stretch for about 2000 km and have been an enormous asset in protecting the ecosystem. A survey by the Agricultural Land Development Panel in the early 1990s found that mining was a dominant cause, among other development activities, of the decline in both the mangroves and the Khazan land system. The panel attributed this to the deforestation in the mine areas that has increased surface run-off and sediment load in the upper reaches of the rivers. This sediment is deposited on the floodplains, increasing their area and pressuring the embankments that were built to withstand an anticipated level of water at high tides. Another reason for the increased sediment load and its downstream deposition is linked to the ore reject dumps in the mine areas. The panel also found that the heavy and continuously increasing barge traffic carrying ore from the mining regions to the port has increased wave energy and weakened the embankments.[15]

Mining has thus had an impact on agriculture, not so much through a movement of agricultural labour to the mining sector for employment, but rather because of the external effects it has had on agricultural activity through the silting of streams that irrigate croplands and in certain areas a silting of the croplands themselves. Moreover, a secondary impact which has been suggested is a change in the perception of cultivators, who have found that receiving compensation is a more rewarding proposition than actual cultivation.[16]

CONCLUSIONS

The mining industry in Goa poses a number of issues for mineral policy. While there is no doubt that the local/regional economy has been given a push through mineral development, there is now evidence to indicate that mine-related practices may be starting to have an adverse impact on other local economic sectors, such as agriculture. If mining is to lead to the sustainable development of the region, it is important that resource development polices have a regional dimension so that mining results in positive local effects. Policy needs to attend to the environmental implications of mining activity. A transport policy needs to be developed so that the sector can be properly regulated, as well as a policy of diversification of economic activity to ensure that some of the income from the mining sector is reinvested in the region, so that the non-mine sector develops more robustly and has a sustainability beyond the life of the mines.

More specifically, a local/regional dimension to mineral policy would require what was referred to earlier as a tiered plan so that the national, the regional and the local all have an adequate voice. Certain axes around which this could be developed are:

1. A land use policy: this will require clear guidelines regarding the land that can be made available for dumping purposes so that cropland is not affected because of run-off from these dumps. This will entail an assessment of opportunity costs involved.

2. An environmental policy: this will require guidelines on dump management and water recycling within mines so that these do not impinge on other economic sectors. There is a need for a more innovative policy to influence the environmental behaviour of agents. Environmental policy in India has so far been very much of the 'command and control' variety. What the policy has emphasized is an alteration of the options open to agents, this alteration almost always involving the restraint of certain practices. As a result, environmental policy has come to be seen as a regime of constraints rather than one of creating positive incentives for environmental change. Policy needs to influence behaviour by altering the costs and/or benefits relevant to agents or through an alteration of the mindset of agents. Such a policy would have a greater chance of promoting a more sustainable development of mineral resources.

3. A transport policy: this will require not only an economic and political evaluation of alternative means of transport to reduce the number of ore handling points, thereby avoiding possible sources of pollution, but also new management systems.

4. A closure policy: this will require attention to the development of alternative opportunities for the mining community, multiskilling, and attention

to the long-term environmental impacts. In general, the impact of closure will be determined by how dependent the community is on mining and the degree of integration of mining activities into the local economy. The diversity – economic, social and demographic – of the mining communities is the crucial element that needs to be taken into account when closure policies are being evolved.

5.   The need for an understanding of the nature of the linked sectors so that regulations are in place from the outset; otherwise, over time the sector can become 'nested' in political terms and change becomes difficult to achieve.

6.   The need to demonstrate the economic advantage to mining companies of environmental improvements, so that improved environmental behaviour becomes self-sustaining rather than having to be continuously imposed by regulations. It is important that regulators themselves are able to perceive (a) the impacts of different environmental management options on the incomes of companies, and (b) the need for policy instruments to differentiate among these options. Such a perception will enable regulators to choose a set of policy instruments that drive home the message of the advantages of being green.

While these factors are recommended, it is not being suggested that attention to these aspects alone can lead to a national policy more sensitive to regional and local concerns, since attention to some could result in conflict between local, regional and national interests. While some of these interests may be complementary, others may conflict, and hence remedying the inadequacy of national mineral policy would require not just a 'representation strategy', that is, one incorporating the interests of each spatial dimension, but also engaging in a trade-off between different interests. Policy making would then move into the realm of politics.

APPENDIX: MAIN FEATURES OF THE NEW MINERAL POLICY, 1993

Elements of policy:

A. Objectives   Scarcity and strategic aspects; development of proper resource inventories, linkage between mineral exploitation and the mineral industry; environmental protection; metals to be exported in more value-added forms.

B. Public sector control — All 13 minerals and mineral-bearing areas listed as reserved for the public sector in 1991 are deleted from this list and opened for private investment.

C. Foreign participation — Foreign equity participation in joint ventures with Indian companies is encouraged. While equity is limited to 50 per cent, this does not apply to the captive mines of mineral-processing industries.

D. Environmental measures — Leases denied to any party, *private or public*, without a proper mining plan that includes an Environmental Management Plan (EMP). An EMP has to include (a) environmental safeguards, (b) restoration of mined areas, and (c) afforestation.

E. Nature of mining agreements — Joint ventures with elements of production-sharing contracts for ores and metals in which the country is deficient.

F. Trade aspects — Emphasis on exports of metals in value-added form; highlights the need for the mineral export industry to be finely tuned to the international market situation; import substitution objectives to be met through increased indigenous exploitation of minerals and through joint ventures in countries with complementary mineral resources.

NOTES

1. This chapter is based on an ongoing study to prepare a regional environmental quality management plan for the mining belt of Goa. The study was commissioned by the Government of Goa.
2. Mineral development in India is regulated by the Mines and Minerals (Regulation and Development) Act 1957. This covers the entire range of minerals in the country. The proprietary title to minerals is vested in the federating states, but legislation to regulate and control mining is a matter for central government. The states can issue mining leases on major minerals only subject to the provisions of the central Act.
3. The mechanics of the manner in which dominant interests influence policy making as well as implementation would be made clear by a political-economy study of the region/industry. This would show not only their greater capacity to acquire and disseminate information and their greater access to the nodal points of state power, but also their greater organizational capacity to respond to changing political and economic contexts.
4. In the 1940s, there was a rush for mining rights in Goa, and the entire mining belt, which extends over an area of 654 sq km or 18 per cent of Goa's land area, was given out as mining concessions by the Portuguese colonial government. The concessions were given to private owners and were for 99 years. Because the demand for mining rights was so high, the Portuguese government had to parcel out small areas of land (hence the small size of holdings). At one time the total number of leases was 868. In 1978 the Indian government terminated 287 concessions on the grounds that they were not being

exploited for mineral production, thus leaving 581 concessions in force. These were converted into ten-year leases which had to be renewed in 1987. In that year only 397 leaseholders applied for renewal; only 108 of these were renewed and have been in operation since then.

5. Goa has 11 administrative units.

6. The total production of iron ore in India was around 67 million tonnes in 1995/6. Of this, 29 million tonnes was in the form of lumps, 31 million tonnes consisted of fines and 6.4 million tonnes consisted of concentrates. Production is expected to rise to 75 million tonnes in 1996/7, to 110 million tonnes in 2001/2 and to 125 million tonnes in 2006/7. Demand for iron ore for the domestic steel industry for the same years is expected to stand at 45, 75 and 85 million tonnes respectively. The balance will be available for export.

7. Income accounts in India are available at the national and the state level, but with one or two exceptions are not available at the level of towns and villages. Net value added for the mining belt was therefore estimated by the 'allocation method', which involved using a state-level average and allocating it to the mining region on the basis of cultivated area or of workers employed in each category of activity. More specifically, it involved: (a) identifying the sectoral composition of economic activity in the mining belt; (b) calculating state-level averages of net value added/hectare in agriculture and gross value added/worker in all other sectors; (c) estimating income from agriculture using cultivated area in the mining villages and the income from other sectors using the number of workers in each economic activity.

8. This is evident in the number of protest groups that are emerging in the region and the setting up of road blocks and other measures employed by the villagers to show their disaffection. This disaffection could be exacerbated by the increasingly competitive politics of the region.

9. The seriousness of this dust problem is evidenced by the fact that a committee headed by the Minister and the local representative was appointed by the Legislative Assembly to study the extent of the problem and suggest possible remedial measures.

10. The larger study of which this chapter is a part is in the process of collecting data to estimate the costs and benefits to the region of the contracting out of ore transportation.

11. In one dense mining cluster, for example, there are about 170 trucks per hour on a 15 km stretch of road. A total of 1700 trips are made per day, and a total of 21 250 tonnes of ore is transported daily to the loading points.

12. Some estimate this amount to be about 0.5 per cent of the tonnage carried. It creates an enormous quantity of ore dust along the road, which is very evident from the surrounding trees and houses and from complaints from local people concerning respiratory problems.

13. Over the period 1980–90, 146.75 million tonnes of iron ore were mined in Goa. With an average stripping ratio of 2.5 cu m per tonne, this implies that 366.88 million cu m of waste was generated during this period, or approximately 37 million cu m per year. The amount of land required for dumping depends on the height of the dump; for example, for an average dump height of 35 m, approximately 3 hectares of land is required in order to dump 1 million cu m of overburden waste. Thus, if annual waste generation is 37 million cu m, this implies that the mining industry has an annual requirement of 111 hectares *outside* the mining concessions in which to dump the overburden. If, for environmental reasons, dump heights have to be less, the amount of land required for dumping will increase. On a long-term basis, this will become an unsustainable demand for land in a state whose total area is only 3702 sq km.

14. There is an ongoing project to study the utilization of waste material for the manufacture of bricks for construction purposes. If this were to succeed, there would be a good market for this material, as construction is an important activity in Goa.

15. In the mining belt there are 54 loading points. About 1500 barge trips per month over a period of eight months are observed from the loading points to the port via the two

arterial rivers. In 1994, there were 136 barges averaging 1020 dead-weight tonnage operating in Goan waters.

16. This needs to be studied, especially given the symbolic importance of land to the individual.

12. The Communal Areas Management Programme for Indigenous Resources (CAMPFIRE) in Zimbabwe

L.T. Chitsike

INTRODUCTION

This chapter discusses a rural economic system based on natural resources – the Communal Areas Management Programme for Indigenous Resources (CAMPFIRE) – in Zimbabwe. This programme originally began by targeting very poor and remote districts that would benefit from their natural resources, such as vegetation, forests, water and wildlife, if they agreed to manage and conserve these resources in accordance with specific guidelines. Altogether there are now 26 out of 57 districts (about half the country) under the CAMP-FIRE programme, which operates according to the following principles:

- all members of the community own and manage resources in their areas, and thereby benefit financially, economically, socially and culturally from them;
- a regulatory system overseen by the government is introduced to control the use of natural resources;
- a land-use system is established to include arable land, pastoral land, wildlife and settlements;
- activities are undertaken in accordance with the already established district, ward and village development committees;
- the programme benefits from technical support from the government, parastatals and non-governmental organizations (NGOs).

MAIN COMPONENTS OF EDUCATION AND SKILLS DEVELOPMENT

Wildlife Management

District councils were provided with management assistance from the Department of Parks and Wildlife Management and from NGOs, through the employment of wildlife monitors and other technical and management personnel at the community level and the construction of supporting infrastructure such as fences and water points.

In collaboration with the Department of Parks and Wildlife Management, the district councils were made responsible for maintaining optimum animal population levels and for controlling problem animals. Locally recruited wildlife monitors and other technical and management personnel were trained and employed by district councils to work at the community level within the project period. Initially, the United States Agency for International Development (USAID) paid for most of the training, but eventually councils used a portion of their wildlife revenues for such training. The monitors shared information with communities on the wildlife situation, and built and maintained infrastructure related to wildlife management.

Expenditure to enhance the use of wildlife through district council activities was to be funded from the programme and would supplement revenues from wildlife utilization. It provided an operating budget in the early years of the programme for capital investment and for technical support for the development of transport and other inputs.

Specific benefits of investments in this area included the establishment and implementation of a self-sustaining wildlife resources management programme and comprehensive land-use plans for each district.

Institutional and Community Development

The responsibility for institutional and community development was assigned to an NGO – the Zimbabwe Trust. The Zimbabwe Trust recruited and deployed a manager in each district after consulting with each district council. The manager's tasks include:

1. strengthening village, ward and district institutions, including wildlife committees, by providing training and assistance in accounting, organizational and problem-solving skills;
2. facilitating the planning and decision-making process, as the above institutions select the best options for development and address issues of distribution and implementation;

3. acting as an adviser, providing information, acting as a negotiator with private businessmen and ensuring that villagers' needs are expressed to councils.

Community Development, Particularly Involving Women

Women are intricately involved in the production economy, assuming responsibility for family well-being in Zimbabwe's rural communities. In the target areas of the programme, up to 65 per cent of households in several districts of western Zimbabwe are headed by women with absent migrant spouses. In general, households headed by women are the poorest in the community; and it is imperative to address the needs of these households.

The CAMPFIRE programme seeks to expand the share of women in the benefits of wildlife production and management. It aims to promote a general increase in the level of economic activities by transferring the technical and problem-solving skills to women; expanding the harvesting and processing of veld crops and products in whose production women might more readily become involved; and providing a mechanism to ensure that women's concerns regarding wildlife management and its impacts are conveyed to district councils.

Education and Training

The widespread introduction of wildlife management and utilization schemes envisaged in the programme requires the participants to have increased environmental awareness, specialized knowledge and skills, and new perspectives on land use and ownership of resources. It was found necessary for support to be given to a wide range of conservation education and training activities, and for that reason to strengthen the capacity of the Zimbabwe Trust and the Department of Parks and Wildlife Management to meet these needs. The Zimbabwe Trust was specifically requested to (a) provide training to local institutions in the necessary skills for planning and implementing project activities; (b) coordinate with other institutions providing conservation education in the districts, such as the Ministry of Education and the Department of Natural Resources; and (c) conduct training through several mechanisms, including informal discussions, presentations, workshops and field trips. A full-time training specialist would be provided, and funding made available for school environment magazines.

Income-generating Activities

The CAMPFIRE programme is planned in a way that allows each community to be free to choose those options for basic income generation that best suit it.

However, some basic guidelines were drawn up to give communities starting points; for example, with wildlife as a form of land use, a management programme was designed which includes international safari hunting, sustainable yield cropping to produce meat and hides, the sale of live animals, crocodile farming, secondary industries, conventional tourism and eco-tourism.

Safari hunting appears to be the most lucrative because it can be implemented with a minimum of development costs. It requires only the leasing of hunting rights to an operator who takes full responsibility for finding clients, accompanying them with a professional hunter, providing accommodation, and other logistic arrangements. Communities earn income from the sale of trophy licences and the lease of hunting areas. Local industry provides scope for the tanning of hides (which increases value added), the manufacture of leather articles, and cottage industries using various wildlife products.

PROJECT IMPLEMENTATION

To begin implementing CAMPFIRE, each district acquired 'Appropriate Authority' status, the legal term used for the transfer of ownership and responsibility for wildlife management from the Department of Parks and Wildlife Management to a district council and its wards and villages. The districts and their communities became responsible for all other resources as well, although the right to exploit forests has not yet been granted.

Support Agencies

The districts under the programme receive technical support from the government, NGOs and a department at the University of Zimbabwe. These meet regularly to coordinate their support services as an agency known as the CAMPFIRE Collaborative Group (CCG) and other specific responsibilities for education and skills training for the districts and their communities at ward and village level are assigned as follows:

1. *The Department of Parks and Wildlife Management* is the statutory body that administers the Wildlife Act (1975) (1982) and provides all basic information on wildlife matters. It also trains game guards, assists in problem animal issues and approves quotas for safari hunting.
2. *The World Wide Fund for Nature and Multi-species Project* is operational in a number of communal and commercial farming areas. Its activities include research to analyse, compare and contrast the economic and ecological consequences of cattle and wildlife production under different tenure systems. Also, it gives advice and assistance to producer

communities on the economic and financial aspects of ecological wildlife management.

3.   *The Centre for Applied Social Science (CASS), University of Zimbabwe*, is responsible for socioeconomic research on CAMPFIRE as well as institutional and policy analysis and postgraduate training. CASS has so far conducted baseline studies for several districts and is also involved in monitoring and evaluation activities with districts.

4.   *The Zimbabwe Trust* is an NGO that supports CAMPFIRE in several districts. In the past, its responsibilities covered capacity-building, that is awareness and training programmes for village committees up to district council level; and the installation of infrastructure with councils, that is earth dams, boreholes and electric fences. At present it focuses on capacity-building and has handed over much of its responsibility for project support to other agencies, including the rural district councils themselves.

5.   *The Africa Resources Trust (ART)* collects information from abroad for CAMPFIRE committees and support agencies on the issues that affect CAMPFIRE's capacity to market natural resources. ART promotes the CAMPFIRE concept to other African countries as well as learning about similar initiatives and policies in other parts of Africa and the rest of the world.

6.   *The CAMPFIRE Association* is a national body made up of all district councils under CAMPFIRE. It collects information from the government, ART and other sources, and transmits it to regions and districts. These organize educational visits within and outside the country for their members.

It is envisaged that other government ministries and parastatals will take an interest and give more technical support to local communities, especially as they enter the phase in which they raise more revenue and engage in more complex projects.

Awareness Campaigns

All promoters of the CAMPFIRE programme agreed that because of the complex problems associated with the CAMPFIRE concept, as well as the complex social, economic and political issues in communal lands, it was necessary to embark on some very effective awareness campaigns throughout villages and wards before trying to implement the programme.

Consequently, a great deal of time was invested in gaining the confidence of councils and communities, and that proved to be a critical but very successful exercise. Councils appointed a CAMPFIRE manager within their administration to work with the NGO promoters, and councillors themselves addressed several meetings in villages together with local chiefs and headmen. Some of the problems the villagers wished to understand were:

- Is CAMPFIRE not an attempt by the government to extend the national parks into our lands, as happened before when Hwange and other parks were established?
- How true or genuine is the government in handing over management and financial benefits to us?

It took between six and twelve months for CAMPFIRE promoters to convince local communities that they had a new and far-reaching approach to conservation and development in their areas using their own resources. Once the villagers and their ward leaders were satisfied, the project began in earnest and on a firm foundation.

Institutional Development

Following the successful awareness campaigns, the promoters of CAMPFIRE – that is, the government through the Department of Parks and Wildlife Management, district council leaders and NGOs – focused attention on institutional and capacity building through appropriately designed training programmes. The objective of such training was to transfer and mobilize knowledge and skills as well as improve the basic conditions for their application, so that the local people and institutions would be able to initiate and sustain solid and independent development processes.

Existing Institutions

Before introducing wildlife committees under CAMPFIRE it is important to present and analyse the institutions in place in the districts. Under the District Council Act (1984) and the Rural District Councils Act (1988), every district had an elected district council, ward development committees and village development committees. The functions of these bodies were to enable villagers to identify and articulate their needs, and to plan and implement development projects at village, ward and district level. However, the institutions could not effectively implement those objectives because they could not produce plans, owing to their low level of education and the lack of support institutions, and because they lacked financial resources to implement plans.

Wildlife Committees

When CAMPFIRE was introduced and awareness campaigns had been completed, communities and district authorities realized that the existing government institutions would be inadequate to perform the functions required to support and sustain the CAMPFIRE programme, for the following reasons:

- the village and ward development committees were weak institutions in terms of project planning, financial resources and administration, and project implementation;
- these committees were already burdened with government administrative responsibilities, such as collecting levies, gathering data for central government and settling local disputes. Setting up wildlife committees was therefore not considered duplication of the responsibilities of existing committees;
- the wildlife committees created would still have to relate to the mainstream development authority within the districts. For example, the ward councillor who chairs the ward committee meetings coordinates wildlife committees and takes up wildlife issues to the district development committee level; and the wildlife committee coopts the village committee chairman;
- communities agreed that the CAMPFIRE programme had a useful role to play in their lives and justified having its own special committee;
- the committees had financial resources of their own from USAID or those they generated from safari hunting in their areas. Programmes should be planned and implemented with technical advice from the government and NGOs and trained local leadership.

Training during and after awareness exposures for committees and communities covered the role and duties of committees and their members; procedures for holding committee meetings; recruitment of game scouts; relations with the council, and representation on the council's wildlife and grazing committee; relations with government development committees; relations with traditional leaders; the rights and responsibilities of programme participants in general; and the participation of women in the programme.

Soon after training, the wards and villages went straight into development issues of great concern to them, and became very active and lively; for instance, in Madhambudzi Ward the committee wished to see CAMPFIRE benefits extended to timber and other resources in their ward. It was pointed out that the district council was selling Mukwa high-quality hardwood from the ward to sawmills, and not passing any revenue down to the villages. In Bambadzi Ward (Plumtree) the wildlife committee began challenging the council to justify stated wildlife management costs. In Hawana Ward (Plumtree) the committee, soon after its formation, embarked on plans to establish a grazing scheme, ostrich egg collection and irrigation farming.

However, despite the successes in the formation of committees and the active participation in CAMPFIRE activities, the wildlife committees in the districts also faced problems. First, some government village and ward committees that were not operating effectively feared, despite assurances, that the new wildlife committees would usurp their powers, authority and influence, since they were economically more powerful and better technically supported from outside. Second, the district councils feared that the vocal ward and village committees knew too much about CAMPFIRE and about their rights in terms of project development, financial benefits and administrative systems based on democratic principles that require consultations upwards and downwards. For these reasons, the district authorities became very suspicious and resentful of wildlife committees and of CAMPFIRE itself.

However, after careful observation, the councils are now very much in sympathy with community empowerment viewpoints. The district CAMPFIRE manager appointed by the council now works well with the NGO support staff. The councils pass CAMPFIRE revenues to the wildlife committees, as outlined in the programme document, and accept that once funds are in local community hands they do not interfere with them. All CAMPFIRE wards are responsible for their own development planning activities, which are discussed at ward general meetings and approved there before implementation. However, owing to illiteracy and a low level of education, wards have difficulty in drawing up and implementing some of their plans on their own. Good working relations with government departments, parastatals and NGOs help overcome the problems.

The councils note that many people who resisted CAMPFIRE at its inception are now vying for posts on the CAMPFIRE committees. Even local politicians, councillors and Members of Parliament are using CAMPFIRE as a way to gain popularity and votes in council elections. In summary, CAMPFIRE institutional development is making good progress on many fronts; the committees are democratically elected and are effective; and decisions are being made by the communities themselves. However, skills in bookkeeping and accounting and in project planning and management still require input from supporting agencies. Women's involvement in decision making is growing but is not adequate.

Networking

From the very beginning of the CAMPFIRE programme, project promoters realized that it was essential to develop sound working relationships or networking with key institutions relevant to CAMPFIRE programmes if serious problems were to be avoided and long-term success achieved. Government institutions were considered crucial, as they could provide technical services outside the scope of CAMPFIRE support agencies (CASS, the Zimbabwe Trust, the Department of Parks and Wildlife Management). In addition, it was important to be in touch with policy-related personnel and institutions, such as provincial administrators and the National Planning Agency offices in the regions. Links were established, and some of the most important ones are outlined below:

- Official contact was established with the Provincial Co-operative and Community Development Officers in order to secure support for the women's officers, who could then work with the Ministry's Ward Community Co-ordinator and the village community workers. Through that linkage, those officers were able to conduct training sessions on needs analysis and other activities successfully and with relative ease.
- An official link was established with the Ministry of Education in order to reinforce the planned efforts to introduce conservation education in schools. The Ministry was able to identify District Education Officers as the appropriate persons for consultation.
- A vital link was created with Agritex, which provided technical input in several districts. Notably, the section responsible for topography and conservation assisted in the production of maps and the insertion of projects on maps. It also assisted by supplying aerial survey profiles, and provided physical input in the determining of sites for water projects.
- The Ministry of Local Government was approached, and its input was in the form of assistance from the provincial promotion and training officers, who help to arrange the initial training of council executive officers and NGO staff with management development programmes.
- The Ministry of Public Service assisted in arranging courses for Zimbabwe Trust staff on 'Training of Trainers'.
- Meetings with the National Planning Commission and Provincial Administrators resulted in a workshop to brief provincial leaders on CAMPFIRE and the inclusion of CAMPFIRE in the Five-Year Development Plans.

Wildlife Management

Once the CAMPFIRE programme had been accepted, communities followed intensive educational and training programmes. The success of these programmes is reflected in various ways.

Physical infrastructure

The Zimbabwe Trust and councils assisted ward and village communities with water projects that are vital for the survival of wildlife, livestock and human beings. In Bulilamangwe District, in which the Maitengwe Area is the centre of wildlife, including birds and fish, support agencies assisted in the repair of the Maitengwe/Masi Dams and their water-holding capacity. A wide variety of animals are attracted to these dams. It is anticipated that a photographic safari project will be in place in the near future. In many other CAMPFIRE districts watering pans and boreholes were drilled.

In Binga the most impressive infrastructure is the solar electric fence blocks between 14 and 24 km in circumference constructed by ward members, the Department of Parks and Wildlife Management and the district council. The fences protect the community crops and residential areas from wildlife. The local community maintains them very well through trained fence monitors.

Game scouts

CAMPFIRE committees select game scout candidates for training with the Department of Parks and Wildlife Management for a one-week period repeatable over several months until the scouts are familiar with their functions. USAID supports the training of these scouts, who go to special training centres in the country. Game guards assist local authorities by supplying information on conservation activities and situations to village and ward wildlife committees, assist and monitor the safari hunters, assist the Department of Parks and Wildlife Management and the district councils on problem animal control matters, and participate in other activities related to wildlife management.

Land-use plans

No district has completed a land-use plan as required in the terms of reference for the programme. Programme support agencies and district councils have called meetings on the matter with communities that are particularly interested, but not much practical action has taken place with the exception of setting up fences that have demarcated wildlife areas from settlements and grazing. The most advanced step taken on district land-use planning was in Binga district, where a wide range of organizations met and produced a plan, which however has not yet been implemented. Agritex is crucial in training districts to understand and produce land-use plans.

Safari contracts and operators

No district council had any experience or skills in safari hunting. The Department of Parks and Wildlife Management and the Zimbabwe Trust assist councils with general information, strategies and tactics for handling the contracts. The wards and villages require the councils to express a wish to be involved. Local communities are trained and participate in quota-setting for each species of wildlife before hunting begins. Most communities make good estimates which are approved and endorsed by the Department of Parks and Wildlife Management.

Community knowledge of natural resources

In a recent survey and evaluation of CAMPFIRE carried out in districts with at least three years' experience of CAMPFIRE, over 96 percent of participants had a good knowledge of basic natural resources. There was, however, very limited knowledge in districts and wards without CAMPFIRE. It was fully understood that wildlife conservation and rural development are intimately related to resources, beginning with the soil, grass, trees and wildlife; this generates the capacity to distinguish resources that can be exploited sustainably. Consequently, communities under the CAMPFIRE programme are now very resource-conscious, with the following results:

- random tree cutting has ceased or been drastically reduced: a resident only cuts trees for a good reason and in a manner that is conservation-friendly;
- bushfire burning has decreased dramatically. Communities voluntarily rush to put out fires if they occur;
- earth dams are being built with community capital and labour resources to conserve run-off water;
- sledge transport is effectively banned;
- conservation committees established in villages are effective and often operate with by-law backing;
- there are increasing cases of planned paddocks to conserve grass and improve pasture;
- there are game scouts everywhere, monitoring wildlife populations and poaching;
- because of the elimination of poaching, wildlife populations are increasing.

Wildlife revenue

Over 90 per cent of CAMPFIRE revenue is from sport hunting, 64 per cent of which is from elephant hunts. It is estimated that districts earn over Z$ 25 million a year from safari hunting. The income to Binga – one of the older districts – is shown in Table 12.1.

Table 12.1 Zimbabwe: Binga district CAMPFIRE income, 1991–5
(Zimbabwe dollars)

1991	1992	1993	1994	1995
237 355	1.24 mn	1.34 mn	1.57 mn	1.57 mn

Source: Binga District Report, 1995.

Communities and their districts decide on the distribution of revenue through open and transparent meetings. However, a guideline which was used by most CAMPFIRE districts split the total amount as follows: 15 per cent as a district levy, 35 per cent for management of the programme and 50 per cent for wards and villages. This was later changed to 20 per cent at the district level for everything and 80 per cent for wards and villages. In the early stages, districts delayed transmitting CAMPFIRE funds until pressure was brought to bear; there have been major improvements.

Having received the money, the ward and village committees call general meetings at which communities decide what to do with the money. Generally, they build schools and clinics and invest in income-generating activities or even household dividends.

Women's and Community Development

The experiences in this sector leave much to be desired, although some progress has been made.

Participation in CAMPFIRE committees

Women were hardly involved in CAMPFIRE committees in the initial stages, because of cultural inhibitions. However, following a number of meetings and workshops, the position began to change and improve. After a preliminary needs assessment, one reason for the lack of active participation noted was women's lack of confidence, especially to address gatherings, raise questions or make a contribution at a meeting.

In order to address these issues, potential resources personnel who could function as training links to target communities were identified. These individuals were to function as a core group through which the needs of communities would be identified. The staff of the Ministry of Community and Co-operative Development were the core personnel and were trained in the project component that requires women's involvement. Following the confidence-building workshops and meetings, women began to participate more actively and were appointed mainly at village committee level, owing in part to their domestic responsibilities. However, one of the best-organized wards in Matebeleland is led by a dynamic woman councillor (ward 7, Tsholotsho).

Women's projects

With regard to women's projects, an officer was appointed to assist in small-scale enterprises, especially in respect of marketing. His specific responsibilities were: to identify natural resource products within CAMPFIRE districts currently being produced which had the potential to be marketed more efficiently; to find lucrative markets for those products in order to get monies flowing into these communities; and to carry out market research on behalf of district councils and producers in CAMPFIRE districts.

Projects selected for support were those that local people had already identified or started but which required outside assistance in terms of skills training, management, finance and marketing. They included:

1. *Mopane worms (amacimbi)* These are said to be a very popular delicacy and rich in protein, and have great potential as money-makers for local communities, especially women. Under CAMPFIRE, mopane trees are well conserved. Local women who harvest and process amacimbi are, however, exploited by middlemen and transport owners who manage to buy these at low prices and resell them in distant markets in the subregion, such as Botswana and South Africa. Funds are being sought to help women to establish amacimbi processing as a viable business. In that connection, research is being conducted to determine ecological sustainability, market value and supply of the product. A processing plant would assist in the preservation, packaging and pricing of the product, and local women would learn all these skills. The women's groups should be able to sell either to wholesalers or directly to the retail market.

2. *Handicrafts* There are numerous handicraft producers who are keen to undertake serious handicraft business individually or in groups assisted by CAMPFIRE. The craft range includes ilala and sisal basketry and woodcarvings. The main producers are women. The quality of the products is already good, although there is room for more refinement. Some NGOs give technical support for management, especially to women with a large volume of business in basketry and crochet work. Binga is well known for its basketry and its financial viability. In 1990, the Kariamwe Basket Weavers were paid Z$ 100 000 for their baskets. There is still scope for expansion with improved market research, product improvement and more capital for women. The project is ecologically sustainable, as special care is taken of the grasses used.

Despite considerable interest expressed by the women and a wide range of possible economic activities, no serious backing was given to the trainer, who became frustrated and left; the post remained unfilled for a long time.

Education and Training

The introduction of wildlife management programmes in CAMPFIRE districts required communities to increase their environmental education and for there to be new perspectives on land use and ownership of resources if such programmes were to be sustainable.

While most components of CAMPFIRE provide appropriate awareness education and training to the adult population, the programme's designers considered it also necessary to focus on young people and on school staff who prepare and train the leaders of tomorrow. If young people were not exposed to intensive environmental education, CAMPFIRE would not be sustainable and would therefore have no future.

It was against the above background and with the above aims that support agencies were to carry out their tasks. The aims were transformed into general objectives, namely to explore teachers' understanding of integrated environmental education; to identify, with teachers, everyday environmental teaching activities; and to produce an awareness among teachers of their environment by effectively using environmental education materials across the curriculum.

Since there were no specialists in the environmental field, an NGO – Action – took up the challenge and is producing a comprehensive range of magazines that are popular in schools. Action is involved in curriculum change and works with teachers and headmasters, hand in hand with the Ministry of Education.

SUMMARY AND CONCLUDING REMARKS

The CAMPFIRE programme is now regarded as one of the most successful resource-based programmes for the poor rural populations in Africa. The role of education and skills development, described below, has been fundamental to its success and prospects for future development.

Awareness Campaigns

Meetings and workshops held under the awareness campaigns conducted by the Department of Parks and Wildlife Management, councillors, NGOs and traditional leaders laid the foundation of the whole CAMPFIRE programme. Local communities would never have accepted and adopted the project without a full understanding of the linkages between environmental resources and the financial and economic benefits accruing to them, and if their suspicions had not been dispelled and confidence not been created. The awareness campaigns helped the councils, the existing ward and village committees, and the traditional leaders to understand what the programme was all about, and people were thus given an informed choice of accepting or rejecting it.

Institutional and Capacity Building

With a full understanding of the programme and the development prospects it offered, it was fairly easy to train local committees to form wildlife or conservation committees at village and ward levels. These committees were in turn vehicles for further and deeper education through various mobilization strategies. Committee members went on training courses and were exposed to more activities on CAMPFIRE, and thereafter acted as trainers at the grass roots.

The education of committee members covered technical skills such as the installation of earth dams and fences, wildlife quota-setting, the drawing up of contracts, revenue distribution, and the construction of schools, clinics and income-generating projects. The CAMPFIRE managers went on more advanced courses involving planning, accounting, general management and marketing products from the districts.

The major constraints relate to low educational levels. The programme began among the remotest, poorest and least literate populations, especially older people. However, the massive education programmes begun throughout the country after independence in 1980 are reducing this constraint. A number of committee members, especially the secretaries and treasurers, are young and have secondary school education.

In conclusion, it may be pointed out that CAMPFIRE support activities consist mainly of educational or skills training either directly or indirectly; and this prioritization of education and training probably forms the cornerstone of CAMP-FIRE's success in developing a resource-based economy in Zimbabwe.

BIBLIOGRAPHY

Bradley, P.N. and K. McNamara (1993), 'Living with trees: policies for forest management in Zimbabwe', Technical Paper 210, Washington, DC: World Bank.

Child, B. and I. Bond (1994), *Marketing Hunting and Photographic Concessions in Communal Areas in Matebeleland*, Harare: Ministry of Environment and Tourism, Department of Parks and Wildlife Management.

Chitsike, L.T. (1995), 'CAMPFIRE programme in Zimbabwe: an approach to environmental conservation and poverty relief', paper presented at CROP/UNCTAD seminar discussion in Sabah, Malaysia, mimeo.

Chitsike, L.T., C. Chinhoyi and N. Mema (1994), 'Natural resources management programme: review report on CAMPFIRE', Harare, mimeo.

Dawe, M. and J.M. Hutton (1994), *An Analysis of the Production and Economic Significance of Elephant Hide in Zimbabwe*, Harare: Africa Resources Trust.

Hutton, J.M. (1996), *Crocodile Management in Zimbabwe: An Example of Sustainable Use*, Washington, DC: Africa Resources Trust.

Jones, M.A. (1994), 'Safari operations in communal areas in Matebeleland', in *Proceedings of the Natural Resources Management Project Seminar and Workshop*, Harare: Ministry of Environment and Tourism, Department of Parks and Wildlife Management, mimeo.

Martin, R.B. (1986), *Communal Areas Management Programme for Indigenous Resources (CAMPFIRE)*, Harare: Department of Parks and Wildlife Management.

PART FIVE

Conclusions

13. Conclusions

Jörg Mayer[1]

This book has brought together cross-country studies which discuss factors that have influenced economic growth in natural resource economies, as well as country case studies which have highlighted policy measures that have contributed to favourable outcomes in a crucial manner. This concluding part discusses salient features of the issues addressed in the preceding chapters, with a view to focusing attention on policy issues which relatively less successful natural resource economies may wish to reconsider. The main lessons are summarized at the end of this chapter.

THE INVERSE STATISTICAL RELATIONSHIP BETWEEN RESOURCE ABUNDANCE AND ECONOMIC GROWTH

The inverse statistical relationship between resource abundance and economic growth has been a recurring theme of economic history. The recent availability of standardized data sets has allowed this relationship to be assessed in more detail as far as the last three decades are concerned (Chapter 2). Regarding the more distant past, Maddison (1982) has shown that the resource-poor Netherlands outperformed Spain in the seventeenth century because of (a) the character of its institutions – 'Dutch views were deeply impregnated with the possibilities for rational manipulation of the human and material environment and a "Faustian sense of mastery over man and nature", which characterizes capitalist attitudes to technological change' (Maddison, 1982, p. 32) – and (b) geographical advantages, since the Netherlands dominated major rivers giving access to markets in the heart of Europe and developed a sizeable volume of entrepôt trade.

On the other hand, in the more recent past – the late nineteenth century – there are several examples of countries with abundant natural resources which grew rapidly. The best documented examples include the United States of America and Sweden. According to Romer (1996), the United States' assumption of economic leadership may be explained on the basis of the interaction between natural resource abundance and scale effects, which was unique to that country at the end of the nineteenth century. Resource abundance was important because the country's great natural advantages in wood, coal and oil enabled it to supply its energy-intensive industrial development from domestic sources, while scale effects from its large domestic market increased the potential of firms to recoup the upfront costs of research and development spending. Similarly, Sweden's rapid growth was founded on resource-based industrialization, namely activities in the timber, pulp and paper, and iron and steel sectors. Many historians, such as Sandberg (1979), with his case of the 'impoverished sophisticate', have asserted that Sweden's rapid growth at the end of the nineteenth century was due to a strikingly large stock of human and institutional capital. Sandberg (ibid., p. 227) argues that the Swedish economy was propelled forward by a large exogenous increase in the international value and economic usefulness of its natural resources and in the availability of technological opportunities related to the use of forests as a source of charcoal and the exploitation of phosphoric iron ore. These opportunities could be seized thanks to the rapid adaptation of new technology to domestic conditions. This process was greatly facilitated by the high level of per capita supply of human capital. However, Williamson (1996, p. 296) argues that human capital was far less important to late nineteenth-century growth than to late twentieth-century growth, and that a series of institutional reforms in agriculture, trade liberalization and a tightening of property rights were equally important factors for Swedish growth.

It is not clear to what extent development experiences in the late nineteenth century can inform today's development strategies in natural resource economies. More research is undoubtedly needed in this area. It could be argued, for example, that the key developmental issue in the late nineteenth century was 'industrialization', while today it is 'technological catch-up within industries'. This could lead to the interpretation that natural resource economies should for preference proceed along a development path of economies which do not have a rich endowment of natural resources, and maximize the extraction of investable funds out of their natural resource sector for industrial development. However, it has been argued, for example by Karshenas (1995), that an important determinant of agricultural surplus outflow is the rate of technical innovation and productivity improvement in agricultural production, while in technologically stagnant agrarian economies the agricultural sector will place a growing financial burden on the rest of the economy. Hence, a part of the financial resources extracted from the primary sector needs to be channelled back in the form of improved technologies and extension services in order to facilitate a balanced development of the natural resource sector and the industrial sector.

The balance between natural resource development and industrial development appears to be determined by the level of human and physical capital accumulation which allows the absorption and incorporation of technology required for industrial production, while at the same time not raising wages beyond the level which impairs competitiveness on the world market, as discussed by Auty (Chapter 4) for mineral economies. Following Leamer (1987) and Wood (Chapter 3), it can be argued in this respect that the development path of an economy is crucially influenced by its endowment with production factors and that, therefore, countries with abundant natural resource endowments may never go through the stage of labour-intensive manufacturing which has been characteristic of industrialization in natural resource poor economies.[2]

The nature of a country's natural resource endowment is crucial for decisions taken to increase this sector's productivity. First, structural changes in world demand may drastically lower the economic value of a country's resources. The partial replacement of natural fibres by synthetic fibres and the swings in the popularity of nuclear energy over the last few years are but two examples. Second, there is the well-known adding-up problem. This means that producing countries will be worse off when several countries increase the supply of the same products at the same time and when this increase leads to a decline in prices on the world market for the product in question; as a result, the countries' export earnings decline in spite of an increase in export volume. On the other hand, there is a group of primary products with high unit value and with income elasticity of demand greater than one which over the past few years has proved to possess a dynamic demand potential, as evidenced in Table 13.1. Such high-value goods include meat and meat products, dairy products, fish and fish products, fresh and processed fruit, vegetables and nuts, feedstuffs, oilseeds, vegetable and animal oils, and spices. The discussion in Chapters 7–10 suggests that several countries have succeeded in imparting growth momentum to their economies through the development of such exports.

It is likely that developing countries will further increase both the absolute level and their share in the world market of such exports. While these countries appear to have a location-specific comparative advantage largely in fishery products, fruit and fruit juices, as well as in vegetable oils and oilseeds, there is also potential for further penetration in the market for meat and meat products. This is because of the gradual decline in developed countries' production and export subsidies and greater market transparency as called for under the Uruguay Round Agreements.

There also seems to be a good demand potential for such products, given that the centre of gravity of the world economy has been shifting towards East Asia, that many of these rapidly growing economies have a very large population base, and that the intensity of direct and indirect consumption of a wide range of food and feedgrains, as well as other agricultural raw materials and minerals and metals, has been low in these countries compared with countries of comparable affluence. For example, the intake of meat, fishery products and other high-value food items in the group of middle-income developing countries

Table 13.1 Exports of selected commodity groups from developing countries and territories, 1970–94 (millions of US dollars)

	1970	1975	1980	1985	1990	1994
Total primary commodities	47 719	183 259	465 544	307 998	367 393	371 938
Primary commodities excluding fuels	29 654	58 780	114 397	104 741	149 318	182 933
Minerals, ores and metals	7 717	13 351	26 764	21 310	34 753	35 156
All food items of which:	16 479	36 961	68 271	69 027	93 285	121 752
Tropical beverages	4 683	7 021	17 636	16 588	12 251	14 981
High-value food products	4 885	9 788	29 023	32 815	52 850	71 247

Note: High-value food products include meat and meat products; dairy products; fish and fish products; fresh and processed fruit, vegetables and nuts; feedstuffs; oilseeds; vegetable and animal oils; and spices. See UNCTAD *Commodity Yearbook* (various issues) for the definition of the other commodity groups.

Source: UNCTAD database.

in Asia ranges from one-third to one-half of that prevailing in the more affluent economies in the region, such as Hong Kong and Singapore, or the group of OECD countries. The respective levels are even lower in the lower-income but equally dynamic and vastly more populous developing countries in Asia. This means that growing prosperity in Asia, combined with the historically observed shifts towards greater animal protein consumption, more variety in the daily diet and a larger intake of cereal-based light alcoholic drinks, is likely to give a significant stimulus to consumer requirements for high-value food items and feedgrains. Moreover, assuming that the energy- and materials-intensive pattern of economic growth in Asian developing countries, which themselves are relatively poorly endowed with natural resources, will continue, a similar expansion in those countries' consumption of agricultural raw materials and of many minerals and metals can equally be expected (UNCTAD, 1996b). Regarding other geographical regions, it can be expected that the level of per capita income in Central and Eastern European countries will continue to rise, and that consumers will demand a wider range of food products, not all of which can be sourced from the local supply base. Hence, there is reason to believe that natural resource economies have a growth and development potential which is better than it may sometimes appear, and that the realization of this potential could be based on increased exports of certain primary products.

ELEMENTS OF A POLICY FRAMEWORK APPLYING TO ALL RESOURCE-BASED ECONOMIES

Basic Policies

With regard to the elements of the policy agenda for resource-rich countries, some elements of a policy framework apply to all natural resource economies, whether these economies are based on renewable or on non-renewable resources. The common elements include standard prescriptions such as sound and sustainable macroeconomic and exchange rate policies; the provision of universal basic education and adequate and well-maintained physical infrastructure; and the presence of a functioning financial sector and of a transparent legal and regulatory framework, conducive to private sector economic activities. As an additional element, close observation of, and provision of information regarding, the evolution of market conditions and the dynamic market potential for different categories of resource-based goods are crucial for capturing market opportunities and for the maximization of revenues from the sustainable exploitation of natural resources. Moreover, policies need to be adjusted as external circumstances change and as an economy evolves along a development path.

Even though many natural resource economies have given effect to at least some of these basic elements, the investment response has been limited. This may be due to domestic and foreign investors' perception that the risk of policy reversals is still high. However, it is none the less timely for those countries which are reasonably advanced in their basic reform efforts to consider developing a broader range of policies. Some key elements of the latter are discussed below.

Trade Policy and Sectoral Policies

There is some controversy regarding the formulation of trade policies in natural resource economies. According to the Heckscher–Ohlin trade theory, countries export goods which use intensively those factors with which they are abundantly endowed and import goods which use intensively factors that are relatively scarce. Trade thus increases the demand for abundant factors, following the expansion of export sectors, and decreases the demand for scarce factors, following the contraction of import-competing sectors. Trade liberalization in economies where natural resources are abundant and skilled labour and capital are scarce will therefore tend to shift the allocation of resources towards specialization in primary products and a decrease in wage differentials between skilled and unskilled workers. As a result, trade liberalization might have an adverse impact on skill upgrading and capital accumulation and maintain the natural resource economy in a low-skill and low-growth trap.

However, these theoretical predictions contrast with the cross-country evidence set out in Chapter 2, which suggests that over the past 25 years the few developing countries which are resource-abundant and have open trade policies have done well, while other natural resource economies – where an industrial policy and an import-substitution strategy were attempted – have done poorly. These predictions also contrast with recent evidence from cross-country studies which examine the behaviour of relative wages in various episodes of trade liberalization in Argentina, Chile, Colombia, Costa Rica, Mexico and Uruguay, and which find almost unanimous evidence for rising rather than falling wage differentials (Robbins, 1996; Pissarides, 1997).

This shift of production towards more skill-intensive products may be explained by trade acting as a channel for the transfer of technology whose assimilation increases the demand for skilled labour in the importing country. High levels of human capital are complementary to physical capital investments and recent technology. In addition, trade liberalization removes price distortions between the tradable and non-tradable sectors and improves access to foreign exchange, thereby improving the incentives for private and foreign investors to become active in sectors for which they perceive market opportunities. More open economies permit better use of human capital through developing profitable innovations for rapidly changing international markets that have positive external effects due to the information they provide to others. However, this shift towards relatively more skill-intensive production does not necessarily have to be reflected in a decrease in resource-intensive exports and an increase in manufactured exports. For example, for Argentina, Chile and Colombia taken together, the share of resource-intensive and low-skill labour-intensive goods in total exports fell by only a small amount (from 90 per cent to 82 per cent) between 1985 and 1994; in Brazil the decrease was from 64 per cent to 58 per cent.[3] By contrast, these four countries have evolved as leading middle- and low-income exporters of high-value food products, as shown in Table 13.2.

Table 13.2 Exports of high-value food products from selected countries, 1980–94 (millions of US dollars)

	1980	1985	1988	1990	1992	1994
Argentina	3 046	3 054	4 256	4 999	55 36	6 200
Brazil	3 963	4 997	5 947	5 636	5 793	6 244
Chile	585	887	1 540	1 840	2 322	2 406
Colombia	201	204	354	505	690	822
Indonesia	769	915	1 701	1 876	2 477	3 524
Malaysia	1 724	2 237	2 558	2 551	3 178	4 488
Thailand	1 369	1 676	3 281	4 231	5 603	6 350
Kenya	79	79	121	125	143	153
Sub-Saharan Africa	1 524	1 403	1 685	1 878	1 877	2 050
All developing countries and territories	29 023	32 819	48 444	52 873	59 419	71 247

Note: Includes meat and meat products; dairy products; fish and fish products; fresh and processed fruit, vegetables and nuts; feedstuffs; oilseeds; vegetable and animal oils; and spices.

Source: UNCTAD database.

The observation that in natural resource rich developing countries a shift towards more skill-intensive production can be accompanied by an upgrading in the skill content of primary, rather than manufactured, products may be explained within a framework of learning sequences. As argued in Mayer (1996), the processes of skill acquisition (through formal schooling and learning) and technological progress (through invention and imitation) are interdependent. This interdependence suggests that there is an infinite continuum of goods ranked hierarchically according to their level of technical sophistication. The technical progress embodied in the process or good being imitated by the labour force is a function of the levels of technology of all lower-ranked goods. This implies that accumulating human and physical capital will not lead to sustainable economic growth and development if this means investing in more of the same machines and shopfloor skills; accumulation needs to have an aspect of innovation to be conducive to sustainable economic growth and development.

An implication of this view is that policy makers should continue making efforts to raise the population's level of formal education and to concentrate the labour force in the production of goods close to their own quality frontier, thus allowing human capital to be accumulated rapidly through high learning rates associated with new activities, as well as to introduce new technologies on a continuing basis in order to avoid cessation of learning effects once the learning benefits of producing with existing technologies start to wear thin. This means that natural resource economies which for historical reasons specialize in sectors with a low level of learning benefits and whose growth potential is therefore low would gain from any policy – for example, subsidies designed to make up for the fixed-cost expenditure associated with the introduction (be it through invention or imitation) of new technology – that induced its producers to switch over to the higher-learning good which is one rung up the skill and technology ladder. Such subsidies would be targeted to sectors where producers could, within a short period of time, accumulate the knowledge required to make up for any deficiency in intrinsic capabilities or experience that had so far prevented them from being competitive in these sectors. The policy intervention would correct for the inefficiency that results from the failure of domestic producers to account for the learning externalities associated with their production decisions. The sectors would be chosen according to the learning potential which they offer – independently of whether they are classified as primary products or manufactures in common trade or employment statistics – taking into account a sector's dynamic demand potential on world markets.

However, it is difficult to choose suitable sectors. With the benefit of hindsight, it appears that high-value food products and other horticulture items have provided a valuable growth stimulus in several natural resource economies. As suggested by the experience of Israel and Kenya (Chapters 7 and 9), export activities need to be organized in the form of integrated agro-businesses in order to tap this potential. High-value food items and other horticultural products, in both fresh and processed form, have dynamic characteristics since a higher level of skills is required in order to master the relatively more sophisticated technical and commercial demands which are associated with their supply, compared with the supply of more traditional products such as tropical beverages.[4] For example, production techniques and organization need to be updated and adjusted on a continuous basis to meet rapidly changing consumer tastes for new products and phytosanitary requirements of importing countries, as well as to fulfil the requirement of just-in-time availability of produce during specific periods of market opportunities.[5] Hence, the procurement of raw material at the right time and of the right quality is crucial. Regarding commercial demands, the fact that only a few countries which enjoy preferential access to the markets of the European Union under the Lomé Convention have made serious inroads into these markets, while market leaders such as Brazil, the Philippines and Thailand have not received such tariff advantages, suggests that the combination of supply and export management, as well as access to international marketing and distribution networks, is crucial, rather than market access as such. Successful exporters need to overcome constraints in areas related to packaging, export logistics, promotional support, product innovation and perceived commitment to becoming a reliable source of import supply, as discussed in Chapter 9. Although many of these problems can be solved only at the level of individual companies, the government can assist by providing public goods, such as research and extension services (see below), as well as education.

Regarding education, it is clear that skill accumulation is a basic issue for development, including in natural resource economies. The conclusions of Chapter 3 suggest that the level of a country's supply of human capital is a crucial determinant of export diversification from unprocessed primary products to processed primary products and manufactures. Similarly, the conclusions of Chapter 4 suggest that the key issue for mineral-based economies is how to evolve from rent-driven to skill-driven development. However, it is less clear how to impart knowledge, and in particular what composition of scientific and other school-based knowledge, and skills acquired through training and learning-by-doing, is required in natural resource economies. For example, it is not clear whether skill upgrading of the labour force in those economies refers to the same type of skills as that of the labour force in other economies. Therefore, whether education policies in natural resource economies need to focus on the same kind of institutions as in other economies is an open question. It is possible, for example, that training and learning-by-doing are a better substitute for advanced schooling in resource-based economies than in other economies.[6] Accordingly, inasmuch as sector-specific policy measures are considered to be an important instrument for human capital accumulation, more conceptual clarity and empirical evidence are needed before specific policy measures can be recommended.

ELEMENTS OF A POLICY FRAMEWORK APPLYING
MAINLY TO MINERALS- AND FUELS-BASED ECONOMIES

An important element in a policy framework specific to economies based on non-renewable resources is a mechanism for the management of mineral revenues. The management of resource revenues is particularly challenging for mineral economies because of the relatively low level of linkages between the mineral sector and other sectors, and because of the fact that mineral resources are depletable, which gives rise to the question of 'how to sow the oil, gold or copper'. Establishing a formal mechanism such as a national mineral revenue stabilization fund can contribute to the efficient absorption of windfall profits during mineral booms, with a view to both minimizing Dutch disease effects and building up savings on which the economy can draw in periods of unexpected earnings shortfalls. Such a fund can play a useful role in earnings stabilization and sterilization, particularly in economies whose domestic financial market is too small to absorb excess funds. Regarding the institutional set-up of such a fund, it is important that the fund's management be isolated from the short-term considerations of political parties and interest groups in order to guarantee that its workings are conducive to the longer-term development of an economy. This may be difficult to achieve in view of the political pressure which a government faces when parts of the mineral revenue are sterilized, rather than injected into the economy, in a period of economic difficulties. However, as suggested by Daniel (1992), separating mineral revenue flows from other revenues makes their management more transparent to policy makers, administrators and the public, and can therefore assist in resisting the build-up of pressure to spend incautiously. Lane and Tornell (1996) explain that revenue windfalls will not give rise to a voracity effect if there are institutional barriers to discretionary redistribution.

Establishing a mineral revenue stabilization fund may not be of equal importance to all mineral-based economies. For example, the need to operate such a fund is less obvious for countries such as Botswana, where the long-term trend in the evolution of revenues is reasonably clear because, *inter alia*, the size of the known reserves allows the economy to buy time with regard to the development of other economic activities (Chapter 5). By contrast, operating a stabilization fund may be very pertinent for small mineral economies such as Jamaica, Trinidad and Tobago and Namibia, where resources are becoming scarce. Equally important, these countries have each experienced a drastic and unexpected drop in revenue from their leading mineral sector, after Dutch-disease-type effects reversed the previous diversification of the economy and made the country increasingly dependent on one mineral resource.

However, even with such a mechanism for the absorption of rents exceeding the economy's absorptive capacity in place, deciding how much of the windfall revenue should be spent and how much saved abroad remains a difficult choice: cyclical swings need to be distinguished from permanent price changes, the risk of structural changes in world demand needs to be assessed, and an estimation of depletion rates is required. In this regard, policy makers need to look at the nature of their particular mineral resources rather than at their mineral endowment as a whole. Governments tend to be overly optimistic regarding the evolution of mineral revenue, whereas caution appears to be called for. On the other hand, deliberately underestimating revenue in order to accumulate reserves can lead to serious credibility problems if this practice becomes institutionalized. Hence, whatever institutional mechanism is in place, ensuring high-quality forecasting and a good understanding of the dynamics of particular minerals markets are crucial for good economic policy.

Stressing the importance of a stabilization fund for minerals may be seen as contradicting the fact that many developing countries have abolished similar institutions (such as *caisses de stabilisation*) for the agricultural sector. However, this issue is far more important for non-renewable resources. First, the utilization of land for agricultural purposes is far more flexible than the exploitation of mineral resources: one can switch from one crop to another relatively easily, whereas a copper mine cannot be turned into an oil well. Hence, reacting to changing prices through shifting economic activities is much easier within the agricultural sector than it is in mineral-based economies. Second, experience has shown that it is much easier for a government to appropriate and squander revenues from minerals. This is probably due to the fact that production and consumption linkages between the mineral and other sectors are relatively small and that, therefore, mineral revenues are first appropriated by the government and then allocated to other sectors by means of transfers, provision of services or public investment.

ELEMENTS OF A POLICY FRAMEWORK APPLYING MAINLY TO AGRICULTURE-BASED ECONOMIES

Economies based on agriculture have a certain advantage over minerals- and fuels-based economies, partly because the possibility of crop substitution offers the former some flexibility, and partly because the employment and skill-upgrading opportunities offered by agricultural activities are greater. None the less, it is imperative for agriculture-based economies to achieve a high level of productivity, in particular in those products which offer a dynamic demand potential on the world market. The development experience of Kenya (Chapter 9) and especially that of Israel and Malaysia (Chapters 7 and 8) suggests that technological upgrading, efficient extension services and indigenous research and development activities play a crucial role in this context. The fact that research and extension are among the few 'green box measures' which may be used to advance growth and productivity in agriculture under the Uruguay Round Agreements, and are therefore not subject to reduction commitments, has further increased the importance of such activities.

Much of the development literature stresses that developing countries do not have a comparative advantage in research and development designed to advance the technology frontier, and that they should therefore limit their research and development activities to imitation and adaptation. On the other hand, agricultural research and development has often been considered a location-specific problem because of different adoption characteristics of farm communities, and because technology employed in agriculture is characterized by a high degree of sensitivity to a specific physical environment. Thus, certain techniques may be optimal solutions with respect to the circumstances in which they were invented and are being used, but may not be optimal in other circumstances.

There is clearly a complementarity between international and national agricultural research systems which is expressed, for example, in the widespread belief that the technologies which led to the Green Revolution and which were developed by international research bodies were able to have such an impact only because the improved germ plasm could be readily moved from a centralized location to competent research bodies in each agroclimatic region for testing and adaptation (Ruttan, 1996). The trade-off between indigenous agricultural research and technology imports has acquired a new facet with the increased integration of the world economy. Substantial improvements in and the more widespread availability of telecommunication, transport and automation facilities have significantly reduced the transaction costs of doing business over long distances. Such transactions have received an additional boost from the move towards better protection of international property rights. Hence, the supply of agricultural technology to developing countries may be expected to have vastly increased compared with a few years ago.

Tabor *et al.* (1996) have conceptualized the factors affecting shifts in the supply of agricultural technology, distinguishing new technology as coming from domestically, regionally or internationally managed research institutes. According to this concept, the supply of domestically developed agricultural technology increases with the stock of human capital and the productivity of the scientists working in the domestic research institutes. Table 13.3 shows that globalization increases the supply of regionally and internationally developed agricultural technology directly through falling transaction costs and greater market integration. Globalization is likely to increase this supply indirectly by increasing potential scale, scope and network economies of regionally and internationally developed technologies. This means that, in principle, a case for indigenous research and development activities can be made only where domestic suppliers are internationally competitive sources of new technology or where, for reasons of location or special capacities, they provide a service that complements global technology outputs or one that is truly unique to local markets (ibid., p. 4), because, for example, it takes account of the growing concerns about the environmental problems associated with agriculture and food production. It would appear that the level of human capital and the chosen institutional set-up have allowed research results in Israel and Malaysia (which were discussed in Chapters 7 and 8) to meet the first condition, while research required for the sustainable production of high-value food and other horticultural products would in most developing countries meet the second condition.

Table 13.3 Factors affecting shifts in the supply of agricultural research and development

	Knowledge	Transaction costs	Market access
Local supplies	***	–	–
Regional supplies	*	**	***
International supplies	*	***	**

Note: * = important; *** = very important; – = base case.

Source: Adapted from Tabor *et al.* (1996, p. 3).

However, even countries for which the trade-off between investing to improve the productivity of indigenous technology services and financing technology imports is skewed towards the latter will have to maintain a minimum research capacity. This is because gaining access to new technology without undue delay requires the presence of a transmission belt, that is, the presence of appropriately skilled scientists and their being effectively linked to global initiatives and networks. In addition, national institutions are required to guarantee that an appropriate diagnosis of the constraints of local farming systems is made, on-farm experiments and validation trials are conducted, and linkages with extension workers are formed.

The appropriate institutional set-up of national agricultural research appears to be characterized by close integration of research, extension services and credit facilities, causing these to interact with individual farmers. Agricultural research will tend to be demand-driven where farmers are included in the determination of research agendas, test runs, technology implementation, and so on, with a view to ensuring wide dissemination and utilization of research results. This can be further strengthened by funding a large part of research through taxes and levies on production or exports of the agricultural product concerned, as well as by including farmers' representatives on the management boards of sectoral commodity bodies. However, such funding needs to be introduced gradually since it requires efficient and profitable production units; otherwise, the imposition of taxes and levies could impair the competitiveness of exporters. Strengthening agricultural research is not just a matter of more money: the financing, organization and management of research and development need to be dealt with in an integrated way. All the participants need to share the goal of developing commercially applicable outputs, and activities designed to achieve this goal need to be appropriately monitored, evaluated and managed, rather than simply administered.

Moreover, there is significant scope for regional and other forms of South–South cooperation among national agricultural research systems of developing countries with similar natural resources and agro-ecological conditions. Reinforcing such cooperation could prove crucial for the efficient use of scarce financial resources and capacities, the maximization of synergies and scale effects, and the furthering of cross-country compatibilities. This could be achieved, for example, through improved cooperation among national research bodies. The recent emergence of such coordinating mechanisms in the form of regional groupings for agricultural research in Africa and Latin America is encouraging. To sum up, although they are still required in the era of globalization and have some roles in common, national agricultural research systems will need to become increasingly different, depending on their size, efficiency, maturity and location.

ELEMENTS OF A POLICY FRAMEWORK FROM A LOCAL AND REGIONAL PERSPECTIVE

While the debate on development in resource-based economies tends to address policy making at the national level, the exploitation of natural resources and the eventual depletion of non-renewable resources are especially important issues at the local level. As discussed in Chapters 11 and 12, greater devolution of development planning and revenue distribution from central to local government is required since the exploitation of natural resources is a socioeconomic activity and an interactive process which involves economic agents, the natural environment and local communities. In order to identify and internalize the social and environmental impacts of resource exploitation, local people need to be involved and provided with the tools that allow them to understand and manage this process. This is important in particular because local communities are usually burdened with the adverse environmental and social impacts of resource exploitation, while the main economic benefits of the latter, such as taxes and foreign exchange revenues, accrue at the national level. Therefore, institutional issues such as the establishment of appropriate rules, the design of incentives to involve local communities and the effective enforcement of policy need to be high on the agenda of sustainable natural resources management.

SOME LESSONS REGARDING DEVELOPMENT POLICIES IN NATURAL RESOURCE ECONOMIES

In this concluding section, the general lessons regarding the five themes formulated in the Introduction are summarized:

1. There is probably a direct relationship between natural resource abundance and low economic growth, since economies whose main activities today are based on the exploitation of natural resources are disadvantaged with respect to early industrializers because they have not been able to benefit from dynamic externalities associated with industrial production. This direct result of not being part of the club of early industrializers has been reinforced by the apparently greater facility of governments in natural resource economies to appropriate and squander resources, or by the tendency of some governments to ignore their economy's endowments with natural resources and to follow a development path similar to that taken by natural resource poor newly industrialized countries. However, given that the development path of an economy is crucially influenced by its endowment with production factors, the key policy issue in natural resource economies is to make the primary sector sufficiently productive to provide the resources for investment in primary and non-primary sectors, with a view to initiating a process of gradual upgrading of skills and technology on the basis of capital deepening in both primary and non-primary sectors.

2. Part of the disappointing growth performance of many natural resource economies is due to insufficient technological upgrading in their agricultural sector. This calls for a strengthening of domestic research capacity, bringing the objectives, nature of resources and available know-how into line with development requirements. Close integration of research, extension services, credit facilities and farming activities is required in order to ensure that research is demand-driven and oriented towards producing results which can be used commercially. Regional integration in agricultural research needs to be strengthened to ensure the presence of a critical mass regarding scientists, investable funds, and so on. Technological upgrading goes hand in hand with skill upgrading through the provision of both learning effects and skill premiums, which act as incentives for individuals to invest more in their own education.

3.   Empirically, trade liberalization has tended to increase the skill premiums in wages. This is probably due to the fact that more open economies permit better use of human capital through developing profitable innovations for rapidly changing international markets, and hence increase the demand for skill-intensive activities.

4.   Establishing a mechanism for the management of mineral resources is an important element of a policy framework specific to mineral economies. The fact that production and consumption linkages between the mineral and other sectors are relatively small facilitates the appropriation and incautious spending of mineral revenues by governments. Separating mineral revenue flows from other revenues makes their management more transparent to policy makers, administrators and the public, and can therefore assist in resisting the build-up of pressure to spend incautiously. Earnings stabilization and sterilization are particularly important in economies whose domestic financial market is too small to absorb excess funds and hence to stem Dutch disease effects.

5.   Greater devolution of development planning and revenue distribution from central to local government is required since the exploitation of natural resources is a socioeconomic activity and an interactive process which involves economic agents, the natural environment and local communities. In order to identify and internalize the social and environmental impacts of resource exploitation, local people need to be involved and provided with the tools that allow them to understand and manage this process.

NOTES

1. This chapter draws partly on the discussion which followed the presentations of Chapters 2–12 at the meeting of the UNCTAD Secretary-General's expert group on 'Development Policies in Resource-based Economies', Geneva, 21–22 November 1996, as reported in document UNCTAD/ITCD/TAB/Misc. 3, 7 March 1997. The opinions expressed in this chapter are those of the author and do not necessarily reflect the views of UNCTAD.
2. This argument can be put as follows: by the time a country with a high ratio between its endowment with natural resources and its labour endowment (N/L) has achieved a high enough ratio between its endowment with human or physical capital and its labour endowment (H/N or K/N) to have a comparative advantage in manufacturing, it must necessarily also have achieved a high H/L (or K/L) and hence have a comparative advantage in medium- or high-skill intensive manufactures.
3. UNCTAD (1996a, p. 116). Resource-intensive and low-skill labour-intensive products include non-fuel primary commodities, wood and paper products, non-metallic mineral products, textiles, clothing and footwear, and toys and sports equipment.
4. For the skill intensity of fresh fruit exports from Chile, see Meller (1995, pp. 39–40).
5. For example, strawberry exports from Costa Rica to the United States are profitable only during one week a year, that is, that week following US imports of strawberries from Mexico and preceding the sourcing of produce from Florida and California. Similarly,

Costa Rican exports of flowers to the United States are profitable only on two days, namely Valentine's Day and Mother's Day. The author is grateful to Ennio Rodriguez (Inter-American Development Bank) for this information.
6. Meller (1995, pp. 30–31), for example, discusses the crucial role of sector-specific training for the development of Chile's fruit exports.

REFERENCES

Daniel, P. (1992), 'Economic policy in mineral exporting countries: what have we learned?', in J.E. Tilton (ed.), *Mineral Wealth and Economic Development*, Washington, DC: Resources for the Future, pp. 81–121.

Karshenas, M. (1995), *Industrialisation and Agricultural Surplus: A Comparative Study of Economic Development in Asia*, Cambridge: Cambridge University Press.

Lane, P.R. and A. Tornell (1996), 'Power, growth, and the voracity effect', *Journal of Economic Growth*, **1**, 213–41.

Leamer, E. (1987), 'Paths of development in the three-factor, n-good general equilibrium model', *Journal of Political Economy*, **95**, 961–99.

Maddison, A. (1982), *Phases of Capitalist Development*, Oxford and New York: Oxford University Press.

Mayer, J. (1996), 'Learning sequences and structural diversification in developing countries', *Journal of Development Studies*, **33**, 210–29.

Meller, P. (1995), 'Chilean export growth, 1979–90: an assessment', in G. Helleiner (ed.), *Manufacturing for Export in the Developing World: Problems and Possibilities*, London: Routledge.

Pissarides, C. (1997), 'Learning by trading and the returns to human capital in developing countries', *World Bank Economic Review*, **11**, 17–32.

Robbins, D. (1996), 'HOS hits facts: facts win evidence on trade and wages in the developing world', Development Discussion Paper 557, Cambridge (Mass.): Harvard Institute of Development.

Romer, P. (1996), 'Why, indeed, in America? Theory, history, and the origins of modern economic growth', *American Economic Review*, **86** (2), 202–6.

Ruttan, V. (1996), 'Global research systems for sustainable development', in C. Bonte-Friedheim and K. Sheridan (eds), *The Globalisation of Science: The Place of Agricultural Research*, The Hague: International Service for National Agricultural Research.

Sandberg, L. (1979), 'The case of the impoverished sophisticate: human capital and Swedish economic growth before World War I', *Journal of Economic History*, **39**, 225–41.

Tabor S., H. Tollini and W. Janssen (1996), 'Globalisation of agriculture research: do winners take all?', Discussion Paper 96–11, The Hague: International Service for National Agricultural Research.

UNCTAD (1996a), *Trade and Development Report 1996*, New York and Geneva: United Nations.

UNCTAD (1996b), 'Commodities: market situation and development opportunities', Geneva: Commodities Division, mimeo.

Williamson, J. (1996), 'Globalisation, convergence, and history,' *Journal of Economic History*, **56**, 277–306.

Index